"Krohn's critical and well-researched analysis of how hermeneutical principles are actually used in interpreting the Bible provides excellent insight into the Church of Jesus Christ of Latter-day Saints. While the LDS claims the Bible as authority, it also sees the biblical text as corrupted. But as revelation is ongoing, what really matters is an experience or word for today. Since this is very postmodern, this study is also useful in considering a philosophy of words and culture."

—**STEVE HARDY**, International Council of
Evangelical Theological Education (ICETE)

"Despite the self-presentation of the Church of Jesus Christ of Latter-day Saints (LDS) since its inception as a fairly monolithic institution, there is a genuine diversity of beliefs (as with any religious tradition). In *Mormon Hermeneutics*, Krohn highlights one particular area of LDS diversity, namely the variety of approaches to reading and interpreting the Bible, and he offers readers a helpful organization and analysis of what individual LDSs do with one of their scriptures."

—**JOHN ANTHONY DUNNE**, Bethel Seminary

"An impressive piece of scholarship. It serves the double purpose of an introduction to Mormon thought as well as a critique of its interpretive practices. When an irenic disposition combines with a sharpness of insight and clarity of expression, something good is bound to happen. I and many others with me will find ourselves much indebted to Jeffrey Krohn not only for elucidating Mormon interpretive practices but also for teaching us many a useful hermeneutical lesson along the way."

—**SVEN SODERLUND**, Regent College, emeritus

"A number of years ago, I was surprised to learn that in the curriculum of the largest university department of religious studies in the world, at the Brigham Young University of the Church of Jesus Christ of Latter-day Saints, not a single class in hermeneutics or principles of interpretation was ever taught. Of course, that doesn't mean that Mormons have no systems of interpretation, and Krohn enlightens us through his creative categorizations and extensive illustrations. A one-of-a-kind study delving into an important topic not covered in book-length fashion anywhere else."

—**CRAIG L. BLOMBERG**, Denver Seminary, emeritus

"Hans-Georg Gadamer meets the *Book of Mormon*! Jeffrey Krohn utilizes the framework of critical realism and the insights of modern philosophical hermeneutics in conducting an insightful analysis of five characteristic but overlapping ways in which the LDSs 'use' (i.e., reinterpret) the Bible, citing numerous textual examples to support his critique. He also helpfully discusses the foundational interpretive assumptions and 'systemic parameters' that guide LDS engagement with biblical texts."

—**RICHARD SCHULTZ**, Wheaton College

"Krohn gives a masterful analysis of hermeneutical approaches in the literature of the LDS from its founder, Joseph Smith, through to modern scholars within the church. . . . Contrary to those who defend the LDS's use of the Bible as legitimate applications of modern hermeneutics, Krohn reveals its deficiency with specific examples."

—**DANIEL S. STEFFEN**, Dallas Theological Seminary

"Anyone who has engaged in serious conversation with a Mormon friend or colleague may well have struggled to understand how a group that claims devout loyalty to Scripture can hold a range of beliefs that seem quite at variance with historic Christianity. This rigorous but fair-minded and accessible analysis of Mormon hermeneutics opens a much-needed window onto an interpretive approach that for too long has remained obscure. I know of no other book like it. It deserves a wide reading."

—**STEVEN M. BRYAN**, Trinity Evangelical Divinity School

Mormon Hermeneutics

Mormon Hermeneutics

Five Approaches to the Bible by the LDS Church

Jeffrey S. Krohn

PICKWICK *Publications* · Eugene, Oregon

MORMON HERMENEUTICS
Five Approaches to the Bible by the LDS Church

Pickwick Publications
An Imprint of Wipf and Stock Publishers
199 W. 8th Ave., Suite 3
Eugene, OR 97401

www.wipfandstock.com

PAPERBACK ISBN: 978-1-6667-1613-9
HARDCOVER ISBN: 978-1-6667-1614-6
EBOOK ISBN: 978-1-6667-1615-3

Cataloguing-in-Publication data:

Names: Krohn, Jeffrey S., author.

Title: Mormon hermeneutics : five approaches to the Bible by the LDS Church / by Jeffrey S. Krohn.

Description: Eugene, OR: Pickwick Publications, 2022 | Includes bibliographical references and index.

Identifiers: ISBN 978-1-6667-1613-9 (paperback) | ISBN 978-1-6667-1614-6 (hardcover) | ISBN 978-1-6667-1615-3 (ebook)

Subjects: LCSH: Bible—Hermeneutics. | Church of Jesus Christ of Latter-Day Saints—Sacred books. | Mormon church—Sacred books.

Classification: BX8622 K76 2022 (print) | BX8622 (ebook)

04/29/22

"That which is new is always exciting, and there is an inevitable tendency for its importance to be overestimated."

—STEPHEN NEILL AND TOM WRIGHT

Contents

Acknowledgments

I OWE A DEBT of gratitude to many people for their assistance in the writing of this book. I thank numerous professors whose passion was evident not in "pyrotechnic," flamboyant expositions, but in deep knowledge of Scripture. My PhD advisor, Dr. Thorsten Moritz, with his vast knowledge of hermeneutics and a notable ability to articulate that knowledge, has steered me toward clearer thinking.

Students and colleagues at USEL (Universidad Seminario Evangélico de Lima) consistently encouraged me and showed interest in my research. I am thankful for the support and patience of my children: Brandon, Jonathon, Nathan, and Sophia. And I am deeply thankful for my loving wife, Stacey, who initially emboldened me to begin the journey, and who has been a faithful conversation partner throughout the process.

Finally, I thank the dedicated and faithful pastors in the province of Apurímac, Peru (as well as my students at Evangelical Theological College in Addis Ababa, Ethiopia), for their friendship and encouragement throughout the years.

Abbreviations

Old Testament/Hebrew Bible

Gen	Judg	Neh	Song	Hos	Nah
Exod	Ruth	Esth	Isa	Joel	Hab
Lev	1–2 Sam	Job	Jer	Amos	Zeph
Num	1–2 Kgs	Ps (*pl.* Pss)	Lam	Obad	Hag
Deut	1–2 Chr	Prov	Ezek	Jonah	Zech
Josh	Ezra	Eccl	Dan	Mic	Mal

New Testament

Matt	Acts	Eph	1–2 Tim	Jas	Rev
Mark	Rom	Phil	Titus	1–2 Pet	
Luke	1–2 Cor	Col	Phlm	1–2–3 John	
John	Gal	1–2 Thess	Heb	Jude	

References Works

AB   Anchor Bible

AoF   *Articles of Faith*

BECNT   Baker Exegetical Commentary of the New Testament

BoM	*Book of Mormon*
CNTOT	*Commentary on the New Testament Use of the Old Testament*
D&C	*Doctrine and Covenants*
DJG	*Dictionary of Jesus and the Gospels*
DLNT	*Dictionary of the Later New Testament and Its Developments*
DOTP	*Dictionary of the Old Testament Prophets*
DPL	*Dictionary of Paul and His Letters*
DTIB	*Dictionary for Theological Interpretation of the Bible*
EBC	Expositor's Bible Commentary
EM	*Encyclopedia of Mormonism*
EMS	*Evening and Morning Star*
ESV	English Standard Version
HC	*History of the Church*
ICC	International Critical Commentary
JD	*Journal of Discourses*
JETS	*Journal of the Evangelical Theological Society*
JST	*Joseph Smith Translation*
JSNT	*Journal for the Study of the New Testament*
JSOT	*Journal for the Study of the Old Testament*
JSNTSup	Journal for the Study of the New Testament Supplement
JSOTSup	Journal for the Study of the Old Testament Supplement
JTI	*Journal of Theological Interpretation*
LDS	*Church of Jesus Christ of Latter-day Saints*
MA	*Messenger and Advocate*
NAC	New American Commentary
NASB	New American Standard Bible
NIB	New Interpreter's Bible
NICNT	New International Commentary of the New Testament

NICOT	New International Commentary of the Old Testament
NIDNTT	*New International Dictionary of New Testament Theology*
NIGTC	New International Greek Testament Commentary
NIV	New International Version
PGP	*Pearl of Great Price*
PNTC	Pillar New Testament Commentary
SHBC	Smyth and Helwys Bible Commentary
SP	Sacra Pagina
TDNT	*Theological Dictionary of the New Testament*
TINT	*Theological Interpretation of the New Testament: A Book-by-Book Survey*
TOTC	Tyndale Old Testament Commentaries
TS	*Times and Seasons*
WBC	Word Biblical Commentary
ZECNT	Zondervan Exegetical Commentary on the New Testament

Introduction

THE CHURCH OF JESUS Christ of Latter-day Saints, otherwise known as the Mormons, casts the interpretive net widely in their reading of the Bible. This book is a brief introduction to Mormon hermeneutics and proposes five LDS approaches to ancient Scripture. I will argue in this investigation that despite implicit and explicit claims by the LDS to the contrary, their uses of the Bible focus on the modern horizon of the interpreter to the neglect of the ancient horizon of the text.

Initially, however, we need to gain a broader understanding of the issues at hand. In the first chapter, I note the danger of oversimplification, the complexity of the LDS church, and the lack of a published LDS hermeneutic. I also introduce Critical Realism, one of the prevailing frameworks in the arena of theological scholarship. In chapter 2, I investigate two LDS presuppositions evinced in their literature. The first is an asymmetrical perspective on the Bible, whereas the second concerns "continuing revelation." Given the conceptual scaffolding afforded by these introductory matters, the subsequent chapters examine the church's five specific hermeneutical approaches to the Bible.

Chapter 3 details a prevalent insistence on "literal" interpretation. Although ostensibly literal, I will argue that these LDS readings are, in fact, "literalistic." Chapter 4 is an examination of LDS allegorical interpretation that is more accurately labeled "allegorization." This is followed by a sociological exploration in chapter 5. In the initial decades of the movement, a sociological reading purported to legitimize the separation of the LDS church (a "new reform movement"), from the existing church of the nineteenth century (the "parent community"). Chapter 6 describes what I have called "emendatory" interpretation, where the *modern* LDS church not only claims to restore the *ancient* biblical text, but also, at times, clarifies the meaning of phrases from the KJV (King James Version). In chapter 7, I investigate a "re-authoring" of the Bible that amounts to "locutionary reassignment," where a phrase or word is lifted from its original biblical context and re-used with a new meaning. Although it is impossible to shoehorn every use of the Bible by the LDS into one of these five approaches—literal, allegorical, sociological, emendatory and "re-authoring"—these offer a general overview of the complex and expansive reality of Mormon hermeneutics.[1] Finally, in chapter 8, I discuss specific insights of the field of "philosophical hermeneutics." This field highlights important aspects of the interpretive process, e.g., the universality of hermeneutics, the unavoidable ontological aspect, presuppositional matters, the community in interpretation, and the importance of application. The hermeneutical insights of Hans-Georg Gadamer will also help me gain clarity.

It is axiomatic that "that which is new is always exciting, and there is an inevitable tendency for its importance to be overestimated."[2] This is frequently illustrated in Bible interpretation, with *modern* application overriding *ancient* meaning. It is seen in several traditions, e.g., the conservative evangelical tradition, as well as the Mormon church. At the outset, it is important to note that the Mormons are not the only tradition that seems to ignore the ancient horizon of the biblical text.

For instance, the conservative evangelical tradition (my own tradition), at times tends to neglect the ancient meaning. First Samuel 17 is taught to merely encourage us "to fight the giants in our lives" (lesson from David and Goliath). The only reason for the story of Peter and the waves (Matt 14:30) seems to be a reminder to "keep our eyes on Jesus in the storms of life." Do we look to Scripture only to extract analogies for memorable Sunday School lessons? Is this the extent of our Bible interpretation? Is this an appropriate response given the depth and richness of Scripture? Stuart Allen writes that there has emerged "a type of believer whose only interest in the Bible is what *he gets out of it for himself and his own comfort* . . . His aim is self and his own particular experience . . . In a

---

1. These five categories are my summary of LDS hermeneutical activity and are by no means reflective of any position, officially sanctioned or otherwise, of the LDS church.

2. Neill and Wright, *Interpretation*, 161.

subtle way it keeps this sort of person *pre-occupied with himself,* instead of being occupied with Christ and God's great and glorious redemptive plan."[3] While the biblical text must be seen as relevant to the modern church (see discussions in chapters 1 and 8), this relevance cannot be at the expense of ancient meaning. Every interpretation of the Bible, LDS or otherwise, should be held accountable. Every interpretation of the Bible that focuses inordinately on the self, LDS or otherwise, should be called into question. I begin with a question for all Bible readers: How serious are we with *correct* biblical interpretation that takes into account the *ancient* meaning?

3. Allen in Thiselton, *New Horizons,* 193, emphasis added.

— 1 —

Mormon Hermeneutics

1.1. Brief Description of the LDS

LDS THINKERS ARGUE THAT a pervasive apostasy occurred after the death of the apostles in the first century, and the church of Jesus Christ needed a complete "Restoration." When Joseph Smith Jr. (hereafter Joseph Smith), purportedly received a personal visit from God in 1820, the Restoration occurred. This divine visitation, referred to as the First Vision, inaugurated the revelatory focus of the Mormon church. Their teaching is based upon the reception of "continuing revelation," with individual as well as prophetic aspects of this revelation. The modern books of the *Book of Mormon* (at times referred to as BoM), the *Doctrine and Covenants* (D&C), as well as the *Pearl of Great Price* (PGP), supplement the Bible as LDS scriptures. Although the church warns against the hazards of a confining creed or statement of faith, basic parameters of their thinking are contained in thirteen "Articles of Faith." These Articles were written by Joseph Smith and are found in the *Pearl of Great Price*. The church states that in 1971 there were three million members, yet today there are more than sixteen million members worldwide. Thus, there has been an "accelerating growth pattern" with "a million new members added every several years."[1] The Association for Religious Data says, however, that in 2010 (the latest date for data) membership in the LDS Church was at six

---

1. LDS, "Growth of the Church."

million, while in 1970 there were two million members.[2] Regardless of the exact figures, there has been significant growth in the LDS Church. Decades ago, based on then-current growth rates, non-LDS sociologist Rodney Stark projected exponential growth for the LDS—estimating as many as 265 million members by the year 2080.[3] Some observers are beginning to speak of the LDS as a *world* religion.[4] In view of such growth, an investigation into their uses of the Bible is warranted.

1.2. Challenges in the Investigation of LDS Hermeneutics

1.2.1. Oversimplification

In some publications, non-LDS authors have succumbed to the temptation of evaluating the LDS with simplistic reductions, caricatures, stereotypes, distortions, and misinformation.[5] Opponents have occasionally pigeonholed their teachings,[6] and given "outdated and inaccurate portraits of Mormon doctrine."[7] Dangers to be avoided in this book, then, include a narrow mindset,[8] a simplistic methodology that fails to do justice to the totality of the evidence,[9] or an oversimplification that presses the evidence to fit a prior theory.[10] My goal is to give the church a fair hearing and avoid a simplistic, reductionistic evaluation of their hermeneutical activity. Although their uses of the Bible are not monolithic, there are patterns of hermeneutical behavior that can be evaluated with some clarity.

2. Association for Religious Data, "Church of Jesus Christ of Latter-day Saints."

3. See Stark, "Rise of a New World Faith," 18–27; Stark, *Rise of Mormonism*, 2; cf. Ostling and Ostling, *Mormon America*, 381; Carl Mosser, in Beckwith et al., *New Mormon Challenge*, 61–71. However, see Dart, "Counting Mormons," 26–29.

4. Huff, "Gentile Recommends," 211; see the title for Givens, *By the Hand of Mormon: The American Scripture That Launched a New World Religion*; cf. Givens, *By the Hand of Mormon*, 11.

5. For reactions by LDS authors, see Arrington and Bitton, *Mormon Experience*, 340. For other responses, see Bitton, *Historical Dictionary*, 3; Millet and Johnson, *Bridging the Divide*, 173; Michaelsen, "Enigmas," 145–53; Jan Shipps in Eliason, *Mormons and Mormonism*, 147.

6. See Barlow, *Mormons and the Bible*, x.

7. See Carl Mosser in Beckwith et al., *New Mormon Challenge*, 29.

8. See Gorman, "Seamless Garment," 122, on the tendency toward narrowness.

9. For an example of a simplistic approach, see Wright, *People of God*, 118–19.

10. For an example of such a theory, see Thiselton, *Hermeneutics of Doctrine*, 39–40.

1.2.2. *The Complexity of the LDS*

According to LDS author Philip Barlow, "Mormonism is extraordinarily complex."[11] Jacob Baker claims that the complexity of their church inhibits straightforward classification.[12] For example, according to one outside observer, "One cannot even be sure if the object of our consideration is a sect, a mystery cult, a new religion, a church, a people, a nation, or an American subculture; indeed, at different times and places it is all of these."[13] Others have concluded that the LDS is "neither a church nor a sect, but rather a near nation, or a 'quasi-ethnic' group in the isolated Intermountain West."[14] Too often Mormonism "has been presented as monolithic and homogenous."[15] The theological language used by the LDS is often distinct from other Bible believers, so that "conventional theological categories do not always accurately translate from mainline Christianity to Mormonism."[16] One author admits, "Any attempt to describe Mormon doctrine is fraught with peril."[17] Additionally, "In the Mormon Church, official doctrines, speculative theories, and personally held beliefs have always co-existed. For many outsiders, this curious phenomenon defies explanation."[18] A specific example, challenging for outsiders, is that "Mormonism's doctrine of God is spread around several works regarded as scripture."[19] In this investigation, I will be focusing on the complex hermeneutical activity of the Salt Lake City, Utah church of Latter-day Saints.

11. Barlow, "Before Mormonism," 739.

12. Baker, *Mormonism at the Crossroads*, xiv; cf. Ericson, "Challenges of Defining Mormon Doctrine," 69–87. For Stephen Webb, it is ironic that many opponents simplistically pigeonhole the LDS, considering this complexity (Webb, *Mormon Christianity*, 24).

13. See Ahlstrom, *Religious History*, 508.

14. Jacobson et al., *Revisiting*, viii; cf. O'Dea, *The Mormons*, 115.

15. Beckwith et al., *New Mormon Challenge*, 21.

16. Givens, *Wrestling the Angel*, x.

17. Southerton, *Losing a Lost Tribe*, 3.

18. Widmer, *Mormonism and the Nature of God*, 157.

19. Beckwith and Parrish, *Mormon Concept of God*, 37.

1.2.3. The Lack of an Official LDS Hermeneutic

The general absence of published academic work on LDS hermeneutics is an added challenge in this investigation. Numerous LDS authors
describe this lacuna. Anthony Hutchinson admitted decades ago that
there was little, if any, official LDS hermeneutical work.[20] In 2013, Philip
Barlow stated, "The majority of Mormons remain in a hermeneutical
Eden, innocent of a conscious philosophy of interpretation."[21] A recent
LDS scholarly article by Julie Smith concurred: "Currently, there is great
debate but no consensus regarding LDS hermeneutics."[22] In another writing, because of the lack of "a formal LDS hermeneutic," Smith describes
members as "plodding along with unexamined assumptions about what
is and what is not legitimate to do when interpreting the scriptures."[23]
Richard Hopkins points to varying opinions on the meaning of differing
biblical passages, thus seeming to question the possibility of accuracy in
hermeneutical reflection.[24] Another LDS author considers it problematic
"to assume that systemic philosophical thought—even the application
of hermeneutical categories—ought to be employed in order to clarify
the content of revelation."[25] The practice of "modern biblical scholarship"
(which presumably includes a theory of interpretation) is disputed by
some in the Mormon tradition: "The Bible need not be subjected to such
rigorous examination; to do so [is] to 'look beyond the mark' or give too
much credence to the philosophies of men."[26] In addition, Ian Barber sees
that "the conservative Protestant hermeneutic proceeded from an unre-
alistic expectation of the revelatory process," since the Bible was recorded

20. Hutchinson, "LDS Approaches," 99.

21. Barlow, *Mormons and the Bible*, 248. Barlow's book is an attempt "to correct
this deficiency" (see Gutjahr, "Measuring Stick," 205). However, Barlow doesn't cat-
egorize LDS hermeneutics, as I am attempting to do here.

22. Smith, "Five Impulses," 2.

23. Smith, "LDS Hermeneutics."

24. Hopkins, *Biblical Mormonism*, 33. One assumes, however, that Hopkins considers his own hermeneutical reflection (as implied in the title of his book) as ensuring
accurate biblical interpretation. This apparent disallowance of hermeneutical activity—amid obvious interpretive actions—causes one to wonder of the extent to which
LDS authors are aware their own hermeneutical activity. For Hopkins, LDS interpreters rely on "common sense, spiritual insight, and respect for the plain language" in
order to produce a "satisfactory hermeneutic" (Hopkins, *Biblical Mormonism*, 34).

25. Siebach, "Dialogue on Theology," 467.

26. See Greaves, "Education of a Bible Scholar," 74. Greaves does not necessarily
agree with such a stance.

by "an imperfect human agent."[27] When Barber questions this "Protestant hermeneutic," he implicitly casts doubt on hermeneutical reflection. Non-LDS observers agree with these observations: "Most Mormons remain aloof from such questions as the philosophy of interpretation or the principles of hermeneutics."[28]

It is necessary to mention, however, some basic hermeneutical guidelines, such as looking at the literary context, knowing the original languages, and application of the text, in some LDS books.[29] Nevertheless, there are various reasons advanced for the lack of a published LDS hermeneutic. Given their views concerning ongoing, continuing revelation from God, they generally avoid official pronouncements, since such declarations could become obsolete. In a sense, "everything the LDS church teaches *now* is official *now*, but that may all change later, as it has in the past."[30] LDS author Terryl Givens explains that "Mormon doctrine is by definition impossible to fix; reflection on the meaning of this living, evolving tradition is, therefore, inescapably a lively and contested theological enterprise."[31] Givens continues: "All attempts to capture the essence of Mormon thought, as is true of any living tradition, are limited and provisional."[32] LDS scriptural corroboration is given in *Doctrine and Covenants*, where God claimed the prerogative to "command and revoke, as it seemeth me good" (D&C 56:4).

The very nature of LDS thinking evades scholarship or official declarations, for, according to James Faulconer, "revelation is *the* Latter-day Saint theology."[33] In another writing, Faulconer discloses that they "may have a greater tendency to morph more than other faiths. Considered diachronously, some accounts of Mormonism and Mormon belief may be contradictory, and there is perhaps no synchronous account without unexplained or nonintegrable gaps. There may be no one, satisfactory

---

27. Barber, "Beyond the Literalist Constraint," 21.

28. Ostling and Ostling, *Mormon America*, 297.

29. Hopkins, *Biblical Mormonism*, 33–34; Fielding McConkie, "The 'How' of Scriptural Study," 51–68; LDS, "How Do I Study Effectively," 17–27; Faulconer, *Scripture Study*, 12–13.

30. This is the viewpoint of non-LDS author Ronald Huggins. See Huggins, "Lorenzo Snow's Couplet," 561.

31. Givens, *Wrestling the Angel*, x.

32. Givens, *Wrestling the Angel*, 22; cf. Barlow, *Mormons and the Bible*, 237–38; Millet, "What Do We Really Believe?," 265–81; White, *Mormon Neo-orthodoxy*, xxi.

33. Faulconer, "Rethinking Theology," 180.

story of Mormon belief."[34] Modern claims may be "inherently inimical" to the articulation of what the church believes, since any such articulation would be viewed as "excessively rigid and unchangeable."[35] There is always "more to know"—consequently, a "complete system of doctrine" cannot be articulated.[36] Sterling McMurrin writes that Mormon theology "is not overencumbered with creeds and official pronouncements."[37] As compared to other religious perspectives, the LDS exhibit "a relative lack of precision and sophistication" and refrain from "a rigorous attempt to systematize" their doctrine.[38] According to LDS author Nathan Oman, their thinking, despite some important exceptions, "has largely eschewed closely reasoned systematic theology."[39] This would include a systematic presentation of their hermeneutic. Sheldon Greaves writes of a surprising lack of LDS scholarship, by noting that a LDS scholar with a "Ph.D. in biblical studies from a major university," eschewed theories of interpretation and biblical criticism in his academic classes at Brigham Young University, and instead emphasized "evangelical gospel teaching."[40] In general, then, the church's scholars are suspicious of any use of theology or philosophy, i.e., the articulation of an official hermeneutic, that would potentially obscure revelation.[41]

A further reason for the absence of an official hermeneutic is a pragmatic, experientially driven ethos. An LDS self-understanding is described as "concerned more with praxis than dogmatic theology."[42] LDS author Charles Harrell points out that "Jesus himself never left a

---

34. Faulconer, "Advice for a Mormon Intellectual."

35. Properzi, *Mormonism and the Emotions*, 5.

36. Brian Birch, in Baker, *Mormonism at the Crossroads*, 52.

37. McMurrin, *Theological Foundations*, 112.

38. Carrigan, "Mormon Mirage," 4. However, according to non-LDS authors Paul Owen and Carl Mosser, the LDS is building a "contextual superstructure necessary for a proper interpretation of the Bible" (Owen and Mosser, "Mormon Scholarship," 200).

39. Oman, "Living Oracles," 1.

40. See Greaves, "Education of a Bible Scholar," 66.

41. See further discussion in Properzi, *Mormonism and the Emotions*, 2–7. Nevertheless, when theology is separated from biblical studies, according to N. T. Wright, one is left with an approach that "lapses into a mere *ad hoc* use of the Bible, finding bits and pieces to fit into a scheme derived from somewhere else," with interpreters "finding a proof-text, or even a proof-theme, from the Bible" (Wright, *People of God*, 138). This *ad hoc* use of Scripture can also be described as privileging the modern horizon over the ancient meaning.

42. Jacob Baker, in Baker, *Mormonism at the Crossroads*, xiii.

systematized theology, but rather it was said of him that he 'went about doing good' (Acts 10:38)."[43] In addition, while Nathan Oman acknowledges "a voluminous body of Mormon writing on many subjects... the overwhelming majority of this work is homiletic and is meant to inspire and motivate its audience rather than provide them with careful conceptual analysis."[44] We will note in this book the importance of this statement: *many LDS works inspire and motivate*, and therefore focus on modern realities to the neglect of the ancient biblical meaning.

To summarize, we see that theological, epistemological, historical, and sociological factors demonstrate the complexity of the LDS. Considering the past tendency of outside observers to oversimplify their conclusions concerning the LDS, a broader approach to methodological aspects must be used.

1.3. Methodological Parameters

Human understanding does not follow strict principles or fixed rules of interpretation.[45] Nonetheless, to a certain extent, methodological *parameters* are helpful, even essential, for any hermeneutical investigation. Such parameters must include what Bernard Lonergan calls a "self-correcting process of learning that spirals into the meaning of the whole by using each new part to fill out and qualify and correct the understanding reached in earlier parts."[46] For example, in chapter 2, the context-providing description of two foundational presuppositions of the LDS will fill out and qualify their specific uses of the Bible outlined in later chapters. Robust assistance, in the form of methodological parameters, is needed to navigate between hermeneutical despair and hermeneutical arrogance. The former could lead to hasty declarations of the impossibility of any discernible meaning, while the latter dogmatically proclaims one's own perspective as the final word, with no dissenting discussion allowed.[47] Jean Grondin comments that Gadamer did not intend any "sharp opposition between truth and method," and neither insisted on nor prohibited

---

43. Harrell, *"This Is My Doctrine,"* 505.

44. Oman, "Living Oracles," 2.

45. Porter and Malcolm, "Remaining Hermeneutical Issues," 159.

46. Lonergan, *Method in Theology*, 159.

47. See Westphal, *Whose Community?*, 10.

the utilization of methodological parameters.[48] Gadamer was against the "dogmatic assertion that there can be no truth outside of method," yet acknowledged that "certainly truth can be achieved by way of method."[49]

Understanding biblical texts, as well as another religious tradition, is a complex process that necessitates a level of interdisciplinary study. Effective methodological parameters would eclectically employ various academic disciplines—including, for example, psychology, with its questions about "selfhood, self-interest, and self-deception,"[50] as well as philosophy and exegetical investigation.[51] Also to be considered are the "many sub-fields of theology, biblical studies and philosophical hermeneutics," along with the sociological issues related to diverse religious communities.[52] The investigation of a specific text would examine matters of "textuality, epistemology, ontology, reference and genre."[53] However, lest I advocate for an over-emphasis on academic approaches,[54] understanding also demonstrates an artistic aspect, as opposed to an exact science. Such an artistic approach will exhibit experiential knowledge and even intuition.[55] Thus, while I expect to utilize varying fields of study in a methodological approach, it is impossible to mandate an overly narrow methodology. My intention is not to offer the LDS a set of rules for interpretation, but rather, a critically well-founded assessment of their hermeneutical activity.

1.3.1. Worldview Investigation

To understand the "other," "patient and attentive listening"[56] is necessary. An empathetic comprehension of the "other" stands at the very heart of

48. See Grondin, *Philosophical Hermeneutics*, 132.

49. Grondin, *Philosophical Hermeneutics*, 132. See also Gadamer, *Truth and Method*, 5–6.

50. Thiselton, *Hermeneutics*, 4.

51. See Porter and Robinson, *Hermeneutics*, 245–46.

52. See Selby, *Comical Doctrine*, 4, 8–9.

53. Selby, *Comical Doctrine*, 236.

54. This is especially the case since hermeneutics has traditionally been seen as a "theory that promised to lay out the rules governing the discipline of interpretation" (Grondin, *Philosophical Hermeneutics*, 1).

55. See Gadamer, *Truth and Method*, 8–9.

56. See Thiselton, *Hermeneutics of Doctrine*, xx.

hermeneutics,[57] and true dialogue presupposes the need for "epistemic humility."[58] Just as the practice of hermeneutics calls for vigilance and critical thinking,[59] so also the evaluation of the hermeneutics of another religious tradition. There should be a "steadfast refusal to take anything for granted," and every axiom must be put to the test and verified.[60] It is difficult to "orient oneself in the vast field of present-day philosophy" and one must "make the attempt again and again."[61] This is true, also, of the investigation into the considerable field of LDS hermeneutics.

Furthermore, I recognize that "all study, all reading of texts, all attempts to reconstruct history, take place within particular worldviews."[62] The LDS worldview will need to be investigated—their deep-level perception of reality and the framework, or grid, through which their world is perceived.[63] Thus, chapter 2 will begin to describe the deep-level perception of Scripture by the LDS church. Published LDS thinking also hints at this study of worldviews: "The doctrinal tenets of any religion are best understood within a broad context, and thoughtful analysis is required to understand them."[64] Another LDS publication concurs: "Getting at the heart of Mormonism is best undertaken not by narrowly focusing on controversy and getting mired in esoteric theological debates, but through a more imaginative examination of the worldview that inspires its members."[65] Thus, at the outset, I recognize the need for worldview investigation, as well as patient, consistent listening, in an effort to avoid simplistic generalization and oversimplification.

I will inquire as to whether the LDS worldview holds to unexamined assumptions that induces "implicit structures of discursive privilege."[66] For example, the foundational LDS presupposition of "continuing

---

57. Ernst Fuchs, in Thiselton, *Hermeneutics*, 6.

58. Donald W. Musser, in Baker, *Mormonism at the Crossroads*, 44.

59. Grondin, *Philosophical Hermeneutics*, 12.

60. Neill and Wright, *Interpretation*, 29; cf. Schweiker, "Sacrifice," 791–810.

61. Grondin, *Philosophical Hermeneutics*, 8.

62. Wright, *People of God*, 137.

63. See Wright, *People of God*, 122–26, for various perspectives on worldviews.

64. LDS, "Approaching Mormon Doctrine."

65. LDS, "A Mormon Worldview."

66. See the discussion of the "discursive privilege" of atheism as the intellectual baseline inherited as an unexamined legacy of the Enlightenment, that has resulted in making "religious belief alone [as] something which is to be explained or defended" (Archer, *Transcendence*, 5).

revelation" may illegitimately privilege their *modern* discourse. On the other hand, other traditions may exhibit a discursive privilege by silencing this LDS perspective on "continuing revelation." Furthermore, I will evaluate the place and impact of "continuing revelation," in comparison to the ancient and fixed state of the Bible. An assessment of an LDS hermeneutic will need to be as comprehensive as possible, since the relationship between the LDS and the Bible has been described as "composite, layered, surprising, evolving, not uniform among adherents or across time, and partially obscure to both believers and observers."[67] The possibility of "hidden scaffolding" in their worldview will be considered.[68] In addition, the acceptance of the BoM, the D&C, and the PGP as *additional* scriptures will be explored as I examine the uses of the Bible by the LDS.[69]

All religious traditions, LDS or otherwise, need to attend carefully to the processes involved in their reading.[70] Every reader brings significant assumptions to the biblical text. Several presuppositions of an LDS interpreter of the Bible will be explored. Relatedly, the role of the LDS community in interpretation will be investigated.[71] Every biblical text comes from an ancient, historical "locatedness." Every modern interpreter and community are similarly "located." Does the LDS sufficiently acknowledge the "locatedness" of the ancient biblical text, as well as their contemporary "locatedness" and worldview? Recognition of my own limited, "located" perspective will be necessary as I approach their hermeneutic.

Many other hermeneutical considerations are at play in this investigation. LDS author James Faulconer writes: "Scripture is more important than rational explanation."[72] There appears to be significant epistemological ramifications and hermeneutical consequences in this ambiguous statement, given that "rational explanation" was used in the assertion. Regarding biblical interpretation, whether by the LDS or a different tradition,

---

67. Barlow, *Mormons and the Bible*, xxviii.

68. See the concept of "hidden scaffolding" in Bartholomew, "Three Horizons," 130.

69. Philip Barlow admits that in the case of Mormonism, the issue of scripture is "complicated by such dimensions as oral scripture, private scripture, noncanonized scripture, [and] temporary scripture" (Barlow, *Mormons and the Bible*, xii).

70. See Wright, *People of God*, 9.

71. Concerning all church communities, Daniel Treier explains that ecclesiology is a "crucial issue" concerning the interpretation of Scripture (Treier, *Theological Interpretation*, 32).

72. Faulconer, "Rethinking Theology," 180.

the question "must always be asked, whether scripture is being used to serve an existing theology or vice versa."[73] Could the LDS (or my own religious perspective), be described as "more of an all-embracing ideology, a Procrustean bed, an *a priori* system that simply discounts or reinterprets any evidence that might call its fundamental veracity into account"?[74]

The assumed influence of the apostasy of the early church, as well as the Restoration initiated by Joseph Smith, will be important considerations. This pervasive apostasy is called the Great Apostasy.[75] The role of the Great Apostasy in LDS thinking and Bible interpretation cannot be exaggerated. An important consideration is whether the Great Apostasy has taken on "a life of its own as a monolithic reification" that "short-circuits the kind of careful textual analysis, empirical study and interpretive synthesis" that is found in the best historical scholarship.[76] Historical investigation is a complex endeavor, and there is no such thing as "mere history."[77] Carl Becker notes that the modern historian does not stick to the facts, but "the facts stick to him."[78] The writing of history is never an impartial recounting of the basic facts. It is rather a *re-presentation* of the past. Human historical actions are "always complex and impossible to reduce to single causes, intentions, or motivations."[79] Thus, we all face increasingly difficult hindrances as contemporary investigators trying to understand documents from the past.[80] According to James Barr, "Historical analysis is not an objective science but produces only hypothetical reconstructions of what might have been the case," as well as, "Far from being scientifically objective, historical analysis may be heavily indebted to ideological factors."[81]

It is possible that an academic, systematic investigation will not be perceived as relevant in LDS thinking.[82] In fact, are outside corrobora-

73. Wright, *Scripture*, 71.

74. See Trueman, *Histories and Fallacies*, 98, 103.

75. Millet et al., *LDS Beliefs*, 46.

76. See the concept of monolithic reification in Trueman, *Histories and Fallacies*, 146.

77. See Wright, *Jesus and the Victory*, 6.

78. Becker, in Ellis, "Perspectives on Biblical Interpretation," 492.

79. Trueman, *Histories and Fallacies*, 106.

80. Porter, "Biblical Hermeneutics," 32–33.

81. Barr, "Allegory and Historicism," 106.

82. This is even more poignant given the "methodological tendency of scholars to systematize ideas as fully as they can, indeed . . . [to] oversystematize them" (Davies, *Mormon Culture*, 71).

tion, verification, and falsifiability legitimate parameters for the investigation of their tradition? LDS author Grant Palmer believes that some observations by non-LDS critics are unreliable, yet he recognizes the need to listen to outsiders, for "your friends don't always tell you what you need to hear."[83] Similarly, D. Michael Quinn states that "primary emphasis must be given to direct evidence from friendly sources. Nevertheless, it is misleading to ignore or reject out-of-hand direct evidence from unfriendly sources."[84] Finally, an approach to LDS thinking must take into account their view that "true religion is a thing of the heart as well as the mind, and when we tread there we tread on holy ground, ground that must not be trampled or harrowed up unnecessarily."[85] Of course, this focus on the heart is not the exclusive territory of the LDS. As non-LDS scholars point out, the Bible was not written as an academic textbook, but "out of a burning experience of the reality of God as made manifest in Jesus Christ, and as a means by which a like experience could be communicated to the readers."[86] These methodological parameters, as well as others, will guide my investigation and evaluation.

1.4. Utilization of Critical Realism

The philosophical framework (i.e., methodological parameter) to be employed is Critical Realism (CR), brought to New Testament studies by Ben Meyer, following the work of Bernard Lonergan.[87] In light of the numerous challenges of this investigation into the complexity of LDS hermeneutics, the "philosophical parameters" of CR translate into a useful framework.[88] CR is a methodology/framework that combines the strengths of a variety of approaches.[89] It demonstrates critical reflection,

---

83. Palmer, *Insider's View*, viii.

84. Quinn, *Early Mormonism*, xvi.

85. Millet and Johnson, *Bridging the Divide*, xxii.

86. Neill and Wright, *Interpretation*, 236.

87. See Lonergan, *Method in Theology*; Meyer, *Critical Realism*; Dunn, *Jesus Remembered*, 110.

88. See Andrew Wright's views on philosophical parameters in Wright, *Christianity and Critical Realism*, 3.

89. Moritz, "Critical but Real," 179–82. Concerning other approaches, Moritz mentions phenomenology and positivism, and to a limited extent, romanticism.

perception of relevant objects and ideas, a search for intelligible patterns, and reasonable, balanced judgment.[90]

In the words of leading proponent Roy Bhaskar, CR includes the three concepts of ontological realism, epistemic relativism, and judgmental rationality.[91] It assumes literary texts, as well as the world, are truly "out there" and are independent of how we would evaluate them. There genuinely exists empirical, "real" data outside of ourselves (hence, "ontological realism") that we investigate and evaluate.[92] Our entire framework is labeled "realism" because of its insistence on the existence of empirical data. Using a framework such as CR allows me to view the LDS worldview as a reality that exists independently of my perception of it. CR also requires the biblical interpreter to view the text as external and independent. As soon as any text is authored, it embodies conceptuality that is "other" than either the author or the interpreter. This external "other" is then interpreted. Ontological realism results in texts having "a *prima facie* claim on the reader, namely, to be construed in accord with its intended sense."[93] This "intended sense" is tethered to the text itself, and must be the controlling factor in interpretation, since the text is the only entity available to the interpreter.

However, because of the epistemic relativism of what it means to be human (Bhaskar's second concept), the intended sense of the text will not be objectively accessible.[94] We can, indeed, apprehend the text—yet only as mediated through our own perspectives and experiences.[95] A theory of reading is needed that does justice both to the reader as a particular human being and to the text as an entity on its own—and not something to be used at the reader's whim.[96] While CR recognizes that, ontologically, there is an "objective world," it admits that there is no truly objective view.[97] We know through our experiences, and "it is inconceivable

90. See these insights of Bernard Lonergan in Thiselton, *Hermeneutics of Doctrine*, 152.

91. Roy Bhaskar, in Wright, *Christianity and Critical Realism*, 9.

92. See, e.g., Archer, *Transcendence*, 1; Meyer, *Critical Realism*, xi; Dunn, *Jesus Remembered*, 110.

93. Meyer, *Critical Realism*, xi. In Meyer's book, see especially chapter 2, "The Primacy of the Intended Sense of Texts," 17–55.

94. See Moritz, "Critical Realism," 149.

95. Westphal, *Whose Community?*, 18; cf. Moritz, "Critical Realism," 147.

96. Wright, *People of God*, 62.

97. See Archer, *Transcendence*, 1–2.

that sound judgment results from looking 'objectively' at the world of experience."[98] Indeed, "Gadamer exposes as fantasy the notion of 'sheer objectivity' wherein one would see, with no expectations or anticipations, what is simply there—'the facts.'"[99] Gadamer is at variance with the "old hermeneutical objectivity."[100] CR, then, is a useful framework as it describes knowledge not as simplistic "reading and seeing," but rather a conjunction of experience, understanding and judging.[101] It emphasizes the locatedness of interpreters, including their communities, and the grid (or lens) that they view reality through.[102] However, the subjective lens used by individuals or communities is not necessarily a negative prejudice or limiting presupposition that distorts the object in view. The "notion of subjectivity in interpretation per se is not an evil to be rejected or lamented; it is to be welcomed as an aspect of human creationality . . . In this sense interpretation has to be subjective to be relevant."[103] In fact, following late modernity's insights on hermeneutical reflection, we are now more conscious of being perspectival and of possessing potentially helpful pre-understandings.[104]

As we approach a perspective other than our own, CR insists that we "be aware of our own viewpoint."[105] Additionally, "human self-knowledge" is not only a "prerequisite of" but also a "continuing factor" in the complex process of interpretation.[106] There should be "a heightened degree of self-reflective awareness, especially with respect to one's own chronic inauthenticity and well-rehearsed habits of self-evasiveness."[107] This self-awareness should then be coupled with an awareness of "historical intentionality." In other words, an "authentic subjectivity" would ensure that an interpreter is not only self-aware, but also cognizant of the historical intention of the ancient text.[108]

98. Moritz, "Critical Realism," 148.

99. Adams, *Oxford Handbook of Theology*, 512.

100. Detweiler and Robbins, "From New Criticisms," 240.

101. Dunn, *Jesus Remembered*, 110.

102. See Wright, *People of God*, 36; cf. Moritz, "Critical Realism," 147.

103. Moritz, "Critical Realism," 149; cf. Meyer, *Critical Realism*, xiii.

104. See Grondin, *Philosophical Hermeneutics*, 17.

105. See Wright, *People of God*, 66, 138; cf. Selby, *Comical Doctrine*, 165.

106. Meyer, *Reality and Illusion*, 92; cf. McLean, *Biblical Interpretation*, 39.

107. McLean, *Biblical Interpretation*, 188; cf. Gadamer, *Wahrheit und Methode*, 274.

108. See Moritz, "Critical but Real," 189.

After an investigation into the ontological realism of external texts, filtered through the epistemic relativity of the interpreter, there follows critical reflection, or a judgmental rationality (Bhaskar's third concept). This includes an empathetic understanding of what was observed.[109] Our framework exhibits its "critical" nature here because of its emphasis on the possibility of located individuals investigating and evaluating data. In addition, it is "critical" by *not* assuming that theological conclusions are exact representations of the empirical data. It is an analysis that attempts to approximate reality, and it recognizes the impossibility of "a final statement of theological truth; the process of validation and improvement never ceases."[110]

As N. T. Wright argues, CR is the theory best suited to doing justice to the complex nature of texts and history.[111] It accomplishes this by "taking seriously the storied nature of knowledge and interpretation."[112] Other methodologies may claim to see a text "straight" with instant access to the raw data of the text and the accompanying ability to make complete, objective judgments about its meaning.[113] Such positivistic, naïve realism ignores the epistemic relativism addressed by CR. This naïve realism is overly optimistic, as it "tends to identify the way things are with the way they appear."[114] Also, an authentic utilization of CR would not obscure the ontological realism of the text or imply that a reader's own sense data is the only concrete, accessible reality in the interpretation process.[115] Neither is CR a full-blown postmodern perspective that exaggerates epistemic relativism by implying that only the interpretations of texts actually exist.[116] Instead, as we have seen, because of ontological realism, it postulates that every literary text exists externally from the interpreter, and therefore, should not be "re-authored" to become an individual's personal interpretation. CR avoids a scientistic mentality that claims epistemic certainty. The empiricist and idealist hegemony

109. See Wright, *People of God*, 36–37.

110. See Osborne, *Hermeneutical Spiral*, 398; cf. Blomberg, "Historical-Critical," 45.

111. See Wright, *People of God*, 64.

112. Moritz, "Critical but Real," 185–86.

113. See Wright, *People of God*, 32–33; cf. Moritz, "Critical Realism," 148.

114. Vanhoozer, *Is There a Meaning?*, 299. We will see further problems with this in chapter 3.

115. Wright, *People of God*, 34–35.

116. See Wright, *Scripture*, 112.

inherited from the Enlightenment denies the ability of the judgmental rationality of CR to make reasoned (though provisional) conclusions.[117] This empiricism claimed that "authentic knowledge" resulted from objective purity that was uncontaminated "by the subjectivity of local place, specific time and particular culture."[118] Yet, "absolute certainty based on objective knowledge," although assumed by many, has been shown to be "castles in the air."[119] Again, CR acknowledges a subjectivity of place and time; an epistemic relativity, given that every interpreter stands somewhere. At the same time, it does not claim to advance "pure objectivity," as if such a construct existed in the realm of interpretive possibility. Instead, it sets forth a qualified rationality based on and aimed at reasoned conclusions and assumptions that are subject to hermeneutical scrutiny.

In sum, a critical realist framework of ontological realism, epistemic relativism and judgmental rationality will be a helpful guide since I am a "located" interpreter seeking to understand a separate faith tradition than my own. For Wright, CR is a useful framework to guide interpreters through the "labyrinths of New Testament study."[120] This also holds true for the complexity of the uses of the Bible by the LDS church.

1.5. Outlook: LDS Hermeneutics as the Object of Investigation

My argument is that despite implicit and explicit claims by the LDS to the contrary, the church's uses of the Bible focus on the modern horizon of the interpreter to the neglect of the ancient horizon of the text. Nevertheless, there are instances of the LDS validation of the ancient text. Julie Smith writes in her commentary on the book of Mark: "The primary question that this commentary seeks to answer is this: What would this story have meant to Mark's earliest audiences?"[121] James Faulconer writes of the need to "always consider the historical and cultural context of a

---

117. See Wright, *Christianity and Critical Realism*, 3, 13.

118. Wright, *Christianity and Critical Realism*, 4; cf. Treier, *Theological Interpretation*, 34.

119. Selby, *Comical Doctrine*, 221.

120. See Wright, *People of God*, 45.

121. Smith, *Gospel according to Mark*, 15. However, throughout the commentary, she admits to giving "multiple options" for the meaning of different biblical texts (Smith, *Gospel according to Mark*, 20)—thus, casting doubt upon the possibility of finding the correct *ancient* meaning.

passage or book."[122] David Wright describes "Isaiah 29 in Its Context," and "Isaiah 48–49 in Their Original Context."[123] However, the contention of this book is that examples such as these are the exception rather than the rule.

In the following chapter, I discuss two foundational presuppositions that appear critical to their worldview. These presuppositions uncover important hermeneutical tendencies. In a broad work such as this, I have tried to be thorough in choosing my conversation partners. These partners include dozens of LDS authors, past and present. In the end, however, I have had to be somewhat selective. Nonetheless, my argument will concentrate on their varied uses of the biblical texts. Therefore, in chapters 3–7, I will consider what appear to be the five most crucial interpretive practices of LDS: literal, allegorical, sociological, emendatory and "re-authoring." Following chapters 5 and 7, I will present a case study of a biblical text, to explore whether the LDS allows for the ontological realism of biblical texts, whether LDS hermeneutical activity is merely inspiring and motivating, and whether interpretation occurs in accordance with its intended sense. Then, in chapter 8, as a final component of my argument, I will examine important facets of philosophical hermeneutics. Since my "locatedness" may obscure a balanced, reasoned judgment, more voices are needed to assist me in this evaluation of Mormon hermeneutics.

122. Faulconer, *Scripture Study*, 102.

123. Wright, "Joseph Smith's Interpretation," 196–99, 186–90.

2

Two Foundational Presuppositions

THE INVESTIGATION OF PRESUPPOSITIONAL matters is the requisite conceptual scaffolding needed to survey more clearly the five categories of biblical interpretation by the LDS. At the same time, these presuppositions matter hermeneutically, and contribute to my argument. The first presupposition is the asymmetry illustrated in their perspective on the Bible. There is a consistent elevation alongside a diminution of the Bible. The second presupposition concerns "continuing revelation," that is, ongoing communication from God to humankind. In our discussion, some features of this chapter touch on theological issues and their ramifications. This theological focus is necessary to help determine the appropriate context of our study. Without these theological matters, it would be difficult to understand the specifics of LDS hermeneutics.

2.1. Asymmetry in LDS Approaches

An important component of LDS hermeneutics is the elevation of, and respect for, the Bible. This elevation highlights a seriousness with which they approach the Bible. However, many LDS writings highlight a negative perspective on the Bible, including the challenge of correct interpretation. Therefore, a diminution of the Bible is also an important aspect of LDS hermeneutics.

2.1.1. Elevation of the Bible

"The Bible stands at the foundation" of the LDS church.[1] Robert Millet proclaims that their "doctrines and practices are in harmony with the Bible."[2] All of their doctrines are "biblical," suggests Richard Hopkins.[3] In addition, "Latter-day Saint doctrines are eminently defensible from the Bible."[4] The ninth President of the LDS, David McKay, spoke of the "harmony of the doctrines of the Church with the Bible."[5] A surprising affirmation by outside observer Harold Bloom is that Mormonism "is truly a biblical religion, whereas Judaism and Christianity never were that, despite all their passionate protestations."[6] Bloom concludes that Mormonism, as the "American Religion," is "unlike Judaism and Christianity" and "is actually biblical, even when it offers and exalts alternative texts."[7] The Bible is seen as the "foremost" and "first among the books" that are used as "written guides in faith and doctrine."[8] The testimony of Joseph Smith is consonant with these acutely positive views: "We teach nothing but what the Bible teaches. We believe nothing, but what is to be found in this book."[9]

Concerning the Book of Mormon,[10] early LDS author James Talmage wrote that its arrival *supported* the Bible.[11] The BoM functioned "as [a] second witness to the Bible's testimony that Jesus [was] the source of

---

1. Ludlow, "Bible," 105.

2. Millet, *Getting at the Truth*, 90.

3. Hopkins, *Biblical Mormonism*, 35.

4. Ricks, "Latter-day Saint Doctrines," 338. Ricks is summarizing Hopkin's view.

5. See Evans, *Gospel Ideals*, 25.

6. Bloom, *American Religion*, 71–72.

7. Bloom, *American Religion*, 72.

8. James Talmage, in Holzapfel and Wayment, *Making Sense*, 523–24. For other positive examples of early LDS use of the Bible, see Irving, "Mormons and the Bible," 473–77, 488.

9. Joseph Smith, in George Albert Smith, *History of the Church*, 4:78.

10. The *Book of Mormon* is "a sacred record of some of the people who lived on the American continents between about 2000 b.c. and a.d. 400" (LDS, *Gospel Principles*, 46; cf. Gutjahr, *Book of Mormon*; Metcalfe, *New Approaches*; Boylan, "On Not Understanding," 181–89; Rees, "Joseph Smith," 83–112; Duffy, "Mapping Book of Mormon," 36–62).

11. See Talmage, *Articles of Faith*, 240, emphasis added.

salvation for all."[12] It even "came forth" to prove that the Bible was true.[13] Underscoring the importance of the Bible in the early years of their movement, Grant Underwood claims that early publications quoted the Bible "anywhere from 19 to 40 times as often as the Book of Mormon."[14] It may seem counterintuitive that the appearance of the BoM would serve to elevate the status of the Bible. Yet, the BoM was considered proof that "the biblical saga had been revived and was continuing in the person of Joseph Smith and the experience of latter-day Israel."[15] The message of the BoM to its readers was clear: "God had spoken again."[16] In many ways, then, the LDS Church elevates the Bible.

2.1.2. Diminution of the Bible

However, the Bible is also "lowered" in their thinking.[17] There exists a deviation and "sophisticated redaction" of it.[18] According to the LDS, the tumult of the nineteenth century precipitated a diminution of the Bible. False interpretations led to "chaos," and the Bible "in the possession of those who misinterpret its true meaning . . . [induced] confusion and misunderstandings."[19] The use of Jas 1:5 at the beginning of the Mormon movement illustrates this diminution (as well as elevation): "If any of you lack wisdom, let him ask of God, that giveth to all *men* liberally, and upbraideth not; and it shall be given him" (Jas 1:5 KJV).[20] On the one hand, fifteen-year old Joseph Smith fervently believed the message of the verse, and earnestly sought the wisdom that James mentions. Years later, Smith recounted the impact of the verse: "Never did any passage of

---

12. Flake, "Four Books," 28.

13. McConkie, *New Witness*, 395; cf. D&C 20:11: ". . . proving to the world that the holy scriptures are true."

14. Underwood, "Book of Mormon Usage," 53.

15. Kenney, "Triumph of Conservative," 163.

16. Barlow, *Mormons and the Bible*, xxxi; cf. Arbaugh, *Revelation*, 98; Flake, "Four Books," 28. Additionally, the LDS routinely emphasizes that they are the "Church of *Jesus Christ*" (emphasis added) with the Bible as their primary source.

17. See Barlow, *Mormons and the Bible*, 110, 242.

18. Flake, "Four Books," 28.

19. Dyer, *Meaning of Truth*, 115.

20. The official version of the LDS is the King James Version. Unless otherwise noted, all biblical references are from the KJV. In the pages that follow, not every verse mentioned receives a comment or reflection.

scripture come with more power to the heart of man than this did at this time to mine. It seemed to enter with great force into every feeling of my heart. I reflected on it again and again, knowing that if any person needed wisdom from God, I did."[21] The remarkable result, according to LDS author Bruce McConkie, was that Jas 1:5 "has had a greater impact and a far more reaching effect upon mankind than any other single sentence ever recorded by any prophet in any age."[22] The elevation of the Bible is clearly evident in these views concerning Jas 1:5. On the other hand, the reason that Smith sought wisdom was because of the many competing, mutually-contradictory interpretations of Scripture during his time. The Bible, although purported to be "plain" and understandable, was found by Smith to be anything but "plain":

> Rather than the balm for all ills and the answer to all questions, the Bible as preached had become the source of Protestant confusion. Each denomination taught that the Bible was clear in its message and was dogmatically convinced of its correct interpretation. Since there was little room for equivocation where the plain Bible was concerned, these multiple versions of truth acted as a deterrent for Smith.[23]

Thus, the possibility of understanding the Bible (other than Jas 1:5) was in serious doubt. Smith's apparent suspicions were confirmed when he received the sought-after wisdom and was told that competing interpretations of the Bible were all in error.[24] Therefore, the LDS was launched by the asymmetrical phenomena of, on the one hand, heartfelt devotion to the Bible (seeking and receiving the wisdom of Jas 1:5),[25] and on the other hand, an accentuation on the limitations of the Bible—specifically on the possibility of correct interpretation.

After the death of Joseph Smith, Brigham Young became the President of the church, and the imbalance and asymmetry concerning the Bible continued. Young attempted to subordinate the importance of the

21. Joseph Smith—History 1:19, PGP. These historical recollections of Joseph Smith are considered scriptural (in contradistinction to the *History of the Church* mentioned earlier).

22. Bruce McConkie, in LDS, *New Testament Seminary*, 230. The hyperbolic nature of many of McConkie's statements will be noted throughout this investigation.

23. Willsky, "The (Un)plain Bible," 20.

24. See Joseph Smith—History 1:12, 19, PGP; cf. Barlow, *Mormons and the Bible*, 110–11.

25. See Arrington and Bitton, *Mormon Experience*, 6.

Bible, while Mormon apostle Orson Pratt consistently endeavored to attach LDS teachings to the Bible.[26] Pratt argued that Mormonism was to be primarily bound to the Bible, in contradistinction to Young's position of Mormonism being led by a Prophet. Indeed, Young was amused by "the exaggerated, almost idolatrous veneration" that the Bible received.[27]

Article of Faith #8 states: "We believe the Bible to be the word of God as far as it is translated correctly."[28] LDS scholars admit this is a "bit of a qualifier" and claim that, although the "essential message of the Bible is intact," errors have been introduced through the centuries.[29] Other authors explain, "we believe in the authenticity of any portion of the Bible only insofar as it is transmitted and then translated correctly."[30] According to Joseph Smith, "ignorant translators, careless transcribers, or designing and corrupt priests have committed many errors."[31] The Bible for Joseph Smith did not come "in its original completeness and clarity."[32] In the process of writing and compiling the Bible, the LDS conclude that "anything placed in the stewardship of human hands" was "susceptible to error."[33] In the translation process, "terms were taken out of context and twisted."[34] Bruce McConkie bluntly asserts:

26. Barlow, *Mormons and the Bible*, 80, 87–90.

27. See Barlow, *Mormons and the Bible*, 87; cf. Young, "Unbelief," *JD* 16:43. The *Journal of Discourses* (*JD*) is a 26–volume collection of sermons of early Mormon leaders. For Brigham Young's *positive* views on the Bible, however, see Young, "Unbelief": "We will start out with the Bible alone taking it as the standard. All that the Bible teaches for doctrine and practice we will take for our guide." For more on Young vs. Pratt, see Bergera, *Conflict in the Quorum*; Turner, *Brigham Young*, 235; England, *Life and Thought of Orson Pratt*, 188–93, 209–11.

28. As indicated earlier, the thirteen Articles of Faith are contained in the *Pearl of Great Price*. Joseph Smith originally prepared these Articles in 1842 in response to a journalist's question concerning the beliefs of the LDS. See, e.g., Bitton, *Historical Dictionary of Mormonism*, 7–8. For Article #8 and the view that Smith probably meant "transmitted" instead of "translated," see Matthews, *Plainer Translation*, 7; cf. Carmack, *New Testament*, 2, 19, 20.

29. Millet, *Getting at the Truth*, 91; cf. Bowman, *Mormon People*, xvii; for the dissenting views of a non-LDS author, see Huggins, "Joseph Smith's 'Inspired Translation,'" 165.

30. Draper and Rhodes, *Paul's First Epistle*, 4.

31. Joseph Smith, in Ludlow, "Bible," 107; cf. Jackson, "Latter-day Saints," 66; Räisänen, "Creative Interpreter," 68–69.

32. Matthews, *Plainer Translation*, 5; cf. Palmer, *Insider's View*, 82.

33. Jackson, "Latter-day Saints," 71–72.

34. Edward Brandt, in Carmack, *New Testament*, 62.

Aside from the sorry state of the text due to scholastic incompetence, there was a far more serious problem, namely, the theological bias of the translators. This caused them to change the meaning or paraphrase texts that were either unclear or embarrassing to them. Concrete terms in Hebrew came out as abstract terms in Greek. Expressions about God . . . were changed or toned down or deleted entirely. Passages . . . were simply assumed by the translators to be false and were translated, paraphrased, and changed accordingly.[35]

Despite this summary by McConkie of the purported hermeneutical conclusions of the ancient translators, he gives no evidence, manuscript or otherwise, for these conclusions. The speculation by McConkie regarding "embarrassing" or "unclear" passages illustrates the LDS tendency to point out the erroneous hermeneutical practices of others, while, at times, excusing themselves from interacting with their own hermeneutical assumptions. In sum, however, a diminution of the condition of the Bible is evidenced by the numerous problems resulting from its translation.[36]

There are additional aspects to the diminution of the Bible by the LDS. The Book of Mormon states that "there are many plain and precious things taken away from" the Bible (1 Nephi 13:28). According to Robert Matthews, the "bigger problem" is not what is in the Bible, "but rather the omissions and the missing parts that constitute the problem."[37] We have noted the alleged impact of the Great Apostasy. Terryl Givens explains that Bible believers added "layer upon layer of accretions to religious institutions."[38] Although some LDS authors allow for limited positive influences during the centuries before the Restoration,[39] the Great Apos-

35. McConkie, *New Witness*, 403.

36. See also Hutchinson, "Mormon Midrash," 13, 28, 29, 30, 49; cf. Barber, "Literalist Constraint," 21; McGuire, "Understanding the Book of Mormon," 176; Barlow, *Mormons and the Bible*, 36, 78, 108–9, 244. In stark contrast to these strong generalizations, see Gibbons, "Paul as a Witness," 27–40. In this chapter, LDS author Gibbons cites *over one hundred* NT scriptures, yet never mentions any potentially corrupt or suspect passage. Gibbons takes at face value the writings of Paul, and refrains from questioning even one of them. Here we note the elevation of the Bible by an LDS author, despite the numerous examples of LDS diminution of the Bible.

37. Matthews, *Plainer Translation*, 8.

38. Givens, in Eliason, *Mormons & Mormonism*, 102.

39. For example, at the end of the third century, "with the return of persecution came an awakening and a renewal in Christian devotion" (Talmage, *Great Apostasy*, 84). Also, "We owe an immense debt to the protesters and reformers who preserved the scriptures and translated them . . . They kept the flame alive as best they could"

tasy negatively impacted not only the condition of the Bible, but also its interpretation. In fact, the ability to "interpret scripture was no longer on earth."[40] In addition, early LDS leaders had "deep misgivings about the ability of human language to capture God's thoughts. Words were too small to convey omniscience."[41] Although the Bible was important, it was not "*all*-important."[42] Neither the Bible, nor any other document or collection was all-sufficient "for redemption, for salvation, for complete enlightenment, or for the perfecting of the soul."[43] As noted, the LDS postulate the existence of other books as scripture, for the Bible merely "constitutes one of its standard works."[44]

A further relativizing example comes from the concept of "derivative revelation" as a description of *written* Scripture. Stephen Robinson writes, "direct revelation to a prophet or an apostle is immediate and primary, and this is the word of God in the purest sense—as *word* and *hearing* rather than as *text*."[45] There are similar notions with LDS author Blake Ostler, who argues that "scripture itself is not, strictly speaking, revelation, but rather a human record of revelatory experience."[46] Concomitantly, the LDS distinguishes between "Scripture" and the Bible, for "Scripture . . . is one thing; the Bible is quite another. Scripture is as broad

---

(Boyd Packer, in Millet, *Getting at the Truth*, 20). Through the centuries, there was still "some light left in the world" (Stephen E. Robinson, in Blomberg and Robinson, *How Wide?*, 72). Finally, "mankind was not left in total darkness or completely without revelation or inspiration" (Millet et al., *LDS Beliefs*, 48).

40. Millet, *Getting at the Truth*, 118; cf. Joseph Smith—History 1:19, PGP; Talmage, *Great Apostasy*, 26–27; Siebach, "Dialogue on Theology," 464. The Great Apostasy was purportedly due, in part, because of the infiltration of Greek philosophy into the church (see, e.g., Hatch, *Influence of Greek Ideas and Usages*; cf. Hopkins, *How Greek Philosophy Corrupted*; Millet, *Getting at the Truth*, 118–19; Robinson, in Blomberg and Robinson, *How Wide?*, 128, 138; LDS, *New Testament Seminary*, 142).

41. Gutjahr, "Measuring Stick," 205; cf. various LDS leaders in *JD* 1:117; 2:314; 3:99–102; 9:311; 16:335.

42. Barlow, *Mormons and the Bible*, 78.

43. See Davies and Madsen, "Scriptures," 1278.

44. Ludlow, "Bible," 105. As mentioned previously, other standard works include the *Book of Mormon*, the *Doctrine and Covenants*, and the *Pearl of Great Price*. Considering such views, it is natural to concur with non-LDS author W. D. Davies, who wrote of the LDS "attitude" toward Scripture as "unusual—undeniably radical if not unique" (Davies, "Mormon Canon," 44).

45. Robinson, in Blomberg and Robinson, *How Wide?*, 57.

46. Ostler, in Owen and Mosser, "Review," 20; cf. Flake, "Translating Time," 507.

as eternity, as comprehensive as the limitless bounds of truth."[47] Indeed, they expand "the definition of scripture itself."[48] LDS scripture states: "And whatsoever they shall speak when moved upon by the Holy Ghost shall be scripture" (D&C 68:4).[49]

The LDS Church maintains that the focus should be on God—not on the Bible. They emphasize that God, not scripture, is perfect.[50] Early LDS author Parley Pratt pointed out that the "central defect" with Alexander Campbell (and other Protestant restorationists in the nineteenth century) was a "narrow fixation on the Bible," because they failed to understand that the "Bible simply pointed beyond itself to the God who was the final arbiter of ultimate things."[51] Lydia Willsky claims that "the Bible itself inspired Smith to seek truth outside its pages, and it was without the plain Bible that he set out for the woods in search of God, spiritual direction and truth."[52] The chief function of the Bible was to "demonstrate the divine power," and thus, the LDS movement "pointed not to a book but to the divine power behind all books."[53] Other Protestant restorationists wanted to get back to the first-century church. Mormonism, on the contrary, "had no interest in patterning their faith and practice after a particular time but looked instead to God who had worked wonders in all times."[54] The message of the Bible "essentially meant soaring with the gods while others groveled on the earth."[55]

Skepticism regarding the process of canonization of the New Testament illustrates an additional diminution of the *current* condition of the Bible. LDS authors assert: "Our understanding remains hazy about

---

47. McConkie, *New Witness*, 395.

48. Givens, *Wrestling the Angel*, 18.

49. This verse from D&C 68:4 initially appeared in the *Evening and Morning Star* (hereafter *EMS*) and was later canonized in *Doctrine and Covenants*. The *EMS* was an early LDS monthly newspaper from 1832–34 that was "commissioned to announce salvation" (see Abanes, *One Nation*, 103; cf. Restoration Branches, *EMS* 1.5:35, "A Revelation, Given November 1831").

50. See Barlow, *Mormons and the Bible*, 117.

51. See Richard Hughes, in Eliason, *Mormons & Mormonism*, 30.

52. Willsky, "(Un)plain Bible," 20.

53. Hughes, in Eliason, *Mormons & Mormonism*, 30.

54. Hughes, in Eliason, *Mormons & Mormonism*, 31.

55. Hughes, in Eliason, *Mormons & Mormonism*, 38. The implication of these abrupt words—others "grovel" while the LDS "soars"—makes dialogue challenging.

how some books were declared authoritative."[56] Canonization was "accomplished unevenly by uninspired men,"[57] who were "hundreds of years removed from the time of Christ."[58] It was a "haphazard process;"[59] accomplished by "disagreement and debate," as well as "contention, compromise, and confusion."[60] In 1877, William McLellin, one of the original twelve LDS apostles, maintained that the process was "all conjecture," and there is now "great uncertainty relative to who wrote the books that are now in our Protestant Bible. We know not who gathered them up and put them together . . . but it was done by uninspired men so far as we now know."[61] The LDS disassociate themselves from other churches that believe in a "closed" and "sterile" canon.[62] However, alongside these negative LDS views, see the more balanced perspective by LDS author James Faulconer, who writes that "canonization wasn't arbitrary . . . It was a combined judgment of many thoughtful people over almost 300 years, and we assume that judgment was led by the Holy Ghost."[63]

I have noted numerous examples of LDS diminution of the Bible. These include the influence of mutually contradictory interpretations, translation discrepancies, removed passages, the Great Apostasy negating the ability to interpret, the limitations of human language, written Scripture as derivative, a focus on God instead of the Bible, and finally, skepticism about the process of canonization. It is important to note, that strictly speaking, some of these concepts are not *interpretive* issues. However, I reiterate, although these are *theological* issues, this discussion is

---

56. Millet et al., *LDS Beliefs*, 91.

57. Bruce McConkie, in Barlow, *Mormons and the Bible*, 210.

58. Paulsen, "Are Christians Mormon?," 50n54; cf. Robinson, *Are Mormons Christians?*, 51–53.

59. Orson Pratt, in Barlow, *Mormons and the Bible*, 95; cf. various LDS leaders in *JD* 7:22–38; 14:257–60; 16:218; 17:268–70.

60. McConkie, *New Witness*, 406.

61. Larson and Passey, *William E. McLellin Papers*, 295, 308.

62. Carmack, *New Testament*, 11. In addition, the LDS position is not "a finalist and minimalist view," i.e., "one canon is enough" (Davies and Madsen, "Scriptures," 1278). This differing canonical understanding and the subsequent argumentation can humorously be described as scholars "firing more than one canon at each other" (see Martin Marty, in Paulsen and Musser, *Mormonism in Dialogue*, vii). Additionally, the LDS seldom utilizes the term "canon"—because of its connotations of finality and completeness. Rather they speak of "the Standard Works of the Church" (see Talmage, *Articles of Faith*, 7; Davies, "Mormon Canon," 63).

63. Faulconer, *New Testament Made Harder*, 487.

necessary to help determine the appropriate context of our study. Without these theological matters, it would be difficult to understand the specifics of LDS hermeneutics. Their regard for the Bible, either positively or negatively, imports for assessing their skill in Bible interpretation.

2.1.3. The Hermeneutical Effect of the Asymmetry in LDS Approaches

The LDS elevates and respects the Bible, illustrated prominently in their interpretation of Jas 1:5. In addition, there is some wisdom in their writings regarding an exaggerated focus on the Bible. Many Bible readers recognize the problem of bibliolatry and would distance themselves from it.[64] A measure of "careful reflection" will prevent an overstated focus on the Bible, for God and the Scriptures "are both authoritative," yet "the latter is an authority because of and on behalf of the former."[65]

The perspective of LDS author Ostler cited above, that "scripture itself is not, strictly speaking, revelation,"[66] seems to align with a "cluster of [mainstream] scholars" who "emphasized the *actions* of God as the focus of his revelation, downplaying the *words* of God."[67] However, D. A. Carson responds: "not many naked events are very significant unless words unpack them," and "words are very frequently required to assign to events their meaning."[68] The detachment of the *words* of revelation from the *event* of revelation does not hold up to scrutiny.

I mentioned previously the assumed influence of the apostasy of the early church. The Great Apostasy appears to be a grid through which they view church history, and through which they interpret the Bible.[69] Careful textual analysis is short-circuited if the Great Apostasy was as pervasive as they claim—negatively impacting the condition, and therefore, the interpretation of the Bible. This perspective strains credibility

---

64. See Goldsworthy, "Relationship," 84; cf. Cole, "God, Doctrine of," 261–62.

65. Humphrey, "Jesus," 360; cf. Grudem, "Scripture's Self-Attestation," 15–60.

66. Ostler, in Owen and Mosser, "Review," 20.

67. Carson, "Contemporary Challenge"; see also Wright, *God Who Acts*.

68. Carson, "Contemporary Challenge."

69. For a non-LDS response to the Great Apostasy, see Craig Blomberg, in Beckwith et al., *New Mormon Challenge*, 318–22.

as most observers maintain that the study of history and its influence on biblical interpretation needs to be more nuanced and balanced.[70]

The LDS has determined that, in the process of transmission, many biblical texts were corrupted. Yet, the method used to arrive at this conclusion represents "a hermeneutic act of the first order."[71] In spite of the lack of a published hermeneutic, then, they are acting hermeneutically by judging the ancient biblical text to be corrupted. This hermeneutical activity is not sufficiently acknowledged.

In an important entry in the *Encyclopedia of Mormonism*, the LDS appears to *partially* respond to this presuppositional matter of the asymmetrical perspective on the Bible:

> Latter-day Saints have continued to trust in the general accuracy of the biblical texts even though they know that the text may not always be correct. Thus, they study and revere the Bible, especially in the context of other scriptures and modern revelation, which have much to say about the Bible and how it is to be interpreted, and as they study they ponder and pray that they may receive inspiration from God and come to understand the Bible's messages as they need to be applied in their lives.[72]

The LDS answer to the asymmetry, then, is found in *modern scriptures* that show "how [the Bible] is to be interpreted," and *personal interpretation* that allows an LDS member to "come to understand" the Bible. Thus, the challenges wrought by the asymmetrical perspective on the Bible are not considered insuperable, given the existence of other LDS scriptures, as well as individualized interpretation. I discussed in the previous chapter the need to be self-aware and even self-critical when approaching a text (or another religious tradition). Although the LDS claims to value the Bible highly, there is also devaluation since "other scriptures" appear to hold an authoritative position over it,[73] delineating "how it is to be interpreted." These modern scriptures are not *only* interpreting the Bible, as any Bible reader does, but, implicit in the words of the *Encyclopedia of Mormonism*, are a type of filter through which correct interpretation occurs. This does not align with their elevation

---

70. See Wright, *Jesus and the Victory*, 6; Trueman, *Histories and Fallacies*, 106; See also p. 11 above.

71. See Grondin, *Philosophical Hermeneutics*, 51.

72. Ludlow, "Bible," 107.

73. McConkie states that the Bible is viewed as a "dim" light—with modern revelation as the "brilliance of the noonday sun" (McConkie, *New Witness*, 411).

of the Bible. In addition, what methodological parameters are in place that help an LDS believer "know" that the biblical text "may not always be correct"? There are problematic notions with such an individualized interpretation. We will note this numerous times in our investigation. In many ways, then, the asymmetrical perspective on the Bible by the LDS yields several questionable implications and seems to direct attention away from ancient meaning and toward modern realities.

2.2. Continuing Revelation as Personal and Prophetic

2.2.1. *Foundational Role of Continuing Revelation*

The second foundational presupposition is commonly referred to as "continuing revelation," "living revelation," or simply "revelation." It is described as ongoing communication from God to humankind.[74] We have already seen the views of LDS author James Faulconer: "revelation is *the* Latter-day Saint theology."[75] Revelation is considered "the chief constituent of Latter-day Saint doctrine."[76] Article of Faith #9 announces: "We believe all that God has revealed, all that He does now reveal, and we believe that He will yet reveal many great and important things pertaining to the Kingdom of God." The BoM concurs: "Unto him that receiveth I will give more" (2 Nephi 28:30). In addition, "Revelation is the rock of Latter-day Saint belief."[77] Early Mormon leader W. W. Phelps mused that "new light" was "occasionally bursting in to our minds."[78] For Kent Jackson, one will stand or fall on this issue.[79] Faulconer agrees: "*Continuing revelation is primary to Mormonism.* Since Latter-day Saints insist on continuing revelation, they cannot have a dogmatic theology that is any more than provisional and heuristic, for a theology claiming to be more than that could always be trumped by new revelation."[80] Given this perspective on continuing revelation, Joseph Smith and others responded

---

74. See Hutchinson, "LDS approaches," 113.

75. Faulconer, "Rethinking Theology," 180.

76. David Paulsen, in Paulsen and Musser, *Mormonism in Dialogue*, 10.

77. Paulsen, "Are Christians Mormon?," 39.

78. Restoration Branches, *Messenger and Advocate*, 1.9:130. The *Messenger and Advocate* was an early LDS monthly newsletter from 1834–37.

79. Jackson, "Latter-day Saints," 81. Also, "If thou shalt ask, thou shalt receive revelation upon revelation" (Restoration Branches, *EMS*, 1.2:9, "Revelations").

80. Faulconer, "Rethinking Theology," 179, emphasis by author.

to their detractors with a pointed challenge—if revelation is dismissed in the present, how "could they defend revelation in the past?"[81] This is reiterated by Givens: "To repudiate divine revelation as a principle would be to undermine the basis of Christianity itself."[82]

The LDS claims that the Father and the Son appeared to Joseph Smith in 1820 as he was seeking for the wisdom mentioned in Jas 1:5. This became known as the "First Vision" (FV), and is the foremost example of continuing revelation.[83] Because of this vision, the LDS concluded that "divinity still communicate[d] with humanity,"[84] and that God was "in fact a literal person such as biblical prophets claim[ed] to see and speak with."[85] As to the idea that, while seeking the wisdom mentioned in Jas 1:5, Smith received knowledge that none of the denominations were correct, the earliest accounts of the FV do not mention this problem with competing churches. Rather, they focused on Smith's sorrow for his sins.[86] Interestingly, this change, far from exhibiting a potentially damaging discrepancy, is proof that Smith "reinterpreted his experience to satisfy institutional needs."[87] We will note the importance of "institutional needs"—and the modern emphasis implied by this—throughout this investigation.

Joseph Smith testified about the FV: "I had seen a vision, I knew it, and I knew that God knew it."[88] Brigham Young also described the epistemological implications of revelation: "I know that Joseph Smith was a Prophet of God, and that he had many revelations. Who can disprove this testimony? . . . I have had many revelations; I have seen and heard for myself, and know these things are true, and nobody on earth can disprove them."[89] Givens explains the significance of the FV: "It is easy to see why [Smith's] personal encounter with a conversing Deity would ground his own sense of epistemological certainty. But he clearly saw his own experience as a prototype to which others could—and should—aspire."[90]

---

81. See Paulsen, "Are Christians Mormon?," 39.

82. Givens, in Eliason, *Mormons & Mormonism*, 110.

83. See Joseph Smith—History 1:12–17, PGP.

84. Shipps, *Mormonism*, 32.

85. Arrington and Bitton, *Mormon Experience*, 6.

86. See Davies, *Mormon Culture*, 22; Palmer, *Insider's View*, 252.

87. Palmer, *Insider's View*, 240.

88. See Jessee, *Joseph Smith Papers*, 218; cf. Jackson, "Latter-day Saints," 78.

89. Young, "Unbelief."

90. Givens, *People of Paradox*, 22.

Therefore, the FV, "with all its epistemological fullness and certainty, betokened an order of knowledge that was the right and destiny of all faithful Saints."[91] Givens also states, "Certainty is a term that frequently appears in the ministry of Joseph Smith . . . [for he] never admitted a particle of possible self-deception."[92] Indeed, in a famous sermon months before his death, Smith proclaimed that it was "the first principle of the gospel, to know for a certainty the character of God, and to know that we may converse with him as one man converses with another."[93] In LDS thinking, then, the reception of revelation appears to be combined with epistemological certainty.

The FV established a basic assumption about how God is known— by revelation—and not known—by disputation and rational enquiry.[94] The FV also underscored that revelation had "replaced the long and in-ordinate reliance on reason."[95] Dallin Oaks claims that "reason can never trump revelation."[96] The early LDS leaders balked at how other leaders, like Protestant restorationist Alexander Campbell, "were rational to the core, applying human reason to the biblical text and limiting authentic religion to that sphere."[97] In contrast, "Mormonism sought to transcend the cognitive and the rational and to soar with the gods in the realm of the infinite and the eternal."[98]

Because of continuing revelation, the LDS claims an advantage over other Bible believers. Joseph Smith boldly proclaimed that other church-es were "bound apart by cast-iron creeds, and fastened to set stakes by chain-cables, without revelation."[99] James Siebach expresses that "in place

---

91. Givens, *People of Paradox*, 23. Givens continues: "the rhetoric of certainty and fullness are still distinguishing features of Mormon religious culture. During testimony meetings that occur on the first Sunday of the month, LDS members "bear a testimony": "I *know* Christ lives"; "I *know* Joseph Smith was a prophet of God"; "I *know* the church is true." Thus, "central to Mormonism is this affirmation of absolute certainty" (Givens, *People of Paradox*, 26). Notice, however, the modern slant of these affirmations.

92. Givens, *People of Paradox*, 22.

93. This sermon is called the "King Follett Discourse." See Smith, "King Follett Discourse."

94. Siebach, "Dialogue on Theology," 464.

95. Maxwell, "From the Beginning."

96. Dallin Oaks, in Baker, *Mormonism at the Crossroads*, 68n61.

97. Hughes, in Eliason, *Mormons & Mormonism*, 32.

98. Hughes, in Eliason, *Mormons & Mormonism*, 32.

99. Smith, in Smith, *History of the Church*, 6:74.

of Nicea I and the disputational manner in which it arrived at a doctrine of the Trinity, the LDS church asserts pure revelation."[100] They do not "limit divine revelation to the past," and are in a "unique position," because God "will yet reveal many great and important things."[101] Other LDS authors speak of their uniqueness: "Mormons find themselves in an isolated position . . . [because] Protestant evangelicals . . . find it impossible to accept the Mormon concepts of an open canon, continuing revelation, or 'inspired' improvements of the sacred text."[102]

There is an interesting argument concerning continuing revelation and the passage of time. According to the LDS, new revelation from God will be needed and expected, as "changing circumstances in the world necessitate new communication from God."[103] They hold to a "profound belief that God has meaningful things to say to humankind in our present age."[104] Early in their movement, Apostle Orson Hyde claimed that words given to one generation did not serve for another.[105] The eleventh President of the LDS, Harold Lee, explained that Noah did not receive the same revelation as Adam, nor the same as Isaiah, Jeremiah, Paul or Jesus—they "all had revelations for themselves."[106] The LDS conclusion, then, is "so must we."[107] Parley Pratt argued that the "old revelations were not suited to the present condition of mankind," and in order to "meet the needs engendered by a more civilized state of society . . . fresh revelations were needed."[108] According to David Paulsen, the Spirit who inspired ancient Scripture also speaks today about contemporary issues "of significant concern, for example, the use of contraceptives, abortion, liberation, ecological irresponsibility, equal rights, euthanasia, nuclear proliferation, global genocide, economic and social justice."[109] It is noteworthy that

100. Siebach, "Dialogue on Theology," 465; cf. Robinson, *Are Mormons Christians?*, 17.

101. LDS, "Divine Revelation in Modern Times"; cf. Oaks, "Scripture Reading and Revelation."

102. Bitton and Alexander, *A to Z of Mormonism*, 18.

103. Jackson, "Latter-day Saints," 63.

104. Paulsen, "Are Christians Mormon?," 52; cf. D&C 124:41; Robinson, in Blomberg and Robinson, *How Wide?*, 71; Holzapfel and Wayment, *Making Sense*, 521–25.

105. See Barlow, *Mormons and the Bible*, 88.

106. See Davies, "Mormon Canon," 58.

107. See Davies, "Mormon Canon," 58; cf. Talmage, *Jesus the Christ*, 778.

108. See Shepard and Marquardt, *Lost Apostles*, 94.

109. Paulsen, "Are Christians Mormon?," 50.

these LDS authors desire, at least implicitly, to be in continuity with the Bible, as modern day revelations ostensibly follow the biblical pattern of revelations given to Noah, Adam, and the other biblical characters.

The LDS also contends that no passage of Scripture explicitly prohibits continuing revelation. In fact, Joseph Smith asserted, "To say that God never said anything more to man than is there recorded [in the Bible], would be saying at once that we have at last received a revelation."[110] Robert Millet asks, "Does the Bible itself suggest that there will never again be revelation and vision and prophecy through God's chosen servants? Does God love the people of our day any less than he loved those to whom he manifested himself in [biblical] times?"[111] The LDS believe it is ill-advised to presume the end of revelation, for only a fool would "close the mouth of God and say his words should cease."[112]

2.2.2. *Personal Revelation and Interpretation*

We have seen that the LDS movement began when Joseph Smith retreated to the woods alone and sought wisdom from God concerning competing scriptural interpretations. As a consequence, the vital importance of *personal* revelation was underscored in LDS religious experience.[113] In fact, "Personal Revelation is a sacred and deeply embedded tradition in the theology, religious practice, and daily life of the Latter-day Saints."[114] It is "for every member of the Church."[115] Stephen Robinson states that "individuals within the Church may receive personal revelation, even on doctrinal matters, for their private benefit."[116] Each member is encour-

110. Smith, in Paulsen, "Are Christians Mormon?," 39.

111. Millet, *Getting at the Truth*, 142. Whether or not God's love can be predicated upon the frequency of manifestations, ancient or modern, is a *non sequitur* beyond the subject of this book.

112. McConkie, *New Witness*, 463.

113. See Riddle, "Revelation," 1225–28, emphasis added.

114. Mould, *Still*, ix.

115. McConkie, *New Witness*, 488; cf. Barber, "Literalist Constraint," 24; as well as passages in the BoM: Moroni 7:30–32, 36–37; Alma 12:9–10; 13:22–26.

116. Robinson, *Are Mormons Christians?*, 17. It is probably no accident that the equality and fairness generated by the concept of personal revelation stimulated early growth in the nineteenth-century LDS, as a reaction to a perceived hegemony on access to the Almighty by professional clergy. Indeed, the "theme of equality appears constantly throughout the Book of Mormon," and Joseph Smith proclaimed the right of everyone to "enjoy a more intimate relationship with God" (see Gutjahr, *Book of*

aged "to independently strive to receive their own spiritual confirmation of the truthfulness of Church doctrine."[117] There is "considerable leeway for individual scriptural evaluation."[118] According to one observer, the "distinguishing feature of Mormon faith" is that "its devotees profess to be in possession of a certain *power of the spirit*, which places them in direct communication with God and his angels, endowing them with the gifts of revelation and prophecy."[119] In addition: "Personal revelation makes every man a prophet, every woman a prophetess, to know the voice of the Lord ... Oh, how personal revelation pulls down intellectual tyranny, priestcraft, and private interpretation of scripture!"[120] McConkie bluntly underscores its importance: "until men receive personal revelation they are without God in the world ... Men may study about religion, about God, and about his laws, but they cannot receive that knowledge of them whom to know is eternal life except by revelation from the Spirit of God."[121]

We have seen that Joseph Smith experienced personal revelation. Other LDS leaders have reported similar experiences. Robert Millet received a revelation and was "filled with the warmth of the Holy Spirit from head to toe."[122] Retired LDS philosophy professor Chauncey Riddle (with a PhD from Columbia University), was devastated as a youth when faced with secular criticism of the church. He was besieged by doubts: "Oh how I prayed to know for myself if there were such a thing as personal revelation. Then ... it came ... I began to feel something special in my breast ... ideas that appeared in my mind. These new ideas told me how to interpret passages of scripture."[123] Lorenzo Snow, the fifth president of the LDS, experienced a "moment of revelation" and a "personal religious

---

Mormon, 41).

117. LDS, "Approaching Mormon Doctrine."

118. Givens and Barlow, *Oxford Handbook on Mormonism*, 127; cf. May, in Eliason, *Mormons & Mormonism*, 63. Givens and Barlow pass over quickly the potential arbitrariness of such "individual scriptural evaluation."

119. Thomas Kirk, in Fluhman, "A Peculiar People," 51.

120. Riddle, "Letter to Michael." The irony apparently is lost on Riddle as "*personal* revelation" is to prevail over "*private* interpretation of scripture."

121. Bruce McConkie, in Draper and Rhodes, *Paul's First Epistle*, 162.

122. See Davies, *Mormon Culture*, 58; cf. Millet, *Within Reach*, 33.

123. See White, *Mormon Neo-orthodoxy*, 133. As a philosophy professor, Riddle only gave the highest grade to his students when he himself received a "revelation that the student had received a revelation or inspiration about the assignment" (see Riddle, "Welcome"). The subjectivity inherent in such an approach demonstrates the length to which personal revelation extends in LDS thinking.

enlightenment" in the woods when he "received by perfect knowledge that there was a God . . . and that Joseph the Prophet had received the authority which he professed to have."[124] Snow knew by "positive knowledge" that the gospel had been restored, for "the Holy Ghost imparted to me a knowledge as physical and demonstrative as that physical ordinance when I was immersed in the waters of baptism."[125] For one LDS author, the "fullest knowledge of God [comes] through revelation."[126] Analysis of these epistemological assumptions is given below.

How does the theological issue of personal *revelation* impact LDS personal *interpretation* of the Bible? As Riddle implies,[127] it is upon the reception of personal revelation that personal interpretation of ancient Scripture occurs. The conduit, as it were, through which personal interpretation of the Bible occurs, is personal revelation. Thus, to obtain an "in-depth, sound understanding of the doctrines of the gospel," LDS authors write of the "personal responsibility" of their members to "search the scriptures."[128] Bruce McConkie agrees with this private searching of the scriptures, to "interpret the Bible by revelation."[129]

To defend this perspective, LDS authors introduce an additional term. Personal understanding of Scripture is through the "*spirit of prophecy.*" The prophet Nephi in the BoM calls his readers to "give ear unto my words; for because the words of Isaiah are not plain unto you, nevertheless they are plain unto all those that are filled with the spirit of prophecy" (2 Nephi 25:4). The LDS conclude from this passage that "the spirit of prophecy" is an essential component in "grasping the correct understanding of scripture."[130] LDS authors often refer to the spirit of prophecy as simply "the Spirit." McConkie asserts that there is "absolutely no way" to

124. See Davies, *Mormon Culture*, 23.

125. Davies, *Mormon Culture*, 23; cf. Williams, *Teachings of Lorenzo Snow*, 193–94. One would prefer to hear some reflections from Snow as to the precise meaning of "perfect knowledge"/ "positive knowledge." However, such reflections do not appear.

126. Bowman, "History Thrown into Divinity," 90.

127. "These new ideas told me how to interpret passages of scripture" (White, *Mormon Neo-orthodoxy*, 133).

128. Millet et al., *LDS Beliefs*, 603.

129. McConkie, in Barlow, *Mormons and the Bible*, 207. However, McConkie qualifies this private interpretation, since individuals should interpret by revelation "only as long as their interpretations and perspectives [are] in harmony with those of Church leaders" (McConkie, in Barlow, *Mormons and the Bible*, 207).

130. Thomas, "Scripture," 1284.

understand the Bible "except by the power of the Spirit."[131] An LDS writing expresses that "as we read, ponder, and pray about the scriptures and ask God for understanding, the Holy Ghost will bear witness to us of the truth of these things."[132] Similarly, Richard Hopkins writes, "acceptance of any interpretation requires the reader to seek spiritual confirmation from the Holy Spirit through prayer."[133] In order to understand the scriptures, the "Holy Ghost" is "the only sure and universal communicator."[134] The Holy Spirit "unlocks the Scriptures."[135]

While personal Bible interpretation through the Spirit is advocated, Dallin Oaks nevertheless cautions against an "over-emphasis on study for interpretation."[136] This can result in a "lesser portion" of the Bible. This phrase comes from a BoM prophet named Alma. Oaks explains, "(i)f we depend only upon our own reasoning or the scholarship or commentaries of others, we will never obtain the understanding that can come only by revelation. Persons in that circumstance will be left forever with what Alma calls 'the lesser portion of the word.'"[137] Oaks warns the reader of the Bible not to "reject continuing revelation," nor to "limit learning to academic study," because such a reader will receive only this "lesser portion."[138] Joseph Smith believed that study and learning were admissible, as long as one did not neglect to "hearken unto the counsels of God."[139] Furthermore, in the early years of the movement, "logical thinking" as well as "analytical thought" were at times rejected

---

131. McConkie, *New Witness*, 399–400.

132. LDS, *Gospel Principles*, 49; cf. Joseph Smith Translation—Matthew 1:37, PGP (a short section of the JST ["Joseph Smith—Matthew"] is included in the *Pearl of Great Price*). According to Joseph Smith, the difference between Mormons and other Christians was "the gift of the Holy Ghost" (Smith, in Smith, *History of the Church* 4:42; cf. D&C 20:27; 42:61; 59:4; 76:5–10; 121:26–32; for BoM corroboration, see Alma 5:45–56; 2 Nephi 25:4). One wonders if understanding here is less about interpretation, and more about confirmation of modern-day church doctrine.

133. Hopkins, *Biblical Mormonism*, 35.

134. Edward Brandt, in Carmack, *New Testament*, 64.

135. Roger R. Keller, in Paulsen and Musser, *Mormonism in Dialogue*, 42.

136. Oaks, "Scripture Reading."

137. Oaks, "Scripture Reading." See Alma 12:10: "And therefore, he that will harden his heart, the same receiveth the lesser portion of the word" (cf. Alma 12:11; Moses 5:58).

138. Oaks, "Scripture Reading." One wonders if his "reasoning" and "commentary" are to be included in this caution.

139. See Wright, "Joseph Smith's Interpretation," 206n53.

in favor of "supernatural experience."[140] Many early converts received confirmation of the LDS faith not through investigation and study, but "through revelations and visions."[141] The *sine qua non* experience was a "manifestation of the Spirit," the still, small voice, i.e., "some kind of inner confirmation."[142] While study and learning are encouraged, personal revelation and its subsequent interpretation, accomplished through the Spirit, remains paramount.[143]

2.2.3. Prophetic Revelation and Interpretation

Prophetic revelation and interpretation also hold prominence. "The First Presidency maintains the exclusive authority to interpret scripture and doctrine for the whole church."[144] The Mormon Prophet "alone can give authoritative interpretations of scriptures that are binding on the Church . . . He alone is the mouthpiece of God to his people."[145] In fact, in "every dispensation, Jesus Christ has sent prophets to teach His gospel to God's children on earth."[146]

The truth of the declarations of LDS authorities is generally unquestioned.[147] However, most LDS members would distance themselves from

140. See Abanes, *One Nation*, 104.

141. Abanes, *One Nation*, 104.

142. Arrington and Bitton, *Mormon Experience*, 41.

143. See Davies and Madsen, "Scriptures," 1280. In other passages, the BoM exhorts its reader to attain knowledge by inspiration, i.e., revelation (e.g., Moroni 10:4) and warns about being learned (e.g., 2 Nephi 9:28; 26:20; 28:4, 15) (see Wright, "Joseph Smith's Interpretation," 206n53).

144. Wilcox and Young, *Standing Apart*, 13. The "First Presidency" is composed of the Mormon Prophet and his two counselors. For the start of the "First Presidency" by Brigham Young, see Abanes, *One Nation*, 209; Robinson, in Blomberg and Robinson, *How Wide?*, 58, 65, 140.

145. Davies, "Mormon Canon," 54; cf. Arrington and Bitton, *Mormon Experience*, 244; Oman, "Living Oracles," 3, 15. Today, LDS members even "celebrate the [prophetic] office with rousing anthems such as 'We Thank Thee, O God, for a Prophet.'" By doing so, they "publicly avow their support of the living tenant of that office of 'prophet, seer and revelator'" (Givens, *People of Paradox*, 15). Not only does the Prophet interpret Scripture for the church, but he also receives new revelations concerning beliefs and doctrine. This is, however, outside the purview of this book.

146. LDS, *New Testament Seminary*, 13. Throughout history, one of the features of a "true church" was the presence of "Living Prophets and Apostles" (LDS, *Primary 5*, 2:7).

147. See Musser, in Baker, *Mormonism at the Crossroads*, 38.

the extreme statements of "When the prophet speaks, the debate is over";[148] or "When our leaders speak, the thinking has been done. When they propose a plan—it is God's plan. When they point the way, there is no other that is safe."[149] On the other hand, they maintain that their prophets provide "authoritative doctrinal and application insights for the Saints," and they "happily defer to them in that divinely appointed role."[150] LDS scholar Robert Millet asserts that "doctrinal truth comes not through the explorations of scholars but through the revelations of God to apostles and prophets. And if such a position be labeled as narrow, parochial, or anti-intellectual, then so be it. I cast my lot with the prophets."[151]

Since Scripture is "frequently misunderstood," the LDS depends on "the prophets' and apostles' interpretations" of Scripture in order to avoid misunderstandings.[152] Without "a living prophetic voice" to interpret the Bible, the "range of possible misunderstanding is significantly increased."[153] Early LDS leaders distanced themselves from other churches, because "without prophets—without authority—the gates were unbolted and thrown open to the whirlwinds of scholarly second-guessing and one-upmanship."[154] Given the LDS view that their church is "a living, dynamic constitution," and even "a living tree of life" (D&C 1:30), they are "commanded to pay heed to the words of the living oracles (D&C 90:3–5)."[155] The Prophet becomes the fulcrum on which the interpretive weight of the church rests, for "what God has said to apostles and prophets in the past is always secondary to what God is saying directly to his apostles and

148. N. Eldon Tanner, in Quinn, *Extensions of Power*, 872.

149. LDS, "Sustaining the General Authorities of the Church," 354. *Improvement Era* was the official magazine of the LDS Church from 1897 to 1970. Concerning the statement of "the thinking has been done," LDS President George Smith later responded that it misrepresents the "true ideal of the church" (see Quinn, *Extensions of Power*, 831–32; cf. Givens, *People of Paradox*, 18; White, *Mormon Neo-orthodoxy*, 129).

150. Holzapfel and Wayment, *Making Sense*, 4.

151. Millet, *Getting at the Truth*, 42. This apparent desire to be anti-intellectual (by intelligible reasoning no less) and "side with the prophets" does not provide much confidence for dialogue. Furthermore, one wonders if *his* words contain "doctrinal truth," considering their source.

152. See LDS, *New Testament Seminary*, 22. Apostles are Mormon leaders that assist the Prophet. See Siebach, "Dialogue on Theology," 464.

153. Davies and Madsen, "Scriptures," 1279.

154. Stephen Ricks, in Black, *Expressions of Faith*, 179.

155. Millet, *Getting at the Truth*, 15; cf. Wilford Woodruff, in Oman, "Living Oracles," 1.

prophets now."[156] A preference for the living prophet is further verified by "the New Testament model":

> For Latter-Day Saints, the church's guarantee of doctrinal cor-
> rectness lies primarily in the living prophet, and only second-
> arily in the preservation of the written text. This is, after all,
> the New Testament model. The ancient apostles and prophets
> themselves were the *primary* oracles. What makes Scripture . . .
> "inspired" . . . is not its *written* character but its *revealed* charac-
> ter. Writing it down preserves the inspired revelation and makes
> it accessible to the wider church, but that is secondary to the
> original revelation itself. The *record* of revelation cannot logi-
> cally be more authoritative than the *experience* of revelation.[157]

The LDS frequently focuses on the Prophet over and against that of the ancient Scriptures, because of their belief that a "living voice is generally richer than any writing."[158] Brigham Young even postulated that books were "nothing to me now" because they "do not convey the word of God direct to us now."[159] Millet states: "We love the scriptures, but ours is a living Church; not all of the mind and will of the Almighty can or should be written down."[160]

Prophetic authority began with the life and ministry of Joseph Smith, who "felt his access to Deity was more direct than the written word itself; his authority was therefore at least as great as the text's."[161] This authority continued throughout his life and ministry.[162] He combined his reading of

156. Robinson, in Blomberg and Robinson, *How Wide?*, 59; cf. Davies, "Mormon Canon," 57; Oaks, "Scripture Reading."

157. Robinson, in Blomberg and Robinson, *How Wide?*, 57–58. These ideas are obviously in consonance with the LDS concept of the Bible as *derivative* revelation, mentioned above (Robinson, in Blomberg and Robinson, *How Wide?*, 57).

158. Davies and Madsen, "Scriptures," 1279. According to the LDS, it is regrettable that other Christian traditions seemingly gag the prophets and hustle them "off-stage" once they have written down their message (see Robinson, in Blomberg and Robinson, *How Wide?*, 58).

159. See Arbaugh, *Revelation*, 3. Brigham Young also asserted, "I would rather have the living oracles than all the writing in the books" (see Davies and Madsen, "Scriptures," 1278).

160. Millet, *Getting at the Truth*, 105.

161. Barlow, *Mormons and the Bible*, 78–79.

162. Anecdotally, a startling event in the early years of the movement captures the authoritative atmosphere surrounding Joseph Smith. In the state of Ohio, after being tarred and feathered by disillusioned former members, Smith was scheduled to preach the following morning. After his wife laboriously scrubbed and cleaned him most of

the Bible with his "appeal to an authority none could challenge—that of
direct revelation from God" in order to "cut the Gordian knot of religious
uncertainty."[163] He "streamlined interpretation and removed the onus
from the individual believer to glean the 'plain' message of scripture."[164]
Therefore, "without Smith and the future Prophets, there could be no way
to know and understand the Bible."[165] According to David Paulsen, in order to arrive at the meaning of biblical passages, instead of using reason
to exegete biblical passages, "Joseph bypassed any such hermeneutical
exercise, instead claiming divine revelation and authority."[166]

The perspective on continuing revelation, then, with its specific
manifestations of personal and prophetic revelation, is a crucial presuppositional matter that illuminates the LDS worldview. After noting several hermeneutical effects of this presuppositional matter, I will explore
how, and why, an "exclusive" prophetic interpretation can exist simultaneously alongside of personal interpretation.

2.2.4. The Hermeneutical Effect of Continuing Revelation

An inordinate focus on the modern is apparent with the examples
given. Joseph Smith claimed to be epistemologically one with God: "I
had seen a vision, I knew it, and I knew that God knew it."[167] Such an
assumption, however, is highly speculative, and despite the words of
Givens,[168] propels Smith to the realm of self-interest and potential self-
deception. The views of Gadamer are instructive: "There is no claim of
definite knowledge, with the exception of one: the acknowledgement of
the finitude of human being in itself."[169] The absolute epistemic certainty

---

the night, he ascended to the pulpit, still carrying scars and bruises: "With a true instinct for the occasion, he thundered no denunciations, but preached as usual, and the
quiet dignity of his sermon added to the aura of heroism fast beginning to surround
him" (Brodie, No Man Knows, 119–20).

163. Winn, Exiles in a Land of Liberty, 51.

164. Willsky, "(Un)plain Bible," 19; 22. It is unknown to what extent individual
Bible readers of Smith's day desired the removal of such onus.

165. Willsky, "(Un)plain Bible," 19.

166. Paulsen, "Are Christians Mormon?," 128.

167. See Jessee, Joseph Smith Papers, 218.

168. Smith "never admitted a particle of possible self-deception" (Givens, People
of Paradox, 22).

169. Gadamer, "The Science of the Life-World," 185.

that Smith exhibits runs afoul of more intuitive thinking on the matter. Since each person in a dialogue is "the not-being of the other," Friedrich Schleiermacher recognized that "it is never possible to eliminate non-understanding completely."[170] In the previous chapter, I mentioned a scientistic mentality that claimed epistemic certainty and an objective purity uncontaminated by subjectivity. This was an empiricist and idealist legacy inherited from the Enlightenment.[171] Smith's strong assertions reflect these negative tendencies. In this chapter, we have seen the claim that the "fullest knowledge of God" comes through revelation.[172] However, this epistemological assertion is passed over quickly. Indeed, significant concerns are collapsed into simplistic declarations, e.g., "I had seen a vision . . . and I knew that God knew it,"[173] or Lorenzo Snow's "perfect knowledge"/"positive knowledge."[174] The lack of engagement with the complexities of epistemology, as well as their strident views on epistemic certainty, illustrate the departure of the LDS from accepted hermeneutical perspectives, and highlight their modern-day focus.

There is a disconcerting comparison between revelation and reason. The foundational belief of knowing God by revelation is the result of a rational conclusion concerning the nature of the FV. That is, the external data of a revelatory event, the FV, is analyzed, summarized and evaluated rationally, with the resulting epistemological judgment that God is known only through revelation, and not reason.[175] This partially responds to the issue mentioned in the previous chapter concerning the epistemological ramifications and hermeneutical consequences of LDS author James Faulconer's seemingly ambiguous statement of "Scripture is more important than rational explanation."[176] The utilization of *rational*

170. See Iser, *Range of Interpretation*, 47; see also the "universal potential for misunderstanding" in Grondin, *Philosophical Hermeneutics*, 71.

171. See Wright, *Christianity and Critical Realism*, 3–4, 13.

172. Bowman, "History Thrown into Divinity," 87–91.

173. See Joseph Smith, in Jessee, *Joseph Smith Papers*, 218.

174. See Davies, *Mormon Culture*, 23; cf. Williams, *Teachings of Lorenzo Snow*, 193–94.

175. However, it should be noted that some mainstream Christians operate under similar assumptions. Priority is given to human reason. Demonstrating a legacy from the Enlightenment, biblical criticism has come to mean an assumption that the critic had a right to pass judgment on the truth claims of the Bible (Silva, in Kaiser and Silva, *Biblical Hermeneutics*, 282).

176. Faulconer, "Rethinking Theology," 180. Similarly, Mauro Properzi writes that "Mormonism makes direct revelation the supreme source of its epistemology" (Properzi, *Mormonism and the Emotions*, 5).

explanation by Faulconer is employed to disparage *rational explanation* and elevate Scripture.

Furthermore, the bifurcation of revelation from reason, far from elevating Scripture over against that of human reason, presents numerous epistemological challenges: "the sharp distinction between the 'supernatural' and the 'rational' *is itself a product of Enlightenment thinking*, and to emphasize the 'supernatural' at the expense of the 'rational' or 'natural' is itself to capitulate to the Enlightenment worldview."[177] This capitulation to a scientistic perspective is an unintended consequence of LDS thinking on revelation. Furthermore, the affirmation of the centrality of Scripture does not automatically discount reason. A simplistic view, at times evident even in historic Christianity, is the "Bible only" perspective. Yet, in response, Richard Hooker, writing as far back as the sixteenth century, insisted that reason was not "an entirely separate source of information, which could then be *played off against* scripture and/or tradition."[178] Hooker concluded, "not that scripture should be judged at the bar of 'reason' and found wanting, but that in reading and interpreting scripture we must do so not arbitrarily, but with clear thinking and informed historical judgment."[179] The priority of revelation by the LDS at the expense of reason is a challenging assertion to maintain.

There are additional hermeneutical ramifications of this presupposition of continuing revelation. Given the need for relevant and timely revelation for contemporary issues, the likely instinct of the LDS is to avoid the meaning of the ancient text and seek contemporary significance. The issue of ancient meaning vs. contemporary significance is a hermeneutical topic that many LDS authors appear to ignore. Furthermore, there may be inherent dangers in the focus on new and novel revelation. As we noted, it is axiomatic that that "which is new is always exciting, and there is an inevitable tendency for its importance to be overestimated."[180] It appears that the LDS assumptions on relevant revelations is at least a partial answer to the question in the previous chapter of how to evaluate the place and impact of "continuing revelation," especially in contrast to the ancient and static state of the Bible. The novelty of modern appears to obscure the relevancy of the ancient.

177. Wright, *People of God*, 10.
178. See Wright, *Scripture*, 82.
179. See Wright, *Scripture*, 82.
180. Neill and Wright, *Interpretation*, 161.

A highly individualized interpretation of Scripture is an integral part of LDS hermeneutics.[181] Nonetheless, we have seen that literary texts exist externally from the interpreter. There is conceptuality embodied in the text that is "other" than the interpreter. Yet, the individualistic interpretation espoused by the LDS engenders a strong possibility of masking the ontological realism of the biblical text. In the previous chapter, I noted a full-blown postmodern perspective that exaggerates epistemic relativism by implying that only the *interpretations* of texts exist.[182] LDS personal interpretation mirrors this postmodern perspective. Similarly, knowledge of the Bible essentially becomes individualized, and is reduced to mere sensory experience. The reduction of the ancient text to sense data (i.e., the "spiritual confirmation of the truthfulness of Church doctrine"),[183] leaves open the question of whether the external world exists—which, as we have seen, is an important aspect of our framework of Critical Realism. Therefore, we note a consonance between the personal interpretation advocated by the LDS and phenomenalism, where the ontological reality of the text is essentially ignored, and the focus instead bends back to the interpreter's perception of the text.[184] The arbitrary subjectivity of LDS personal interpretation presents numerous problems.

The ability of Joseph Smith to "bypass" hermeneutical activity reflects a surprising lack of awareness of many current hermeneutical notions.[185] For instance, although not commenting on anything directly related to the LDS faith, George Stroup wrote decades ago that "to confess Christian faith is to engage in a hermeneutical activity—an exercise of reason and intellect that entails interpretation and understanding."[186] Furthermore, the "process of reconstructing personal identity in the context of the faith narratives of the Christian community is a hermeneutical activity."[187] LDS views are in direct contradiction to Stroup. The

---

181. The LDS is not alone here, given the "common [individualistic] devotional reading by thousands" in conservative Christian traditions, as well as the "cavalier approaches to interpretation"—in typical church Bible studies (see Silva, in Kaiser and Silva, *Biblical Hermeneutics*, 291, 310).

182. See problems with this in Wright, *Scripture*, 112.

183. LDS, "Approaching Mormon Doctrine."

184. See the perspectives on phenomenalism in Wright, *People of God*, 34–35.

185. Paulsen, "Are Christians Mormon?," 128.

186. Stroup, *Promise of Narrative Theology*, 200.

187. Stroup, *Promise of Narrative Theology*, 200.

possibility of bypassing hermeneutical activity in the interpretation of the Bible is an unsustainable premise.[188]

It is important to note the striking priority of prophetic revelation, and the resultant subordination of the biblical text—precisely because of an interpretive use of the text itself—"the New Testament model."[189] The Bible itself is used to point to something else—the "living prophet." The "New Testament model" purportedly describes the "experience of revelation" of the living prophet as more authoritative than the "written text."[190] This assertion, however, as the result of a *biblical* interpretation, supposedly curtails the legitimacy and relevancy of the Bible.

I noted the views of Millet: "doctrinal truth comes not through the explorations of scholars but through the revelations of God to apostles and prophets. And if such a position be labeled as narrow, parochial, or anti-intellectual, then so be it. I cast my lot with the prophets."[191] Interpretation seems to be suppressed, or at least minimized, by this freedom of personal revelation. In fact, Millet's statement implies an avoidance of interpretation since he eschews "doctrinal truth"—which would presumably result from interpretation. He desires to avoid the constricting confines of "doctrine," which is impossible for any Bible believer. In addition, the modern thrust of Millet's statement—at the expense of the ancient—is patently clear.

An additional difficulty evidenced here is the stark subject-object distinction implied in both personal and prophetic interpretation. The "subject," whether the individual or the prophet, receives what is considered the "object"—a revelation or an interpretation. Yet, the emphasis remains on the subjecthood of the prophet or individual interpreter. While this notion would be acceptable as part of a reader-response hermeneutic,[192] for critical realists, it does not show appropriate respect for the rights of the text. This idea of a sovereign subjecthood is a "myth of the Enlightenment."[193] It represents a discredited model of biblical interpretation where an interpreter acted as a "detached subject" who could

---

188. This will be further explicated in chapter 8 under the section: "The inescapability of interpretation."

189. See Robinson, in Blomberg and Robinson, *How Wide?*, 57–58.

190. Robinson, in Blomberg and Robinson, *How Wide?*, 58.

191. Millet, *Getting at the Truth*, 42.

192. E.g., see Detweiler, "Reader Response," 8; cf. Osborne, *Hermeneutical Spiral*, 478–82; McKnight, "Literary Criticism," 476.

193. McLean, *Biblical Interpretation*, viii.

survey the past, including biblical texts, "from a great height."[194] The all-knowing subject was seen as controlling a passive object. However, a detached subject is not in dialogue, but rather, carrying on a monologue. A true dialogue, strongly advocated by current hermeneutical thinking, occurs when modern interpreters are addressed by the ancient texts. Both the interpreter and the text have their own roles to play in dialogue.[195] A responsible hermeneutic will avoid a stark subject-object distinction.

2.2.5. An Additional Hermeneutical Effect: Priority of Prophetic Interpretation

Prophetic interpretation apparently overrides personal interpretation. This discrepancy, however, is acknowledged by LDS authors: "In an inexplicable contradiction, Joseph was designated as the Lord's prophet, and yet every man was to voice scripture, everyone to see God. That conundrum lies at the heart of Joseph Smith's Mormonism."[196] Roger Terry comments: "the modern Church, as it was initially established, was both a theocracy and a democracy."[197] Givens notes the paradoxical nature of their faith being "founded on the radical premise that direct revelation is the province of every individual, [although] Mormonism quickly ordered the flow of revelation in a kind of federal channeling of prerogatives that remain rigidly hierarchical even as every person is invited to seek unmediated access to God."[198] LDS authors ponder: "How can Mormonism simultaneously be authoritarian yet individualistic, orthodox yet creedless, objectively imposed yet subjective, unified yet endlessly pliable and diverse?"[199] Every believer may read and interpret the Bible, yet "doctrinal finality rests with apostles and prophets, not theologians or scholars."[200] Notwithstanding these tensions, both personal and prophetic interpretation of ancient Scripture are foundational in their thinking. It is noteworthy that LDS authors admit this conundrum as an unavoidable aspect of their worldview. However, the issue is passed over quickly. The

---

194. McLean, *Biblical Interpretation*, 55.

195. Gadamer, in McLean, *Biblical Interpretation*, 187.

196. Bushman, *Rough Stone*, 175.

197. Terry, "Authority and Priesthood," 13.

198. Givens, *Wrestling the Angel*, 41–42.

199. Shepherd and Shepherd, *Kingdom Transformed*, 5.

200. Millet et al., *LDS Beliefs*, 463. This is curiously written since it is from scholars.

prophets are granted ultimate authority to interpret, yet all LDS members are encouraged to strive for their own personal revelations. The simple acceptance by the cited LDS authors of this "inexplicable contradiction"[201] is another indication of the lack of hermeneutical and epistemological reflection by the LDS.

2.3. Potential Label of a Hermeneutical Filter: "Systemic Parameters"

At this point in our investigation, and before concluding our evaluation of the two foundational presuppositions, it is important to introduce the concept of "systemic parameters." This final piece of conceptual scaffolding is needed to survey more clearly the five categories of uses of the Bible by the LDS. This term describes the phenomenon of a multi-faceted LDS "system," composed of numerous overlapping, yet underlying matters—epistemological, historical, theological, ecclesiological, and sociological—all of which are crucial to the maintenance of the system and fuel the interpretive process itself. These foundational matters enable their hermeneutical activity and could be described as a hermeneutical filter of the LDS. Both the lack of a published hermeneutic and the scarcity of discussion of many hermeneutical issues are challenges that involve an element of speculation in many of my assessments, hence, the phrase "systemic parameters."

This comprehensive system, or "system-in-place," means that, while the LDS is neither monolithic nor homogeneous, there are aspects that are indicative of a closed system. The system can be viewed as a structure upheld by several supporting columns. Each column is crucial to the viability of the system itself. Such columns include the Great Apostasy and the subsequent need for Restoration, the supposed possession of the "fullness" of the Gospel, as well as continuing revelation and modern scriptures. Other columns include the following. The Bible remains one of their "Standard Works," although, as we have seen, it has been tainted. The existence and legitimacy of the Book of Mormon is essential. Also included is the life of Joseph Smith, along with the First Vision, his prophetic authority, his later plural marriage, his murder, and the influence of the nineteenth-century context on his life.

---

201. Bushman, *Rough Stone*, 175.

The nineteenth-century context evidenced, among other realities, a frontier mentality, and a freedom from authority, not only ecclesiologically, but also politically.[202] The nineteenth century also evinced an anti-institutionalism, an anti-creedalism, and an unstable American religious culture that was "contentiously pluralistic, eclectic, and syncretistic from the outset."[203] This lack of stability created widespread denominational infighting. All these nineteenth-century realities played a part in the life of Joseph Smith and the early LDS. Additionally, at the time of the inception of the movement, the resolution of painful issues was urgent—whether high mortality rate for infants, the question of the salvation of the indigenous peoples in the Americas (which was partially resolved with the publication of the BoM), or the question of a "capricious" God sending people to hell. The ability to provide answers was a significant aspect of early recruitment of members.[204] Therefore, the nineteenth century-context is an important column in the LDS system.

Also, indispensable is the priesthood, which only male LDS believers possess. In addition, "legal administrators" are needed to lead the church and direct a centralized headquarters. The Temple ordinances and sealing power are also integral to their system. Finally, there is a focus on the pragmatics of faith.

The system, then, labeled as "systemic parameters" and composed of several essential columns, is a hermeneutical filter that drives much of their interpretation of the Bible. LDS author Philip Barlow elucidates the views of Brigham Young, who implied the existence of a Mormon system: "Unless one understood Mormon theological insights, one did not really understand and believe the Bible."[205] That is, if one does not comprehend the characteristics of the system before interpreting the Bible—proper understanding will not occur. Early Mormon leader Lowell Bennion said that a requisite for understanding the Bible was being "consistent with

---

202. "The bases of social order were in a state of disarray, and as a result of the nation's having cut its ties with England and her history, a clear lack of grounding in the past was evident" (Shipps, *Mormonism*, 34).

203. Shepherd and Shepherd, *Kingdom Transformed*, 15.

204. See Beckwith et al., *New Mormon Challenge*, 43–48.

205. Barlow, *Mormons and the Bible*, 104. Barlow then gives a surprising assessment: "From one angle of vision, this is merely a case of blatant scriptural eisegesis" (Barlow, *Mormons and the Bible*, 104). Such "blatant" eisegesis needs to be put to the test. This eisegesis demonstrates a modern-day focus at the expense of the ancient.

gospel fundamentals."[206] These are implicit admissions by LDS authors of the need for a hermeneutical filter. The structure supposes that all columns are in place, and all features of the system are assumed to be true, relevant, and valid. We will note the modern system of "systemic parameters" numerous times in our investigation.

2.4. Hermeneutical Dynamics of LDS Presuppositions

I have attempted to establish the external data of two important LDS presuppositions. I have demonstrated an asymmetry concerning the Bible as well as the doctrine of continuing revelation. These presuppositions give us important insights into their worldview.

In sum, several hermeneutical dynamics are present with these presuppositions. As I wrote in chapter 1, presuppositions are not necessarily negative or an indication of a distorting prejudice. However, we have seen how continuing revelation leads directly to interpretive assumptions about how ancient scripture speaks specifically of modern, continuing revelation. This is problematic, as it reflects a simultaneous validation and relativization of ancient scripture. We have also encountered hermeneutical inconsistencies that are partly explained by the church's asymmetrical view of the Bible. An interpretive posture is manifestly evident—at times irrespective of the ancient context of the biblical text. In chapter 1, we noted the need for "patient and attentive listening."[207] However, with these presuppositions, it appears the LDS Church does not listen to the ancient realities of the biblical text. For example, it is declared that the text is corrupt—and that translators were not concerned with accurate translations.[208] We also saw in chapter 1 that comprehension of the "other" stands at the very heart of hermeneutics.[209] With the sustained focus on modern continuing revelation, the ancient biblical text as "other" is not sufficiently taken into consideration.

Following this inquiry into presuppositional matters, the following five chapters describe specific uses of the Bible by the LDS.[210] The first four

---

206. Bennion, in Barlow, *Mormons and the Bible*, 223.

207. See Thiselton, *Hermeneutics of Doctrine*, xx.

208. For a response, see Cole, "Myths about Copyists," 132–51.

209. Ernst Fuchs, in Thiselton, *Hermeneutics*, 6.

210. See the Appendix for a succinct summary of the biblical examples of these categories.

categories (literal, allegorical, sociological, and emendatory interpretation) illustrate a more concise focus on the *interpretive* realm. However, the fifth category of "re-authoring" is characterized by an implicit claim to be interpretive, but that amounts to a *de facto* creation of a completely new text. A biblical word or phrase is lifted from its context and re-used in a different context with a new meaning, with no mooring or connection to its original context. Strictly speaking, then, the fifth category of "re-authoring" merely *parades* as interpretive practice. In other words, it only *appears* to be interpretive. Nonetheless, it reveals a use of the Bible by the LDS, and thus warrants an investigation.

---------- 3 ----------

Literality and the LDS Church

THE LDS FREQUENTLY CHAMPIONS a literal interpretation of the Bible. Before I explore numerous examples of these interpretations, however, we need to gain clarity on the topic of literality. I will first investigate the contrast between literal and figurative interpretation. Secondly, I will detail the difficulties of defining literality, LDS or otherwise. I believe that LDS authors have overlooked this difficulty when they assert that literal interpretation is their predominant approach. Finally, I will describe my understanding of what is occurring when the LDS "literally" interprets the biblical text. As will become apparent, what they maintain is literal, I suggest is *literalistic*.

3.1. Considerations, Questions, and Concepts of Literality

Our first examination is the conceptual comparison of literal and figurative aspects of interpretive practice. This will be the first step of an exploration into various nuances of the term "literal," and will orient us in this complex topic.

3.1.1. Literal vs. Figurative

While there are similarities between literal and figurative interpretations, there are also significant differences. An important issue is the extent to

50

which a text connotes a one-to-one correspondence between the reality described and the locutions used to describe that reality. This demonstrates the process of how things are represented by words. The correspondence between the locution and its referent, or how things are represented by words, is seen more acutely in literal interpretation, in contrast to a figurative interpretation. A literal claim is advanced if there is a direct correspondence between the text and the empirical world. This comports even in fictional writing—a literal door means a physical door, even in the world of fiction. James Barr comments: "To understand the text literally is to suppose that the referents are just as is stated in the text, the language of the text being understood in a direct sense."[1] LDS author Richard Cummings recognizes this concept, since literality is "a distinct mind-set which presumes facticity in scriptural accounts, interprets scripture at face value, and by extension, tends to favor one-to-one equivalence over ambiguous multivalence."[2] Barr introduces a term to emphasize the convergence of the text with its referent: "*Physicality* affords a simple, commonsense, one-to-one correspondence between the entities referred to and the words of the text."[3] Kevin Vanhoozer concurs: "the literal sense has been identified with 'the sense of the letter,' which in turn has been identified with the objects to which individual words refer."[4] When there is a one-to-one correspondence, then, between the words and the entities represented by those words, a literal sense is advanced.

However, there are additional considerations. Because of the various nuances of literality, we must "resist reducing the literal sense to its most primitive level, namely, the empirical objects named by individual words."[5] A simplistic view is the claim that every biblical word says what it means.[6] If ostensibly the language is about something else—then the meaning is figurative/metaphorical. For example, the colloquial phrase "hit the road" does not illustrate a one-to-one correspondence between the language used and the reality the language refers to (e.g., physically pounding the street with hammer in hand). Rather, it deploys a metaphorical catalyst for the reader (or hearer) to advance quickly. If then, a

1. Barr, *Bible in the Modern World*, 171.

2. Cummings, "Quintessential Mormonism," 93.

3. James Barr, in Vanhoozer, *Is There a Meaning?*, 305, emphasis added.

4. Vanhoozer, *Is There a Meaning?*, 304.

5. Vanhoozer, *Is There a Meaning?*, 304.

6. See Cummings, "Problem of Protestant Culture," 182, 195.

speaker says, "let's hit the road," an audience is expected to understand this figurative meaning of rapid advance. Biblically, for example, the "cross" has both literal and figurative senses. It refers to the physical, wooden cross of the crucifixion of Jesus,[7] yet also connotes a figurative sense that centers on the climax of God's redemptive work.[8] A direct, one-to-one correspondence, then, presupposes an understanding of the standard meaning of the locution. However, words often have more than just a "standard meaning." In other words, "a statement is literal if the primary or conventional meanings of the terms are intended, and metaphorical when associative meanings cause a semantic interplay between the terms that creates a dynamic new understanding of the subject."[9] Words are flexible, and often have different connotations, as illustrated by their literal or figurative senses.

There exists an all-too common assumption that "literal" is the opposite of "figurative." Hans Frei makes the important point that, although the Reformers set the literal sense in opposition to allegory, they were not opposed to figural interpretation: "Far from being in conflict with the literal sense of biblical stories, figuration or typology was a natural extension of literal interpretation. It was literalism at the level of the whole biblical story and thus of the depiction of the whole of historical reality."[10] Relatedly, G. B. Caird recognizes a confusion between "literal" and "real," as well as an assumption in many dictionaries that literal simply means "not figurative or metaphorical."[11] In fact, "literal and figurative language can refer to real entities, and both can refer to fictional entities. There is no logical correlation between literal and 'true,' or between metaphorical and 'false.'"[12] In spite of this, as we will see, LDS thinkers seem to equate "literal" with "real" or "true" or "correct." They appear to assume that if a biblical text is not taken "literally," the reader would not be interpreting correctly.

---

7. "When they had carried out all that was written about him, they took him down from the cross" (Acts 13:29 NIV).

8. "For the message of the cross is foolishness to those who are perishing" (1 Cor 1:18 NIV).

9. Osborne, *Hermeneutical Spiral*, 388–89.

10. Frei, *Eclipse of Biblical Narrative*, 2; cf. Vanhoozer, *Is There a Meaning?*, 119.

11. Caird, *Language and Imagery*, 133.

12. Blomberg and Foutz Markley, *Handbook of New Testament Exegesis*, 228n32. Also, "the 'truth' of an utterance does not depend on its literal nature" (Osborne, *Hermeneutical Spiral*, 389).

Authorial intention is also an important component of literal *and* figurative meanings. According to Wright, the *literal* sense is the sense originally intended—whether the statement is literal or figurative.[13] Specifically for Wright, the literal sense of a parable of Jesus "involves recognizing it *as* a parable, not an anecdote about something which actually happened."[14] A literal interpretation, then, "can include figurative senses, if they are intended [as such]."[15] In light of many LDS interpretations explored below, LDS thinkers appear to overlook the fact that "the biblical text, literally interpreted, may itself point to a figural sense."[16] Indeed, for Wright, "the 'literal' sense actually means 'the sense of the letter'; and if the 'letter'—the actual words used by the original authors or editors—is metaphorical, so be it."[17]

To summarize: a literal claim is illustrated if there is a direct correspondence between the text and the empirical world—if there is a one-to-one relationship between the locution of speech and the empirical reality that the language is applied to. On the other hand, if, evidently, an audience is expected to understand that a phrase or word does not exhibit a one-to-one correspondence between the language used and the reality the language refers to (e.g., "hit the road" referring to something other than a physical road), the sense is figurative/metaphorical. Furthermore, "literal" is not opposed to figurative, nor should it be automatically equated with what is "real" or "true." Finally, a literal interpretation could include a figurative sense if the author intended it in this way.

3.1.2. The Challenges of Determining a "Literal" Interpretation

The meaning of "literal," LDS or otherwise, is debated. We have just briefly explored this with a comparison between literal and figurative interpretations. According to David Graham, the literal sense of a text "is itself not an unproblematic notion."[18] Wright writes of "residual problems" as to the exact contours of "what the literal sense might be."[19] Anthony Thisel-

---

13. Wright, *Scripture*, 135.
14. Wright, *Scripture*, 135.
15. Vanhoozer, *Is There a Meaning?*, 117.
16. Vanhoozer, *Is There a Meaning?*, 117.
17. Wright, *Scripture*, 73.
18. Graham, "Defending Biblical Literalism," 173.
19. Wright, *People of God*, 19. For example, Bible believers insisted on "the *literal or*

ton comments that "literal" is, in fact, "a slippery term that people use in many different ways."[20] Vanhoozer admits that the "literal sense" is "by no means straightforward."[21] Furthermore, there is a misleading assumption that "literal" always signifies "plain." Some posit that the "literal meaning is the 'plain and ordinary' meaning."[22] Simply put, a "plain sense [is] not the same as literal. For literal might indeed be anything but plain, if the passage was itself complex and convoluted."[23] We have already seen that a literal claim is advanced if there is a one-to-one correspondence between the locutions and the empirical reality referred to in the locutions. Nonetheless, there are further suggestions regarding the exact identification of a "literal" interpretation.

Kathryn Greene-McCreight postulates that the "literal sense" might indicate "the verbal sense," i.e., "the givenness of the words."[24] This echoes my discussion of a one-to-one correspondence between locutions and their referents. For Graham, a literal interpretation occurs when "one works out the meaning of the text while taking its verbal signs according to their proper usage."[25] Watson summarizes: "The notion that texts have a single, literal, *verbal meaning* ascribes a certain stability and solidity to the phenomenon of the text."[26] Watson also posits a reading where the "referential claim implied by the text" is "inseparable from its literal sense."[27] Problems arise, however, with a narrow definition of "literal" as "the verbal sense." For one, words form meaning with "an author's particular use of language in a specific context."[28] For Gadamer, "the meanings of words depend finally on the concrete circumstances into which they

---

historical sense of scripture as the arbiter of the meaning of the text," to keep "allegorical" interpretation "at bay" (Wright, *People of God*, 19).

20. Thiselton, *Hermeneutics*, 4.

21. Vanhoozer, *Is There a Meaning?*, 303.

22. See Vanhoozer, *Is There a Meaning?*, 116. Wright mentions an obvious difficulty with this: "The word 'plain' inevitably introduces a subjective element, inviting the riposte, 'Plain to whom?'" (Wright, *Scripture*, 79).

23. Wright, *Scripture*, 79.

24. Greene-McCreight, "Literal Sense," 455; cf. Watson, *Text and Truth*, 110–15.

25. Graham, "Defending Biblical Literalism," 187.

26. Watson, *Text and Truth*, 107, emphasis added.

27. Watson, "Toward a Literal Reading," 211.

28. See Brown, *Scripture as Communication*, 173; cf. Barr, *Semantics of Biblical Language*; Thiselton, *Hermeneutics*, 203, 210; Wright, *People of God*, 116.

were spoken."[29] Meaning "is construed not at the level of the individual terms but at the level of the whole utterance or speech act."[30] Words have histories and are flexible.[31] The given sense of a word does not remain static.[32] McLean writes that words do not always "say" what they mean, for they transmit meaning beyond the literal.[33]

Greene-McCreight also postulates that the literal sense might mean "the historical sense," i.e., "what really happened."[34] Graham writes of "literal interpretation in terms of the referentiality of the text, in which the interpreter discerns how the text narrates past events."[35] For instance, the Antiochene interpreters insisted that God's revelation "was in history," and therefore, "this history was the referent of the biblical text when interpreted literally."[36] According to Barr, there can "be no doubt about the importance of the historical dimension."[37] Vanhoozer writes that literality as historical reference "means identifying the events and persons to which it refers."[38] Problems arise, however, with a narrow perspective on "literal" meaning as the historical referent. For example, Hans Frei asserted that in centuries past, literal interpretation was equated with a text's historical reference, yet today such a restrictive reading of Scripture is difficult to sustain.[39] Neil MacDonald comments, "Frei is absolutely right in his claim that literal sense is not to be equated with historical reference."[40] Barr points out that the historical dimension may mean different things: the intention of the writer "at the time of writing or editing," "the earliest known form of the text," or even a determination of

29. Gadamer, *Philosophical Hermeneutics*, xxxii.

30. Osborne, *Hermeneutical Spiral*, 388. For example, Osborne comments on the isolated word "bear" when referencing a man, and its possible meanings at the level of a "whole utterance": "does the man look like a bear, or is he as strong as a bear, or is he a 'bear' of a grader?" (Osborne, *Hermeneutical Spiral*, 388).

31. Neill and Wright, *Interpretation*, 86.

32. See the discussion in Thiselton, *New Horizons*, 192–95; cf. Brown, *Scripture as Communication*, 21–22; Hicks, Review of *Scripture as Communication*, 817.

33. McLean, *Biblical Interpretation*, 229.

34. Greene-McCreight, "Literal Sense," 455.

35. Graham, "Defending Biblical Literalism," 174.

36. See Vanhoozer, *Is There a Meaning?*, 115.

37. Barr, "The Literal," 9.

38. Vanhoozer, *Is There a Meaning?*, 307.

39. See Frei, *Eclipse of Biblical Narrative*.

40. MacDonald, "Illocutionary Stance," 319.

"what really happened."[41] Graham writes that literal interpretation "is not less an inquiry into the text's reference to actual things or historical events, [but] it must transcend profane, reductionist literalisms in which the letter's referent is understood exclusively within a mundane historical framework."[42] A "literal interpretation," then, "is more than a univocally descriptive and exact presentation of historical factuality."[43]

Greene-McCreight postulates that the literal sense might mean "the authorial meaning," i.e., "what the author really meant."[44] We have already noted authorial intention in our discussion contrasting literal and figurative interpretations. The literal sense could connote what "the first writers intended," i.e., "the whole expressed mind . . . of the human writer."[45] The interpreter, then, seeks "to put himself in the writer's linguistic, cultural, historical, and religious shoes."[46] The impact intended by the author (the illocutionary force) is a crucial component in a literal meaning. Vanhoozer writes that the "literal sense" is "not a matter of locutions alone; every utterance has an illocutionary force as well."[47] I mentioned earlier that Critical Realism requires the biblical interpreter to view the text as external and independent. The ontological realism of texts results in "a *prima facie* claim on the reader, namely, to be construed in accord with its intended sense."[48] This "intended sense" is authorial and is tethered to the text itself. Watson offers a defense of "authorial intention":

> To construe a series of marks as a series of words is already (in normal circumstances) to assume that these words are combined with the intention of communicating an intelligible meaning; and if the words objectively embody an intention to communicate, then that intention can only be that of the author . . . To disregard authorial intention would be to refuse to strive for intelligibility and to allow the text to fall into relative or complete opacity and thus to lose the communicative function without which it is nothing.[49]

41. Barr, "The Literal," 9.

42. Graham, "Defending Biblical Literalism," 190.

43. Vanhoozer, *Is There a Meaning?*, 307–8.

44. Greene-McCreight, "Literal Sense," 455.

45. Wright, *Scripture*, 74.

46. Packer, "Infallible Scripture," 345.

47. Vanhoozer, *Is There a Meaning?*, 312.

48. Meyer, *Critical Realism*, xi, 17.

49. Watson, *Text and Truth*, 112–13.

A problem emerges, however, if literal meaning is limited to what was understood by the author's "original audience," with the result that "the literal meaning of the text is perfectly stable and univocal, and its meaning in the past is its only meaning."[50] In addition, as we have discussed, how do we equate literality with authorial intention, if the "intention" was metaphorical? While authorial intention needs to be included in the discussion regarding "literal sense," it should not be reductionistically used to encompass the sole component of a literal interpretation.

A further aspect of the literal sense of the Bible focuses on its theological content. Childs writes that a problem arose with "a severe tension between a flat, formalistic reading of the text's verbal sense" that was, in fact, "deaf to its theological content."[51] Since the authors of Scripture proclaimed faith convictions, Schneiders writes, "the literal meaning of the text was understood to include primarily theological material in kerygmatic form."[52] Thus, "theological concerns were an integral part of the literal sense of the text."[53] This is similar to Moberly, who sought to "take with full seriousness the integrity of the biblical text on its own terms: that is, to find the 'spiritual meaning' precisely in the 'literal sense.'"[54] He wrote, "what the words of the biblical text say and mean," i.e., the literal sense, should be contrasted with an "understanding at a deeper level that of which they speak," i.e., the "spiritual" sense.[55] He saw the literal sense as a combination of the "letter" and the "spirit" of the biblical text, even defending a "holding together of 'spirit' and 'letter.'"[56] Thus, "the text is read literally when this spiritual sense is taken into account."[57] Relatedly, Graham speaks of the literal sense being conveyed through the text's theological content:

> Scripture refers to a mysterious, transhistorical reality which
> exceeds its own textual, historical form. Human words cannot

50. See Schneiders, "Faith," 721.

51. Childs, *Biblical Theology*, 724–25. The converse was also problematic, when "a theological and figurative rendering of the biblical text . . . ran roughshod over the language of the text to its lasting detriment" (Childs, *Biblical Theology*, 724–25).

52. Schneiders, "Faith," 723.

53. Schneiders, "Faith," 723.

54. Moberly, *Bible*, 232.

55. Moberly, *Bible*, 228.

56. Moberly, *Bible*, 229.

57. Moberly, *Bible*, 229. Thiselton considers Moberly's views an "excellent discussion of the complexity of a 'literal' meaning" (see Thiselton, *Hermeneutics*, 4n7).

contain the Word, nor can a historical scientific framework adequately account for the text's theological reference. The whole of Scripture, therefore, functions as an improper sign, its letter always pointing beyond itself.[58]

This theological focus on the content of Scripture evinced here illustrates another component in a literal interpretation.

Before summarizing this discussion on literality, we note that Greene-McCreight speaks for many when she considers how the role of the reader as well as of the community have become "of greater interest than any concept of fixity in the literal sense of the text as once understood."[59] In addition, Stephen Fowl argues for a "multivoiced literal sense," and writes that as far back as Thomas Aquinas many authors recognized that "literal" did not incontrovertibly signify "only one meaning."[60] These observations emphasize the complexity of the topic under discussion.

To summarize what we have seen, the "literal sense" can encompass verbal meaning, the historical referent, authorial intention, and/or the theological/spiritual component. Literality cannot be limited, however, to any one of these categories. For my purposes, I reiterate my earlier conclusion: a literal claim is advanced if there is a one-to-one correspondence between the locutions and the reality that the locutions refer to. Other aspects can now be added. The verbal meaning of individual words remains important, since words are the "raw materials" of language. However, it must be emphasized that entire locutions make up a communicative act, and therefore, meaning comes from phrases, not isolated words.[61] Furthermore, while the historical referent cannot be *equated* with a literal sense, it is *aspect* of communicative action and, therefore, of a literal interpretation. The impact intended by the author is a crucial component in a literal meaning. For Watson, the literal sense includes an illocutionary and perlocutionary force that is tied to the author's intention.[62] Since texts are "communicative actions," they "seek to convey a meaning to evoke a particular response."[63] Therefore, "to grasp the verbal

58. Graham, "Defending Biblical Literalism," 197.

59. Greene-McCreight, "Literal Sense," 455–56.

60. Fowl, "Importance of a Multivoiced Literal Sense," 35.

61. Vanhoozer, *Is There a Meaning?*, 310.

62. Again, an illocutionary force is the impact intended by the author, and a perlocutionary force is the expected action taken by the reader/hearer.

63. Watson, *Text and Truth*, 123.

meaning and the illocutionary and perlocutionary force of a text is to understand the authorial intention embodied in it."[64]

Considering these additional insights, I can now give a fuller explanation. A literal interpretation is illustrated with a one-to-one correspondence between the locutions and the empirical reality that such locutions refer to. However, if, ostensibly, the locutions do not describe an empirical reality, then the sense is figurative. A literal interpretation could include a figurative sense if the author intended it as such. In addition, there is determinate meaning tied to the illocutionary intent of the author. The goal of the careful interpreter will be this determinate meaning.[65] Taking into consideration these aspects of literality will militate against indeterminacy in the interpretive process.

3.1.3. Literalistic Interpretation by the LDS

As a final introductory matter before viewing specific LDS interpretations, I propose that the literal interpretations by the LDS are better characterized as *literalistic*. I believe the LDS is insufficiently critical of their perspective on literality. Their interpretations presuppose a self-evident understanding of the empirical referentiality of the text with a direct correspondence between the text and external realities of the text. As I will detail with numerous relevant examples, their literalistic interpretations assume a one-to-one correspondence between the locution and the reality described—yet without consideration of authorial intent.

A *literalistic* sense, in contradistinction to a literal sense, occurs when the illocutionary aspect of the text is ignored—when an interpreter fails to appreciate the author's intention in giving the utterance a certain force. Often, it is a wooden, thin interpretation that fails to go beyond the lexical meanings of words and expressions and is a "word-for-word" translation that yields verbally exact versions.[66] A *literalistic* interpretation occurs when an interpreter detects a one-to-one correspondence, yet from the perspective of the author, it was never intended. For example, no one literally interprets Jesus' words of "I am the door" (John

---

64. Watson, *Text and Truth*, 123.

65. Vanhoozer, *Is There a Meaning?*, 302. Considering this determinate meaning, the interpreter will judge as "inadequate or incorrect" other interpretations of the same communicative act (Vanhoozer, *Is There a Meaning?*, 302).

66. See Vanhoozer, *Is There a Meaning?*, 311.

10:9)—in the sense of imagining Jesus being composed of wood and a doorknob.[67] In other words, for our purposes, a *literalistic* interpretation does not consider the ancient intention of the author, but instead centers on modern realities.

In the first chapter, I maintained that Critical Realism requires the biblical interpreter to view the text as external and independent, with a conceptuality embodied in the text that is "other" than the interpreter. In addition, we have seen an "intended sense" of the text that must be a controlling factor in interpretation. I can now add the concept of literality, as a contrast to *literalistic* interpretation. The intended sense of a biblical text may be literal (a one-to-one correspondence between the locutions and the empirical reality represented by them) or figurative. In both, the interpreter must recognize the illocutionary impact of authorial intention. By considering these aspects, determinate meaning can be gleaned from the text. In the following section, along with detailing LDS *literalistic* interpretations, I will argue, among other things, that a one-to-one correspondence between the words used and the reality described by the words is not the intent of the ancient author, but of the modern LDS interpreter.

3.2. LDS Authors and Literal Interpretation

The predominant interpretive practice by the LDS appears to be literal interpretation. Parley Pratt was an early LDS apologist who set the tone for later writers by attacking those who "spiritualize" the Bible, "rather than read in the plain, literal sense."[68] In his book *Voice of Warning*, he compared dozens of biblical passages and concluded that the LDS believed in the "Doctrines of Christ," (i.e., the literal meaning), while other churches believed in the "Doctrines of Men," (i.e., the spiritualized meaning).[69] Pratt also bemoaned the illegitimate hermeneutical posturing of other churches:

> Having lost the Spirit of Inspiration, they began to institute their own opinions, traditions, and commandments; giving constructions and private interpretations to the written word, instead of believing the things written. And the moment they departed

---

67. Vanhoozer, *Is There a Meaning?*, 117.

68. See Givens, *Wrestling the Angel*, 18, 321; cf. Restoration Branches, *EMS*, 1.2:14, "Hosea Chapter III."

69. Pratt, *Voice of Warning*, 206–20.

from [Scripture's] literal meaning, one man's opinion, or interpretation, was just as good as another's.[70]

Brigham Young, the second LDS president, reprimanded the Christian
world "for failing to believe [the Bible] in its literal sense."[71] Literal interpretation is "firmly rooted in LDS history."[72] Indeed, the early LDS
"out-Bibled the biblicists" as a result of "their marked literalism in scriptural interpretation."[73] Contemporary LDS author Richard Hopkins contends that when interpreting the Bible, literal interpretation "is always
preferred."[74] For Richard Cummings, "literalism . . . lies at the core of the
Mormon belief system."[75] The LDS keeps "symbolic, figurative, or allegorical interpretation to a minimum," instead maintaining that Scripture
is "literally true."[76] Other LDS authors call this an "entrenched literalism,"[77]
and assert that "Mormons were strikingly literalist."[78]

This literal interpretation, however, is a selective literalism. Early
leaders of the LDS "selected their texts carefully" to emphasize doctrines
that convinced those outside of their church.[79] Such doctrines included
apostasy, the restoration, the millennium, and the special role of Israel.
Echoing the teaching of continuing revelation, "Joseph Smith's expanding theological understanding at any given time dictated which biblical
materials he took literally and which less literally, [or] not literally at all."[80]

70. Pratt, *Voice of Warning*, 3–4.

71. Young, in Barlow, *Mormons and the Bible*, 95.

72. Barber, "Literalist Constraint," 25; cf. McMurrin, "Some Distinguishing Characteristics," 35–46; Wright, "Historical Criticism," 28–38.

73. Underwood, *Millenarian World*, 58.

74. Hopkins, *Biblical Mormonism*, 34.

75. Cummings, "Quintessential Mormonism," 92.

76. Robinson, in Blomberg and Robinson, *How Wide?*, 55. Here we note the erroneous concept that literal is in opposition to figurative. The way Robinson would
interpret a passage where the authorial intention is figurative is unclear.

77. Shepherd and Shepherd, *Kingdom Transformed*, 5; cf. Mauss, "Refuge and Retrenchment," 34; White, *Mormon Neo-orthodoxy*, 58.

78. Arrington and Bitton, *Mormon Experience*, 30.

79. Barlow, *Mormons and the Bible*, 10, 49; cf. Irving, "Mormons and the Bible,"
483–87; Arrington and Bitton, *Mormon Experience*, 30; Craig Hazen, in Beckwith et
al., *New Mormon Challenge*, 36.

80. Barlow, "Before Mormonism," 759.

As the LDS movement grew, there was a careful selection of texts to take seriously, and a careful selection of texts to neglect.[81]

As we have seen, some observers, LDS or otherwise, contend that the "plain meaning" of the biblical text is in consonance with a "literal" interpretation. This, in fact, holds acute prominence in LDS thinking. The deciphering of the "plain meaning" is "a leading principle in LDS exegesis."[82] Early LDS leader Sidney Rigdon presented "plain scripture facts" and was "contemptuous of 'spiritualizing' the prophecies.'"[83] The BoM prophet Nephi declared that his "soul delighteth in plainness" (2 Nephi 25:4). Nephi was referring to the "plainness" of the interpretation of the book of Isaiah, as well as to his own prophecy.[84] Similar to many Bible believers in the nineteenth century, early Mormons "looked to a common-sense reading of the KJV for their spiritual understanding."[85] These Mormons "prided themselves on the self-evident biblical premises of their faith."[86] On account of the "religious confusion engendered by priestcraft," many restorationists, including the early leaders of the LDS, insisted that Bible believers "should shun the priests and become their own ministers. Any person with a Bible and the ability to read could learn the plain self-evident truths of Christianity."[87] These LDS thinkers, then, assume that a literal interpretation is equated with the "plain," or "straightforward" meaning. This "straightforward" reading, however, seamlessly assumes a one-to-one correspondence between the biblical locutions and the empirical realities that the locutions refer to, regardless of authorial intention.

81. See Barlow, *Mormons and the Bible*, 220.

82. Davies and Madsen, "Scriptures," 1280.

83. See Arrington and Bitton, *Mormon Experience*, 30.

84. See also 2 Nephi 31:3; D&C 1:24. A positive aspect of the BoM during the early years of the LDS was its supposed "plainness" and "straightforwardness." For its "rural audience," this was a "mark of its genuineness" (O'Dea, *The Mormons*, 30).

85. Givens and Barlow, *Oxford Handbook on Mormonism*, 130. Indeed, Joseph Smith "sought, in short, to restore the Bible's perspicuity" (Smith, "Hermeneutical Crisis," 87).

86. Fluhman, *"A Peculiar People,"* 66.

87. Winn, *Exiles in a Land of Liberty*, 50.

3.2.1. *James 1:5 and the Straightforward, Literal Call to Seek Wisdom*

We have seen the use of Jas 1:5 as an example of diminution and eleva-tion of the Bible: "If any of you lack wisdom, let him ask of God, that giveth to all men liberally, and upbraideth not; and it shall be given him" (Jas 1:5). According to Cummings, "Joseph Smith took literally the words of James 1:5."[88] Smith needed clarification because of competing Bible interpretations. However, there appears to be a one-to-one correspon-dence imposed on the text that was not intended by the author: "wisdom" for Smith was an aid for personal decision-making. Other interpreters, however, note a dissimilar intention by the author. Contextually, wisdom was needed "in order to achieve the programme set out in [Jas] 1:2–4."[89] This "programme" was the "maturing toward moral perfection" through afflictions.[90] There is a connection between the "perception" of v. 2 con-cerning "trials of many kinds," and the need for wisdom and prayer in v. 5, in order to gain the proper perspective. Wisdom was "the lack most critical to remedy," and was "practical rather than theoretical, enabling not only true perception, but also proper action in the world."[91] Wisdom was for comprehension and correct perception related to the trials and "life's testings" of v. 2.[92] If these mainstream thinkers are correct in their interpretation of Jas 1:5, then Joseph Smith literalistically interpreted the text. The illocutionary aspect of the text was ignored, for Smith failed to appreciate the author's intention concerning wisdom amid trials. Al-though Smith legitimately focused on the verbal meaning of "wisdom," he neglected the illocutionary force of authorial intention.

3.2.2. *Joseph Smith and the "True Meaning" of Genesis 1:1*

In the King Follett Discourse, Joseph Smith interpreted the first verse of the Bible and gave its "true meaning."[93] Commenting on what "sort of a

---

88. Cummings, "Quintessential Mormonism," 94.

89. See Cheung, *Genre*, 63.

90. Dibelius, *James*, 77.

91. Johnson, *Letter of James*, 179.

92. See Johnson, *Letter of James*, 182–84.

93. Smith, "King Follett." Again, the King Follett Discourse was an important sermon delivered near the end of his life. At least one statement in the sermon has attained "quasi-official" status in the LDS (Robinson, in Blomberg and Robinson in *How Wide?*, 85–86).

being" God was in the beginning, Smith preached, "Open your ears and hear all ye ends of the earth; for I am going to prove it to you by the Bible."[94] He continued: "God himself, the Father of us all, dwelt on an earth the same as Jesus Christ himself did, and I will show it from the Bible." Later in the discourse, he expressed that "I suppose I am not allowed to go into an investigation of anything that is not contained in the Bible."[95] Summarizing this sermon, LDS author Richard Bushman adduced that Smith spoke "as if he was giving the obvious meaning of the Bible."[96]

Smith claimed that in Gen 1:1 the Hebrew word (בְּרֵאשִׁית) *berēʾšît* (also commonly written as *bereshit* and translated as "In the beginning") was actually composed of three words: "*baith*–in, by, through, and everything else. *Rosh*–the head. *Sheit*–grammatical termination." He explained that originally "*baith*" was not present but was added by "a Jew without any authority." Turning to *Rosh*, he expressed that Gen 1:1 originally read "The head one of the Gods brought forth the Gods."[97] Smith concluded, "that is the true meaning of the words."[98] He attempted to remain in the interpretive realm with this "plain" reading, and even included text-critical issues and manuscript histories. His hermeneutical intuition demonstrated that meaning was locatable in the smallest linguistic unit.

Smith's straightforward (read: literal) interpretation, however, does not receive support outside of LDS circles. In contrast to "*Rosh*" ("head") as the subject of the sentence, Charles Hummel remarks: "God is not only the subject of the first sentence, he is central to the entire narrative. It

---

94. Smith, "King Follett."

95. Smith, "King Follett."

96. Bushman, *Rough Stone*, 534.

97. I.e., רֹאשׁ בָּרָא אֱלֹהִים (*rōʾš bārāʾ ʾelōhîm*) "The head one (of the Gods) brought forth the Gods."

98. Smith, "King Follett." The standard LDS defense is that Smith used Hebrew "as an artist, inside of his frame of reference, in accordance with his taste" (Zucker, "Joseph Smith as a Student," 53). Yet, another LDS author admits to Smith's "apparent garbling of the Hebrew" (Barney, "Joseph Smith's Emendation," 106). Barney does defend, however, Smith's idea of a scribal error ("a Jew without any authority") with the apparent dittography of the Hebrew letter (ב) *bet*. Supposedly the scribe noticed the *bet* of the second word (בָּרָא) *bārāʾ* and added *bet* to (רֵאשִׁית) *rēʾšît*, which again, according to Joseph Smith, was really *Rosh*—"the head" (רֹאשׁ). Barney adds that the lack of vowels for an ancient scribe would have contributed to this error. However, Barney admits that this error "would have been highly unlikely at the beginning of the text" (Barney, "Joseph Smith's Emendation," 110–11). In response, this is not only highly unlikely, but seemingly impossible, given the seriousness with which scribes worked in the ancient world, as well as being the very first words a scribe would copy.

mentions him thirty-four times."[99] The Hebrew word "*Rosh*" is not found in any Hebrew manuscripts. Paul Kissling writes that the Bible simply doesn't explain or defend the existence of God. He was there "in the beginning" and "nothing precedes him and everything in the cosmos finds its origin in him."[100] Although Kissling admits to "disagreement on the translation of the verse," the "traditional translation" of "in the beginning" is "the only one which does justice to the original intention of the author and the wider 'canonical context.'"[101]

However, LDS scholar Kevin Barney responds, "Revelation often results after wrestling with ideas."[102] He states: "Joseph's struggle with the Hebrew of Gen 1:1 seems to have yielded six concepts," two of which are "a plurality of gods," and "a head God."[103] To support the former, Barney simply declares there is an "essentially accepted idea in scholarship today," that "the ancient Hebrews of the patriarchal age believed in a plurality of Gods."[104] As regards the latter, Barney states, "One can argue that the existence of a pantheon implies the presence of a supreme God who rules the pantheon."[105]

Non-LDS scholar Ronald Huggins disagrees with Barney on the translation of Gen 1:1.[106] He mentions two earlier translations *by Joseph Smith*: "in the beginning I created the heaven, and the earth upon which thou standest" (Moses 2:1, PGP); "they went down at the beginning, and they, that is the Gods, organized and formed the heavens and the earth" (Abraham 4:1, PGP). These translations differ significantly from the interpretation under consideration. Huggins also mentions a sermon by Smith given on June 16, 1844—months *after* the King Follett Discourse—when he did, in fact, include *bereshit*: "In the begin[ning] the heads of the Gods organized the heaven & the Earth."[107] Huggins then points out the problems in the King Follett Discourse that treats God/gods as a direct

99. Hummel, "Interpreting Genesis One," 179.

100. Kissling, *Genesis*, 1:82.

101. Kissling, *Genesis*, 1:82.

102. Barney, "Examining Six Key Concepts," 107.

103. Barney, "Examining Six Key Concepts," 107.

104. Barney, "Examining Six Key Concepts," 112. This is not as "accepted" as Barney claims.

105. Barney, "Examining Six Key Concepts," 114.

106. Huggins, "Joseph Smith and the First Verse," 29–52.

107. Huggins, "Joseph Smith and the First Verse," 30, 33, 40.

object (contra the works just cited of the Book of Moses, Abraham and the June 16 sermon).[108]

I noted above that Smith's hermeneutical intuition was to locate meaning in the smallest linguistic unit. However, the legitimacy of this approach is a matter of some debate. The "true meaning" of biblical passages is rarely, if ever, found by *exclusive* focus on word studies and contextual linguistic investigation. Hermeneutically, an exaggerated focus on etymology has dangers, since it may take the reader outside of the text itself, in search for the history of the word. The views of Wright echo this caution, although he doesn't foreclose all etymological investigation: "Historical exegesis is not simply a matter of laying out the lexicographical meanings of words and sentences. It involves exploring the resonances those words and sentences would have had in their contexts."[109] In actuality, the LDS infrequently focuses on the minutiae of the biblical texts. Rather, it seems that Smith and the Mormon church desire flexibility and interpretive freedom, as is witnessed in the divergent translations by Smith of the verse under question. Smith appears to exhibit a thin veneer of scholarly work, as evidenced with such words as "I am going to prove it to you by the Bible"; "I will show it from the Bible"; "I suppose I am not allowed to go into an investigation of anything that is not contained in the Bible." In fact, however, he closes down the interpretive practice. On one hand, Smith reduces interpretation to detailed linguistic investigation, yet on the other hand, he seeks to maintain freedom and flexibility and does not consider the authorial intention of biblical texts. Given the different translations of Gen 1:1, two of which are included in LDS "Standard Works" (cited above), the "literal" and "straightforward" interpretation of Gen 1:1 by Joseph Smith in the King Follett Discourse does not hold up to scrutiny. These disparate translations exhibit a modern freedom with ancient words. In addition, Barney's view that "Revelation often results after wrestling with ideas" illustrates a problematic emphasis on the modern interpreter.[110]

108. Huggins, "Joseph Smith and the First Verse," 45.

109. Wright, *Jesus and the Victory*, xvii. We noted this above in our discussion on literality.

110. Barney, "Examining Six Key Concepts," 107.

3.2.3. *Literal Interpretation and the Deification of the LDS Believer*

The LDS teaches that "men and women have the potential of evolving literally into gods themselves."[111] Paulsen writes, "Biblically, Peter, John, and Paul all spoke of the idea that man can become God (2 Pet 1:4; Rom 8:16–17)." He continues: the phrases "participating in the divine nature" (2 Pet 1:4) and becoming "heirs" of God and "co-heirs with Christ" (Rom 8:16–17) describe deification.[112] Benjamin Huff cites 1 John 3:2, and comments: "Mormons take very seriously the New Testament promises" that "when (Christ) shall appear, we shall be like him; for we shall see him as he is (1 John 3:2)."[113] The phrase "we shall be like him," is taken to mean, literally, that we will become god-like.[114] Millet cites the call to be perfect in Matt 5:48 as support for the doctrine of deification.[115] Millet also uses a straightforward reading of 1 Cor 2:16 and gaining "the mind of Christ" for a similar defense.[116] Robinson notes that the LDS "take seriously and literally the scriptural language about becoming children of God (Rom 8:16)."[117] According to Blake Ostler, there are "four biblical texts most often cited to support deification": 2 Pet 1:2–4, John 10 (citing Ps 82), John 17, and 1 John 3.[118] An interpretive focus on the "plain" meaning of these biblical texts leads to these LDS conclusions.

111. Cummings, "Quintessential Mormonism," 95.

112. See Paulsen, "Are Christians Mormon?," 80; cf. Paulsen, in Paulsen and Musser, *Mormonism in Dialogue*, 527. Paulsen believes that in contrast to the Orthodox church in the East, Western theologians have given marginal attention to the doctrine of deification, although he notes some exceptions: Mosser, "Greatest Possible Blessing," 36–57; Rakestraw, "Becoming Like God," 257–69 (see Paulsen, "Are Christians Mormon?," 84).

113. Huff, "Theology in the Light," 484; cf. Smith, *Essentials in Church History*, 725; Carmack, *New Testament*, 17.

114. However, for John Painter, the point of the passage was not the ontological deification of the believer, but "the question of why the author thought that to see him is to be like him" (Painter, *1, 2, and 3 John*, 221). I. Howard Marshall equates this verse with glorification (see 2 Cor 3:18) and not deification (Marshall, *Epistles of John*, 172–73).

115. Millet, in Baker, *Mormonism at the Crossroads*, 257. To the LDS Church, this "admonition of Jesus," frequently quoted in sermons and writings, "would be strange indeed were it impossible to fulfill" (White, *Mormon Neo-orthodoxy*, 74; cf. LDS, "Be Ye Therefore Perfect," 236–42).

116. Millet, in McLaughlan and Ericson, *Discourses in Mormon Theology*, 275.

117. Robinson, in Blomberg and Robinson, *How Wide?*, 80; cf. Ing, "Ritual as a Process," 349–67.

118. Ostler, *Of God of Gods*, 616–66. Furthermore, in his King Follett discourse,

However, do these interpretations unequivocally assert "human-kind becoming godlike"? Although supposedly *literal*, these examples on deification appear to be literalistic interpretations, i.e., "wooden, thin" interpretations that fail to go beyond the standard meanings of words and expressions.[119] A "word-for-word" interpretation seamlessly connects "perfect" (Matt 5:48) with deification. A literalistic reading of "becoming children of God" becomes evidence for humankind becoming god-like. The locution of being "like him," is taken as a one-to-one correspondence regarding deity, and being "like him" becomes a "verbally exact version"[120] of god-likeness. This is unwarranted. Additionally, "participation in the divine nature" assumes that the empirical realities of both "participation" and "divine nature" correspond to a human perspective. Regardless of authorial intention in the passage, the plain meaning of "participation" is effortlessly connected to a human ability to not only "take part in"/"participate," but also *possess* divine nature. These interpretations appear to ignore the illocutionary impact of authorial intention. Instead of an investigation into the conceptuality embodied in these texts, and an attempt to find the intended sense, these literalistic interpretations appear to override any ancient, contextual meaning.

3.2.4. *Literal Interpretation and Divine Corporeality*

As regards divine corporeality, David Paulsen seems to advocate for literal interpretation to release "biblical passages from the shackles of merely figurative interpretation."[121] Although this quote has only a tangential connection to the topic at hand, it does merit comment, for there appears to be a bias against "figurative" here. Why would a figurative interpretation be a "shackle"? This is especially noteworthy, since, as we have seen, it is undeniable that authorial intention can be figurative. Other LDS authors admit this—for, as I will note, Richard Hopkins sees figurative interpretation in the book of Psalms with God having

---

Joseph Smith challenged his hearers to strive for their eventual godhood (Smith, "King Follett"). Modern LDS scriptural support for deification is found in D&C 132, the revelation on plural marriage. Also, Givens chides the Protestant tradition for neglecting and even rejecting the "patristic teaching on theosis" (deification)—"only to see it raised in such venues as *Christianity Today*" (Givens, "Mormons at the Forefront," 20).

119. Vanhoozer, *Is There a Meaning?*, 311.

120. See Vanhoozer, *Is There a Meaning?*, 311.

121. Paulsen, in Paulsen and Musser, *Mormonism in Dialogue*, 516.

"wings." At the very least, Paulsen's view underscores the fact that the LDS does not seem interested in authorial intention. Paulsen appears to assume, irrespective of the contextual intention by the author, that "literal" is in opposition to "figurative."

Nonetheless, Paulsen believes there is "considerable biblical evidence" for divine corporeality (e.g., Gen 1:27; 5:1; 9:6; 32:30; Exod 24:10; 31:18; 33:11; Luke 24:39; John 14:9; 2 Cor 4:4; Phil 3:21; 1 John 3:2; Rev 22:4).[122] Passages that appear to depict an embodied God should be interpreted "in a straightforward, literal sense."[123] A "very human God" walked with Abraham.[124] Further evidence is that the "Israelites see God's feet; Moses sees his back; he is 'seen face to face' by his people, and so on."[125] Dwight Monson claims that there "are more than thirty references to specific body parts of God," for example, face (Gen 32:30; Exod 33:11), mouth (Num 12:5–8) and finger (Deut 9:10). In addition, there are references "to functions associated with a body such as sitting (Ps 47:8), walking (Gen 3:8; 5:24) and standing (Acts 7:56)."[126]

The body of the incarnate Christ is also used as evidence. Since Christ is the "image of the invisible God" (Col 1:15); is in the "form of God" (Phil 2:6); is the "express image of the [Father]" (Heb 1:3); and had a "glorified body of flesh and bones" after his resurrection, "inescapable logic requires the conclusion that God the Father has a glorified body of flesh and bones."[127] God is spirit, according to LDS thinkers, yet is not

122. Paulsen, in Paulsen and Musser, *Mormonism in Dialogue*, 519. Paulsen also asserts that the early Christians believed in divine embodiment. See Paulsen, "Early Christian Belief," 105–16; Griffin and Paulsen, "Augustine and the Corporeality of God," 97–118. He does write, however, that "Modern Revelation" is the "bedrock" for this belief (Paulsen, in Paulsen and Musser, *Mormonism in Dialogue*, 520). Relatedly, for Stephen Robinson, divine embodiment cannot be proven or disproven by the Bible, but instead comes from modern revelation (Robinson, *Are Mormons Christians?*, 88; Robinson, in Blomberg and Robinson, *How Wide?*, 91). An example of such modern revelation is D&C 130:22, which states the Father has a "body of flesh and bone as tangible as a man's and the Son likewise." Blake Ostler writes that the Father, Son, and Holy Spirit each "possesses a unique material body" (Ostler, *Of God and Gods*, 411).

123. Paulsen, in Baker, *Mormonism at the Crossroads*, 216.

124. Faulconer, "Rethinking Theology," 191. This "human God" in Genesis 18 is presumably embodied.

125. Givens, *Wrestling the Angel*, 90.

126. Monson, *Shared Beliefs*, 23.

127. See Hopkins, *Biblical Mormonism*, 60. However, regarding other views of Heb 1:3, Attridge writes that the passage cannot refer to physical realities, "since the context, especially vs 2b, clearly refers to the pre-existent Son" (Attridge, *Epistle to the Hebrews*,

limited to being spirit: "God's being a spirit doesn't necessarily preclude him from also having a body."[128] God is "a glorified person with a tangible body."[129] Indeed, only those unduly influenced by Greek philosophy, with its spirit/body dualism, viewing "spirit and matter [as] mutually exclusive, opposing categories" will fail to see how God could be both spirit and embodied.[130] It is important to note that the very idea of an embodied God supposedly holds difficulties for non-LDS Bible readers—who are under the influence of Greek philosophy—while the LDS claims to remain free from such difficulties.

The notion of an embodied Father, however, is the result of *literalistic* interpretation. The figurative meanings of God's face, mouth and finger are given a one-to-one correspondence to a physical, human body. Authorial intention in these passages is not a concern for the LDS authors. An important perspective concerning this issue is from Nicholas Wolterstorff. For instance, he recognizes a fundamental distinction between the locutionary and illocutionary content of the biblical texts, with emphasis on the latter.[131] Biblical narrative is not simply declarative, for "stories were being told to make a point."[132] For example, Wolterstorff stresses the majesty of God as the illocutionary intent of Ps 93: "The Lord reigns, he is robed in majesty; the Lord is robed in majesty and is armed with strength. The world is firmly established; it cannot be moved" (Ps 93:1 NIV). The main point of the psalm is the illocutionary content— God and his majesty. Yet, this illocutionary intent apparently obscures the locutionary content of the "world/earth is firmly established"—for we know that "the earth cannot be moved" is not true, since the earth is

---

44). Koester relates how the Son was the "impress" of the Father's "substance." Therefore, there was "congruence between God and the Son in terms of their "substance" or "being" (Koester, *Hebrews*, 189; cf. deSilva, *Perseverance in Gratitude*, 89).

128. Harrell, "*This Is My Doctrine*," 132.

129. See LDS, *New Testament Seminary*, 143.

130. See Robinson, *Are Mormons Christians?*, 80–81. In addition, according to Bruce McConkie, if God was only a spirit, he is "a spirit nothingness that fills the immensity of space" (McConkie, *New Witness*, 23). McConkie also asks how "a three-in-one spirit essence that is everywhere and nowhere in particular present," can "either see or hear or eat or smell, all of which things the true God does?" (McConkie, *New Witness*, 525). Also, because of a "Cartesian dualism," which was influenced by "the Platonic tradition . . . Christianity gave priority to things spiritual over things physical" (see Park, "Salvation through a Tabernacle," 4).

131. See Wolterstorff, *Divine Discourse*, 20.

132. Wolterstorff, *Divine Discourse*, 214.

rotating and constantly in motion. However, we can "discard the psalm-ist's particular way of making the point as of purely human significance."[133] Wolterstorff summarizes that some locutionary content is left behind (e.g., "earth cannot be moved") because of the illocutionary intent—God as majestic and everlasting.[134] To relate this to our discussion, we can "leave behind" the content of a "very human God" who walked with Abraham (Gen 18:16), because of the illocutionary emphasis on God's presence—in solidarity with Abraham and in judgment against Sodom and Gomorrah. We can "leave behind" the content of "being like Christ" (1 John 3:2) to stress the illocutionary content of the passage—the onto-logical reality of Christ himself—for to "see him" is to be "like him." In addition, the transcendence of God appears to be the illocutionary intent of Gen 1:1. He created everything "in the beginning." While not all the complexities of creation are answered in Gen 1:1, the illocutionary intent conveys a transcendent, creator God. Smith's translation of the "head (one of the Gods) brought forth the gods" neglects this illocutionary intent.

For Wolterstorff, language about God's "body" (e.g., ears, eyes) is an example of metaphorical/figurative speech.[135] The main intent in biblical interpretation is to "move from our interpretation of the human discourse to our interpretation of the divine discourse mediated by that human discourse."[136] The "divine discourse" of God's speech often results in an illocutionary force, rather than exhibiting a literal character. Addi-tionally, the frequent references to God's "mouth" (Num 12:8; Deut 32:1; Isa 55:11; Lam 3:38), exhibit anthropomorphism. God does not physical-ly communicate like human beings, with sounds emanating from vocal cords.[137] To summarize Wolterstorff's perspective, language about God's body, if taken in a literalistic manner, ignores the illocutionary intent of passages that communicate a "divine discourse." The passages describing God's "mouth" or citing the "voice of God" are intended metaphorically to emphasize that God communicates with his creation—that there is "divine discourse."

Vanhoozer advances similar notions. The *literal* sense of "the eyes of the Lord are on the righteous" (Ps 34:15) is figurative. This is because

---

133. Wolterstorff, *Divine Discourse*, 210.

134. See Wolterstorff, *Divine Discourse*, 211.

135. Wolterstorff, *Divine Discourse*, 211.

136. Wolterstorff, *Divine Discourse*, 227.

137. Wolterstorff, "On God Speaking," 8; cf. Henry, *God*, 3:409.

of the intention of the author to highlight God's "oversight" of his people. "The author intends that the reader recognize his expression as a
metaphor."[138] Far from describing divine embodiment, "the communicative act of metaphorical assertion" in this passage conveys the meaning
of divine care and providence.[139] With the phrase of "eyes of the Lord" an
established metaphorical figure of speech is literalized by the LDS to de-
note physical, human-like eyes. However, similar to "hit the road" mentioned earlier, the biblical reader is expected to understand the figurative
meaning of "the eyes of the Lord." The illocutionary intent communicates
divine care.

3.2.5. Literal Interpretation and the Image of God

The LDS doctrine of the image of God follows naturally from their teaching on divine corporeality, for "by definition, an image is the representation of physical qualities."[140] Since God has a body, male and female
humans will literally and physically "image" him (or her). Arrington
and Bitton claim that "it is possible for Mormons to take quite literally"
that male and female were made in the image of God (Gen 1:26–27).[141]
Cummings confidently states that "surely in the entire Judeo-Christian
tradition there has been no more literal interpretation than that of the
basic doctrine set forth in Gen 1:27 that 'God created man in his own
image.'"[142] Physicality is assumed with the terms in Gen 1—(צֶלֶם) ṣĕ·lĕm
for "image" and (דְּמוּת) demûṯ for "likeness," with human beings as "exact
duplicates who 'look like' God and the gods."[143] Ostler's argument centers
on Gen 5:3 and its contextual proximity to Gen 1:26–27. If Adam's son,
Seth, was "in [Adam's] own likeness (דְּמוּת) demûṯ," and "in [Adam's] own
image (צֶלֶם) ṣĕ·lĕm" (Gen 5:3), then this physicality would apply to Gen

---

138. Vanhoozer, Is There a Meaning?, 312.

139. Vanhoozer, Is There a Meaning?, 312.

140. Robinson, in Blomberg and Robinson, How Wide?, 80.

141. Arrington and Bitton, Mormon Experience, 186.

142. Cummings, "Quintessential Mormonism," 94. Of course, as Vanhoozer comments, "One's view of God . . . will influence which biblical statements about God one
considers literal and which statements one takes as figurative" (Vanhoozer, "Theological Interpretation?," 19).

143. Ostler, Of God and Gods, 422.

1.[144] Ostler also speaks of the "image" as "visual representation."[145] Philip Davies believes that, unlike the LDS perspective, other traditions read Gen 1 as an "over-interpretation, inspired by the presence of a theological agenda, which in many cases appears reluctant to allow that God has a shape that is the same as a human one and wishes to allegorize the 'image' and 'likeness' in some way."[146] This is echoed by Richard Hopkins who sees non-LDS readers as "unwilling to accept" the literal meaning of Gen 1:26–27.[147]

Non-LDS author Gordon Wenham does admit that a "physical image is the most frequent meaning of [*ṣĕ·lĕm*]." He does point out, however, that challenges emerge with the equivalency of the image with physical representation, since "the OT's stress on the incorporeality and invisibility of God makes this view somewhat problematic (cf. Deut 4:15–16)."[148] Thiselton relates the image of God to humankind's reasoning capacity, ability to relate to others, and dominion over creation.[149] G. C. Berkouwer laments that the biblical witness "never gives us any kind of systematic theory about man as the image of God," although the terms used, *ṣĕ·lĕm* and *demût*, "obviously . . . refer to a relation between man and his Creator; a 'likeness' between man and God, with no explanation given as to exactly what this likeness consists of or implies."[150] John Frame cautions his readers: "We should not try to identify the image with something *in* us, maybe intellect, emotions, or will. The Bible doesn't say that there is an image of God *in* man; rather, it says that man *is* the image of God . . . Everything in us—intellect, emotions, will, even body—reflects God in some way."[151] Frame speaks of how the image relates to dominion, to ethics, and more importantly for our purposes, to a physicality element:

> The image of God is physical, bodily. The human eye is an image of God's power to see . . . God doesn't have literal eyes, but our eyes reflect his power of sight. Similarly, Scripture speaks of God's "arm" and "hand," indicating his power to act, and

144. Ostler, *Of God and Gods*, 422.

145. Ostler, *Of God and Gods*, 456–57n6.

146. See Philip Davies, in Ostler, *Of God and Gods*, 657.

147. Hopkins, *Biblical Mormonism*, 55.

148. Wenham, *Genesis 1–15*, 30.

149. Thiselton, *Hermeneutics*, 223.

150. Berkouwer, *Man*, 67, 69.

151. Frame, *Salvation Belongs to the Lord*, 88.

> showing that our arms and hand are also images of him . . . God
> doesn't have a body, but our bodies certainly reflect his power.[152]

Neither divine corporeality nor a literal, physical imaging of God in the
believer is advocated by Frame. According to Francis Watson, the discussion of the image should not be isolated to the Genesis passage but should
include the New Testament: "It is impossible to explain how humankind
is created in the image of God without explaining how the image of God
is Christ," for "we learn from Jesus what it is to be human."[153] Watson
continues: "the notion of a visual likeness between God and humans . . .
is not simply to be rejected. It is to be understood as a prophetic anticipation of the incarnation. The incarnate, human Jesus is the image of God."[154]

These possible meanings of the image of God put forward by
non-LDS authors are not compatible with the LDS notion of physicality. For authors such as Frame and Watson, there are different nuances
of meaning regarding the physicality of the image, although it is not
the direct, one-to-one correspondence that the LDS authors assume,
i.e., God's literal, physical body, including (presumably) height, weight,
eye color, etc., as physically replicated in humankind. Specifically, the
physicality of the image emphasizes our bodies as representing God's
power and authority (Frame), or as being represented in the bodily incarnation of Jesus (Watson).

One final comment is necessary. To those who point out that God is
described in the Psalms as having "wings" (e.g., Pss 17:8; 57:1; 91:4), LDS
author Richard Hopkins responds that in such a context, the meaning is
figurative. This is determined by using "simple rules of hermeneutics."[155]
This is a surprising assertion from Hopkins, given his perspective already
referenced, that hermeneutical reflection does not seem to automatically ensure accuracy in interpretation.[156] For our purposes, it would be
helpful to know the "simple rules" that Hopkins utilizes to determine a
figurative meaning. It is disconcerting when an LDS author uses phrases

---

152. Frame, *Salvation Belongs to the Lord*, 88–89.

153. Watson, *Text and Truth*, 282–83. See 2 Cor 4:4; Col 1:15; cf. Heb 1:3, Col
3:9–11.

154. Watson, *Text and Truth*, 291.

155. Hopkins, *Biblical Mormonism*, 56.

156. Hopkins, *Biblical Mormonism*, 33.

like this, thus allowing for implicit, hermeneutical principles, while at the same time, appearing to disallow hermeneutical reflection.[157]

3.2.6. Literal Interpretation and "the Spirit"

I have discussed the "spirit of prophecy" as an important component of personal revelation. Several straightforward interpretations of NT passages corroborate this perspective. LDS authors Draper and Rhodes summarize 1 Cor 2:6–13: "For Paul, the Spirit is the key that opens up proper understanding and makes it possible to judge the truthfulness or falseness of all things."[158] Delbert Stapley affirmed that "the Holy Ghost is required to interpret correctly the teachings of holy men. Therefore, those who do not possess the Spirit of God cannot comprehend the things of God." Stapley also referenced 2 Pet 1:20–21, and concluded that just as the ancient prophets were moved by the Spirit, so also modern interpreters need the Spirit for biblical interpretation.[159] Similarly, for Robert Matthews, the scriptures were written by holy men moved by the Holy Ghost (2 Pet 1:20–21; D&C 68:3–4), and therefore, "inspiration from the same Holy Ghost is required in order for anyone else to perceive the true meaning and intention of a scripture."[160] Also citing the text of 2 Pet 1:20–21, and defending its plain meaning, LDS authors state that "to understand the scriptures, we must study them with the Spirit."[161] In like manner, Dallin Oaks cites the "ministration of the spirit" of 2 Cor 3:8 so that Bible readers will avoid "trusting in [their] own interpretations of written texts."[162] Because there are "too many ambiguous sections of scripture to let the Bible speak for itself," LDS authors cite 2 Peter 1:21 so their readers will be "in tune with the Spirit enough to understand what the scripture intends."[163]

---

157. Again, for Hopkins, "common sense, spiritual insight, and respect for the plain language" of the text produces a "satisfactory hermeneutic" (Hopkins, *Biblical Mormonism*, 34). This view by Hopkins, however, is overly simplistic.

158. Draper and Rhodes, *Paul's First Epistle*, 162.

159. Stapley, "Gift of the Holy Ghost."

160. Matthews, in Black, *Expressions of Faith*, 121; cf. Joseph Smith—History 1:73–74, PGP.

161. LDS, *New Testament Seminary*, 239.

162. Oaks, "Scripture Reading." See 2 Cor 3:8: "How shall not the ministration of the spirit be rather glorious?"

163. Millet et al., *LDS Beliefs*, 463.

Commenting on 1 Cor 2:9–12, non-LDS scholar Victor Paul Furnish notes that God's wisdom has been revealed to all believers through the agency of the Spirit.[164] Furnish also sustains the "Spirit's role as mediating the knowledge of God" in 1 Cor 2:10–15.[165] Some of the LDS conclusions referenced above appear to be reasonable interpretations that take into account not only the illocutionary force of the biblical passage, but also its referentiality. However, there is no hermeneutical or epistemological framework in place that will help LDS members differentiate between their own interpretation of the Bible, and one performed "by the Spirit." It seems that interpretive rigor is abandoned in favor of interpretation "by the Spirit." Since the Bible cannot "speak for itself," one must be "in tune with the Spirit."[166] This is a concept derived from a literalistic interpretation of 2 Pet 1:21. In addition, it is unclear if the LDS provides any hermeneutical categories that assist interpreters when they read "the many ambiguous sections of scripture."

3.2.7. Further Examples of Literalistic Interpretations by the LDS

The LDS literalistically interprets additional passages. The notion of a "burning bosom" comes from a passage in Luke: "Did not our heart burn within us, while he talked with us by the way, and while he opened to us the scriptures?" (Luke 24:32). This "burning bosom" seems to be crucial for proper interpretation,[167] and is, in fact, the confirmation that a textual interpretation is correct.[168] Thus, according to these LDS authors, a

---

164. Furnish, *Theology of the First Letter*, 40.

165. Furnish, *Theology of the First Letter*, 45; cf. Thiselton, *First Epistle*, 252–76; Garland, *1 Corinthians*, 90–103.

166. Millet et al., *LDS Beliefs*, 463. Also, it is unclear how LDS interpreters can decipher whether they are "in tune with the Spirit enough."

167. See LDS, *Preach My Gospel*, 18; cf. LDS, *Gospel Principles*, 127; D&C 9:7–9.

168. See Bushman, *Rough Stone*, 291; cf. Arrington and Bitton, *Mormon Experience*, 34. Besides a burning bosom, there are other confirmations of a correct interpretation of the Bible (or confirmations for other life issues): a nagging thought, a vague feeling, a prompting, a dream, a strong impression, a peaceful feeling, or even "a booming voice or vision" (Mould, *Still*, ix, 390–91; cf. Smith, "LDS Hermeneutics"). This is also described as "whisperings of the Spirit" (Faulconer, "Dialogue on Theology," 469); a "strong and clear" perception (Ostling and Ostling, *Mormon America*, 154); a "stupor of thought" (Arrington and Bitton, *Mormon Experience*, 34); "a knowledge of what needs to be done or said" or "an insight" (Faulconer, "Advice for a Mormon Intellectual"); a "still small voice, which whispereth through and pierceth

"burning bosom" occurs throughout the process—*before* interpretation, to interpret, and *after* interpretation, to confirm. This criterion for interpretive veracity is also found in LDS modern scriptures: "if it is right I will cause that your bosom shall burn within you; therefore, you shall feel that it is right" (D&C 9:8).[169]

However, in contradistinction to this individualistic and experiential "burning bosom," Francois Bovon writes that the Lucan passage emphasizes the opening of the eyes (v. 31; cf. v. 16); the intelligence (vv. 31, 35; cf. v. 45); and the heart (v. 32; cf. v. 25). The result of this "opening" activity is that "the Scriptures are explained by the Risen One (v. 32c)."[170] Joel Green points out that "burning" was used in a figurative sense, "connoting the divine presence (e.g., Exod 3:2; Deut 4:11; 9:15)."[171] Non-LDS authors, then, see the passage not as a confirmation of a personal experience before and after biblical interpretation. It also appears that the LDS perspective is immune to criticism, precisely because of its individualistic focus. Outside critique faces insurmountable obstacles in evaluating a "burning bosom." We note here a literalistic interpretation, with the notion of a "burning bosom" connoting a one-to-one correspondence between the phrase and the physical hearts of interpreters.

I have previously referenced the perspective on prophetic authority and revelation. This derives from a "plain" reading of the Bible: "Surely the Lord God will do nothing, But he revealeth his secret unto his servants the prophets" (Amos 3:7). Several sources take this passage at face value to establish modern-day LDS prophetic authority.[172] The passage of 2 Pet 1:19–21 is also cited to defend biblical interpretation "by the Prophet," just as it was used to argue for biblical interpretation "by the Spirit." Scripture is "best interpreted as it was given—when holy men of God (apostles and prophets) are moved by the Holy Ghost. Far from prohibiting prophetic interpretation of the texts, this Scripture [of 2 Pet 1:19–21] mandates it."[173] The Prophet will "authoritatively interpret"

---

all things" (LDS, *New Testament Seminary*, 121). These modern occurrences tend to overshadow ancient realities.

169. See Givens, *Wrestling the Angel*, 81; LDS, *New Testament Seminary*, 106; Millet et al., *LDS Beliefs*, 537.

170. Bovon, *Luke*, 375.

171. Green, *Gospel of Luke*, 850n38.

172. See LDS, *Gospel Principles*, 39; LDS, *New Testament Seminary*, 13; LDS, *Primary 5*, 2:7; cf. 2 Nephi 27:11; D&C 128:18.

173. Robinson, in Blomberg and Robinson, *How Wide?*, 205n10.

the Bible, and this is "the real intent of 2 Peter 1:19–21."[174] Millet writes
that 2 Peter shows the "final word on prophetic interpretation rests with
prophets."[175] Another biblical text that corroborates prophetic interpretation is Eph 4:11–16.[176] For the LDS, this passage states that the Prophet
can "give authoritative interpretations of scriptures that shall be binding
on the Church."[177] The book of Acts demonstrates "the Lord directing
Peter, the President of the Church, to take the gospel to the Gentiles."[178]
The LDS maintains that God continues to give direction—including interpretation of the Bible—through the LDS Prophet, in consonance with
the "plain" meaning of these passages. This perspective on prophetic authority illustrates a literalistic interpretation. It does not account for the
illocutionary force of the passages under consideration, nor for the text's
historical referentiality. Instead, it accentuates the Mormon prophet's
ecclesiological authority.

Modern-day prophetic authority and interpretation is also related
to the biblical practice of plural marriage (polygamy). This practice operated in the early decades of the LDS movement. A defense of plural
marriage was based on "the lives of noble and faithful men and women in
the Old Testament," that included "Abraham, Jacob, and Moses" (see Gen
16:1–11; 29:28; 30:4, 9, 26; Exod 2:21; Num 12:1).[179] Joseph Smith "knew
the Bible backward and forward," and therefore, recognized the importance that plural marriage had for "Old Testament figures as Abraham,
Jacob, Moses, and King David."[180] Robinson writes that the OT "explicitly
sanctions polygamy."[181] The practice of plural marriage was rescinded in

174. Robinson, in Blomberg and Robinson, *How Wide?*, 58, 205n10.

175. Millet, *A Different Jesus?*, 51.

176. See especially Eph 4:11–12: "And he gave some, apostles; and some, prophets . . . For the perfecting of the saints, for the work of the ministry, for the edifying of
the body of Christ."

177. J. Reuben Clark Jr., in Millet et al., *LDS Beliefs*, xi.

178. LDS, *New Testament Seminary*, 141.

179. Millet et al., *LDS Beliefs*, 494. Importantly, for these LDS authors, "there is no
indication that God disapproved of their actions in any way" (Millet et al., *LDS Beliefs*,
494; cf. Barlow, *Mormons and the Bible*, 91n21; Givens, *Wrestling the Angel*, 279).

180. Beam, *American Crucifixion*, 84. Even a well-known critic of the LDS Church
admitted that Smith had a thorough knowledge of the Bible and studied it as an "earnest and perceptive reader" (see Walters, "Use of the Old Testament," 1).

181. Robinson, *Are Mormons Christians?*, 92. For Robinson, the biblical support
is found in Gen 16:4; 25:6; 30:4, 9. Robinson also writes that the NT "does not forbid"
plural marriage (Robinson, *Are Mormons Christians?*, 92). Joseph Smith practiced

1890, however, by the LDS prophet Wilford Woodruff. As Woodruff announced the end of the practice, he disclosed that the "Lord will never permit me or any other man who stands as President of this Church to lead you astray. It is not in the programme. It is not in the mind of God."[182] Woodruff claimed this authority based on his literalistic interpretation of 2 Pet 1:20–21 and Amos 3:7. Thus, we note the striking phenomena of literalistic readings of the Bible, pre–1890, to advocate for plural marriage, alongside the post–1890 institutional and doctrinal change—on account of a prophetic pronouncement. Overall, the LDS maintains that no misunderstanding will occur as God communicates to the Prophet. This is applicable to new revelation or, for our purposes, to Bible interpretation.[183]

The proposed literal interpretation of Amos 3:7 ("Surely the Lord God will do nothing, But he revealeth his secret unto his servants the prophets"), receives a measure of support from mainstream scholars. Shalom Paul writes that this verse reflects a notion "rooted in biblical concept of prophecy. The prophet stands in the presence of God (Jer 15:1, 19), is privy to the divine council (Isa 6; Jer 23:18, 22), and as the spokesman for the Deity is apprised in advance as to the plans of his God."[184] He continues: "the institution of prophecy is founded on the basic premise that God makes his will known to chosen individuals, as is already clearly stated in

---

plural marriage and was "doing the works of Abraham" (Givens, *Wrestling the Angel*, 281; cf. D&C 132). Since Abraham was promised a posterity "as plentiful as the dust of the earth, the stars in the sky, and the sands of the seashore (Gen 13:16; 16:10; 17:6; 18:18; 22:17)," so also Smith sought an extended family through plural marriage (see Compton, *In Sacred Loneliness*, 10–11).

182. Woodruff, "Official Declaration 1," in *Doctrines and Covenants*; cf. Bowman, *Mormon People*, 124–51. The LDS prefers to call the practice "plural marriage" in contradistinction to "polygamy."

183. A similar occurrence of prophet authority is seen in a revelation in 1978 to President Spencer Kimball on the acceptance of black males into the "priesthood." The "priesthood" is a vital LDS doctrine. Before 1978, LDS black male members did not have the same privileges as white male members (see Southerton, *Losing a Lost Tribe*, 8–9). For this revelation, see Kimball et al., "Official Declaration 2," in *Doctrines and Covenants*; cf. Bringhurst and Smith, *Black and Mormon*; Harris and Bringhurst, *Mormon Church & Blacks*; Millet et al., *LDS Beliefs*, 505–8; Bowman, *Mormon People*, 212–15. The potential for a forthright declaration, i.e., the LDS admitting errors with their former policy of prohibiting the priesthood from black males, is discussed in Martins, Review of *All Abraham's Children*, 423–24. According to an early LDS publication, "reason and analogy" showed that God caused some people to be cursed with black skin (Phelps, "Letter No. 5"). Current LDS thinking does not agree with this strong view.

184. Paul, *Amos*, 113.

Gen 18:17."[185] Other authors concur, admitting the possibility that "the idiom here means that the Lord will not execute a decree without first telling a prophet and having him announce it."[186] However, there is not an all-encompassing formula concerning God's communication to prophets: "Obviously God does most things without first telling a prophet."[187] At times the biblical context alludes to a "specific course of action in response to an unusual situation, one requiring forethought and planning."[188]

Concerning the passage of 2 Pet 1:19–21, Peter Davids mentions the most perplexing question of the passage: whether it "refer[s] to the prophet's own interpretation or to the contemporary reader's own interpretation."[189] The most probable answer is the "prophet's own interpretation of his visions."[190] Charles Bigg agrees, and points out that Peter was not describing modern-day, "right interpreters of Scripture," but he was "thinking solely of the Hebrew Prophets."[191] For Daniel Harrington, "genuine prophets served as instruments of the Holy Spirit, and so their prophecies had a divine origin ('spoke from God') rather than only a human origin."[192] Therefore, far from granting an all-encompassing, modern-day prophetic authority, the passage is a "reflection on the OT as Holy Scripture, its divine origin, and its proper interpretation."[193]

One wonders about the legitimacy of President Woodruff's statement concerning plural marriage and included in the LDS scripture of D&C: "The Lord will never permit me or any other man who stands as President of this Church to lead you astray . . . It is not in the mind of God."[194] This statement appears to equate the "mind of God" seamlessly with that of the LDS president. The President is claimed to be a spokesperson for God who, without impediment or obfuscation, transmits the commands of God. We have seen the questionable epistemological judgment of being "one with God." The LDS would buttress this idea

185. Paul, *Amos*, 113.

186. Andersen and Freedman, *Amos*, 398.

187. Andersen and Freedman, *Amos*, 399.

188. Andersen and Freedman, *Amos*, 399.

189. Davids, *Letters of 2 Peter and Jude*, 210.

190. See, e.g., Davids, *Letters of 2 Peter and Jude*, 211; cf. Watson, *Second Letter*, 343.

191. Bigg, *Epistles of St. Peter and St. Jude*, 270.

192. Harrington, *1 Peter, Jude and 2 Peter*, 258.

193. Harrington, *1 Peter, Jude and 2 Peter*, 259.

194. Woodruff, "Official Declaration 1," in *Doctrines and Covenants*.

with their interpretation of Amos 3:7. However, this passage does not justify epistemological oneness between God and the Prophet, nor the unfettered ability to communicate directives from God. An inordinate amount of weight is placed upon locutionary expressions by LDS prophets. Therefore, the historical event in 1890 concerning plural marriage, with its example of a prophetic announcement, illustrates one of our stated objectives—to demonstrate the most significant sociological factors that account for apparent inconsistencies in the interpretive methods deployed in LDS uses of the Bible. In sum, the literalistic interpretations of Amos 3:7 and 2 Pet 1:19–21 appear to ignore the illocutionary intent of the passages and advocate an overly optimistic direct correspondence between the concept of biblical prophetic authority and modern-day LDS prophets.

3.2.8. *The Canon and Literalistic Interpretation*

We have seen theological arguments against the canon as examples of diminution of the Bible.[195] The LDS perspective on canonicity is also determined by interpretive methods—by taking several passages at face value. An "incomplete biblical canon" is advanced, given the (presumably) lost Pauline letter mentioned in 1 Cor 5:9, as well as the (lost?) "epistle from Laodicea" (Col 4:16), along with numerous references to other books mentioned but not included in the Bible, e.g., "Book of kings of Judah and Israel" (2 Chr 16:11; 25:26; 27:7; 32:32); "Book of the Wars of the Lord" (Num 21:14); "Book of Jasher" (Josh 10:13; 2 Sam 1:18).[196] In 1877, LDS Apostle William McLellin spoke of ten lost books of the NT, including the letter mentioned in 1 Cor 5:9, the "Epistle of the common salvation" mentioned in Jude 3, and the "Commandments to the Thessalonians" of 1 Thess 4:2.[197]

---

195. Further theological arguments are as follows. Even the *possibility* of canonization is questioned, since "the notion of a finite, strictly defined biblical canon is itself an extrabiblical conclusion" (Paulsen, "Are Christians Mormon?," 48), and "there is no biblical statement closing the canon" (Robinson, *Are Mormons Christians?*, 48). Since the Bible itself does not explicitly "close the canon," apparently the Bible must be taken at face value—and not be "closed." This echoes the assertion that the Bible does not prohibit continuing revelation. Here we note an argument from silence. We also see that it does have bearing on hermeneutical notions, by highlighting an LDS focus on the content (or lack thereof) of the biblical text.

196. Millet et al., *LDS Beliefs*, 91.

197. See Larson and Passey, *William E. McLellin Papers*, 312. For example:

The LDS acknowledges that other Christian traditions quote Rev 22:18–19 and its words against "adding to" the Bible as an argument for a closed canon. Millet, in turn, responds by quoting Deut 4:2: "Ye shall not add unto the word which I command you." According to Millet, if this passage of Deuteronomy is taken at "face value," i.e., literally, then "61 books in the Old and New Testaments should be jettisoned."[198] However, Robinson points out that in the passage of Deuteronomy "obviously Moses was referring here to the specific revelation then being recorded," so likewise, John was referring to the book of Revelation in Rev 22:18–19.[199] It is important for our purposes to point out the seriousness with which these LDS authors read these passages—both Deut 4:2 and Rev 22:18–19—appearing to interpret them according to their intended sense. The LDS position on the canon yields insights into their hermeneutical perspective because of their approaches to these verses.[200]

Concerning 1 Cor 5:9 and Paul's comment of "I have written you in my letter", most commentators simply believe that the letter referenced by Paul is lost.[201] There is little doubt that some correspondence from the apostles has, indeed, been lost, and 1 Cor 5:9 holds no importance for the issue of canonicity, despite the assertions of LDS authors. Regarding Col 4:16 and "the letter from Laodicea," Edward Lohse admits, "There is no trace of the Epistle to the Laodiceans."[202] David Pao writes that "most are convinced . . . that this letter remains lost."[203] T. K. Abbott agrees that it could be a "lost Epistle," although he remarks: "the Epistle referred to

---

"Beloved, when I gave all diligence to write unto you of *the common salvation*, it was needful for me to write unto you, and exhort you that ye should earnestly contend for the faith which was once delivered unto the saints" (Jude 3, emphasis added); "For ye know what *commandments* we gave you by the Lord Jesus" (1 Thess 4:2, emphasis added).

198. Millet, in Millet and Johnson, *Bridging the Divide*, 119; cf. Millet et al., *LDS Beliefs*, 91.

199. Robinson, *Are Mormons Christians?*, 47.

200. Other thinkers also ponder the effect that the process of canonization plays on interpretive issues: "What role do events (i.e., the process of canonization) occurring after the original composition play in interpretation?" (Porter and Stovell, *Hermeneutics*, 21; cf. Treier, *Theological Interpretation*, 18).

201. See Orr and Walther, *1 Corinthians*, 120; Robertson and Plummer, *Critical and Exegetical Commentary*, 105. Some, however, surmise that it "is imbedded in II Cor 6:14—7:1" (Orr and Walther, *1 Corinthians*, 190).

202. Lohse, *Colossians and Philemon*, 175n48.

203. Pao, *Colossians and Philemon*, 321.

was one to which some importance was attached by St. Paul himself, so that he himself directs that it be read publicly in two distinct Churches."[204] Therefore, contra Lohse,[205] he believes it to be the "Epistle to the Ephesians, which we know to have been written about the same time as the Epistle to the Colossians, and conveyed by the same messenger . . . [and] regarded as a circular letter."[206] This would call into question the citation of Col 4:16 to argue for an incomplete canon. With these examples, LDS interpretations illustrate a neglect of the illocutionary intent of the author of individual biblical texts. This is done, apparently, on account of modern institutional motivations—casting doubt on the ancient canon will open the door to modern additions to Scripture.

3.2.9. LDS Literality as a Claimed Non-interpretive Virtue

We note an extremely unusual perspective by the LDS regarding literality. Joseph Smith claimed that they "believed what the Bible foretold" while the "sects of the day only held to 'interpretations' of the book."[207] Both Joseph Smith and Brigham Young posited that other churches "interpret" the Bible, while the "Mormons alone take it just as it stands."[208] When asked by an opponent about his belief in the Bible, Brigham Young replied,

> *I believe it just as it is.* I do not believe in putting any man's interpretation upon it, whatever, unless it should be directed by the Lord Himself in some way. I do not believe we need interpreters and expounders of the Scriptures, to wrest them from their literal, plain, simple meaning.[209]

These strong statements have significant hermeneutical ramifications. We note LDS thinkers appearing to *avoid* interpretation. There appears a self-evident notion that interpretation is not even needed. In other words, meaning is both obvious and undisputed. Both Smith and Young

204. Abbott, *Epistles*, 305, 306.

205. "No stock can be put in considering Eph as that letter to the Laodiceans" (Lohse, *Colossians and Philemon*, 175n48).

206. Abbott, *Epistles*, 306.

207. See Irving, "Mormons and the Bible," 477.

208. See Barlow, *Mormons and the Bible*, 95; cf. Givens, *Wrestling the Angel*, 15; Alexander, *Mormonism in Transition*, 283–85.

209. Young, "Effects and Privileges."

simplistically separate literal interpretation by the LDS from those that "interpret." Their statements highlight the lack of awareness regarding their own hermeneutical activity. Smith and Young imply that *literality is non-interpretive*. For both, *believing* the Bible, or reading it "just as it was" (i.e., literally), was contrasted to others who "interpret" the Bible.[210] Both Smith and Young placed interpretations *in opposition to* reading the Bible. This is perplexing and is difficult to reconcile with accepted hermeneutical thinking. To place interpretation as the direct opposite of a literal reading leads to numerous unresolved questions.

3.2.10. LDS Authors and Literality

Philip Barlow recognizes the challenge of defining "the proper meaning of literalism."[211] He maintains, however, that Joseph Smith exhibited a "selectively applied literalism" throughout his life and ministry."[212] LDS author Ian Barber also acknowledges the potential problems of literalism and reacts against the "Mormon obsession of literalist interpretation" to advocate for the "complex LDS scriptural tradition" to be "a fresh Christian doctrine of dynamic development and transformation." For Barber, the literalist tendency "has become a largely inward and unproductive commitment of Mormon intellectual and theological resources." Thus, they "must look beyond evidentiary debate and an inflexible literalist framework."[213] James Faulconer writes against those who "assume that meaning, biblical or otherwise, is essentially referential/representative" and advocates an incarnational reading of scripture, to go beyond a strict literalism. Faulconer argues that "we can understand scripture as an incarnation or enactment of history rather than a representation of it," and "the scriptures are literal history, but their history is incarnational rather than representational." He continues against the aspect of historical referentiality: "such a theory of history is problematic, for to the degree that a historian can be successful there is, ironically, no real history, only

210. See Young, "Effects and Privileges"; cf. Irving, "Mormons and the Bible," 477; Barlow, *Mormons and the Bible*, 95. We also note that if other churches "interpret" and the Mormons "take Scripture as it is," they are using interpretive language—yet are excusing themselves from the need to interpret. This idiosyncratic use of interpretive language should be questioned.

211. Barlow, *Mormons and the Bible*, 35.

212. Barlow, *Mormons and the Bible*, 71.

213. See Barber, "Literalist Constraint," 20, 25.

the repetition of something that is always the same."[214] In response, it is unclear how these views illuminate the complex issue of literality. There is a general omission by LDS authors to provide practical reflections on the meaning and outcomes of literality. Barber simplistically calls for a looking "beyond" literality. Faulconer introduces another term in need of definition: "incarnational" reading. He is not explaining the interpretive process but appears to be avoiding its complexities by introducing an ambiguous term.

3.3. The Hermeneutical Effect of Literalistic Interpretation

We have seen a consistent emphasis by LDS authors concerning a simple, plain, literal hermeneutic. This illustrates the positive way the LDS, at times, values the Bible. However, the LDS appears to be unable or at least unwilling to articulate the hermeneutical parameters that would guide literal interpretations. My stated argument is that despite implicit and explicit claims by the LDS to the contrary, the church's use of the Bible, as illustrated in the five interpretive categories, emphasizes modern realities at the expense of ancient meanings. LDS interpreters would undoubtedly assume alignment with accepted norms of hermeneutical principles with their explicit claims of correct interpretation (e.g., finding "the true meaning").

However, several LDS interpretations are literalistic, by assuming a straightforward understanding of the verbal sense of biblical locutions. In addition, their literalistic reading ignores the illocutionary force of the text. They presuppose not only a self-evident understanding of the empirical referentiality of the text, but also a direct correspondence between the text and external realities of the text. This is an overly optimistic, one-to-one correspondence between the text and the empirical realities projected by the text. We saw in the first chapter that some methodologies claim to see a text "straightforwardly" with instant access to its locutionary meaning and the accompanying ability to make judgments about its meaning. The LDS not only fails to acknowledge the challenges of a "literal" interpretation but appears to advocate a simplistic equation of literality with the "verbal sense of the words." Literalistic interpretations are the result. While the verbal sense of biblical locutions does, in fact,

214. Faulconer, "Scripture as Incarnation."

retain some importance in the interpretive process, it should not be at the expense of the illocutionary intent of the author.

4

Interpretation by Allegorization

A SECOND INTERPRETIVE PRACTICE relates to allegory. In contrast to their literal interpretations, the LDS does not explicitly acknowledge this allegorical approach. As a preliminary exercise, I will introduce basic aspects of allegory. I will also make the important distinction between *allegory* and *allegorization*, specifically how both relate to the historical referent. This concept of the historical referent will be explored with particular emphasis on the parables of Jesus. Finally, I will describe my understanding of what is occurring when the LDS allegorically approaches the biblical text. I will argue that their "allegorical" interpretations, are, in fact, *allegorizations*.

4.1. The Complexity of Allegory in the Mainstream Academy

4.1.1. The Identification of Allegory

As an introduction to allegory, we note that "metaphor" refers to a general category where one object is identified and/or contrasted with another object.[1] A metaphor could also be described as "a comparison between two dissimilar things that creates unexpected associations in one's mental

---

1. See Tate, *Handbook*, 256.

image of the things compared."[2] While metaphors can be, in fact, "mini-stories,"[3] I am using allegory as a more detailed, "extended" metaphor. In other words, an "allegory paints a series of pictures in metaphorical form."[4] In this way, allegory is more than a simple metaphor, as it exhibits details and more narratival characteristics. Allegory, then, is "an extended metaphor in which actions, objects . . . and/or persons in a narrative correspond to or suggest meanings outside the narrative."[5] According to Grondin, the interpretation of an allegory results in the discovery of "something more profound behind" the literal sense.[6] A deeper meaning is found in an allegory when a textual character, place or event represents real-world issues and occurrences. An allegory addresses "insiders," who can "work out the code," and who are "in the know."[7] Given that allegory "presupposes shared understanding"[8] between the implied author and the implied reader, real-world issues are vividly imaged by these textual characters, places or events.[9]

4.1.2. The Distinction between Allegory and Allegorization: The Historical Referent

There is an important distinction between allegory and "allegorization." In an allegory, a deeper meaning is found when a character, place or event represents *ancient* real-world issues, occurrences, or perspectives. Furthermore, the deeper meaning in a biblical allegory, with its *ancient* historical referent, was the intention of the author. Two examples include Hagar and Sarah representing two covenants in Gal 4:21–31, and the parables of Jesus concerning Israel's history (to be covered below). However, a deeper meaning in an allegorization is found when a character, place or event represents *modern* real-world issues, occurrences, or perspectives. This deeper meaning, with its modern historical referent,

---

2. Brown, *Scripture as Communication*, 142n9.

3. See Wright, *People of God*, 135.

4. Osborne, *Hermeneutical Spiral*, 293.

5. See Tate, *Handbook*, 11–12.

6. Grondin, *Philosophical Hermeneutics*, 24. For Gerald Bray, an allegorical reading occurs when the literal sense conceals a hidden meaning (Bray, "Allegory," 34).

7. Thiselton, *Hermeneutics*, 38.

8. Thiselton, *Hermeneutics*, 38.

9. See chapter 8 for a discussion on implied authors and implied readers.

is entirely the invention of the interpreter. When this occurs, there is, effectively, a "re-doing" of the text's referentiality. Interpreters find hidden, deeper meanings where there were none from the perspective of the author. The result of this type of interpretation is the disclosing of "deep secrets and arcane significances that were never there to begin with and never entered the mind of the author."[10] Non-LDS allegorizations include the following. Leah and Rachel, the wives of Jacob, represent the layperson and monk, respectively.[11] The twelve precious stones of Rev 21:19–20 represent the twelve tribes or the twelve apostles.[12] The escape of the soul from the limitations of the body was seen as a representation of the biblical Exodus.[13] Again, allegorization is the practice of a modern interpreter imposing a deeper meaning on the text, by assuming that the historical referent represents a modern real-world issue.

4.1.3. *The Historical Referent and the Parables of Jesus*

To illustrate the impact of the historical referent in allegory, I will briefly discuss the parables of Jesus. According to Wright, "at least some of Jesus' parables," are to be read as allegory.[14] They have "an intended figurative meaning"[15] that presupposes a shared understanding between authors and interpreters. The use of the parables by Jesus was subversive. This, at the very least, implicitly acknowledges a historical referent. In other words, his parables were designed "to break open his contemporaries' worldview."[16] Specifically, by representing "different elements in the 'real' world," the parables of Jesus told "the story of Israel herself."[17] That is, the parables were "Jesus' telling of the Israel-story in order to undermine

---

10. See Hughes, "Truth of Scripture," 188.

11. See Barr, "The Literal," 4.

12. See Osborne, *Hermeneutical Spiral*, 284.

13. See Trebilco, "Diaspora Judaism," 296. These examples, strictly speaking, do not necessarily highlight *modern* issues or occurrences, despite my definition of allegorization. However, they illustrate deeper meanings that reflect issues or perspectives that are *later* than the text. For my purposes, the emphasis on the *modern* is due to contemporary LDS allegorizations of the ancient text.

14. Wright, *Scripture*, 66.

15. Gaipa and Scholes, in Vanhoozer, *Is There a Meaning?*, 312.

16. Wright, *People of God*, 433.

17. Wright, *Jesus and the Victory*, 177.

the present way of understanding the nation's identity."[18] One specific example (referencing Matt 21:33–46) is the following:

> In the parable of the wicked tenants, Israel is the vineyard, her rulers the vineyard-keepers; the prophets are the messengers, Jesus is the son; Israel's god, the creator, is himself the owner and father. But this "allegorical" meaning allows fully for much wider implications. Jesus is claiming to be developing a story already used by Isaiah (5:1–7).[19]

Wright demonstrates how powerfully these parables would have impacted the worldview of his hearers, as well as subvert their religious outlook. Jesus was telling the story of Israel in allegorical form—with deeper meanings reflected in the real-world (ancient) realities of his hearers. They would have "heard," then, what he was attempting to communicate—precisely because of their shared understanding. A true allegory assumes this shared understanding between authors and interpreters. In the following examples, I will argue that the LDS interpretations are ostensibly allegorical, although, in reality, are allegorizations. Only with the insider information afforded by "systemic parameters" could an interpreter understand the deeper, hidden meanings. The ancient historical referent in the biblical passages to be studied (i.e., the shared understanding between the ancient interpreters and authors), is not considered. Rather, the LDS deploys allegorization to promote modern real-world issues.

4.2. Examples of Allegorization by the LDS

4.2.1. The Book of Mormon and Allegorizations of Ezekiel 37 and Isaiah 29

Ezekiel 37 refers to two "sticks": "take thee one stick . . . then take another stick . . . And join them one to another into one stick; and they shall become one in thine hand" (Ezek 37:16, 17). From the LDS perspective, these two "sticks" represent the Bible and the BoM.[20] It is claimed that the Bible and the BoM "come together as witnesses" when they are joined

---

18. Wright, *Jesus and the Victory*, 179.

19. Wright, *Jesus and the Victory*, 178.

20. See McConkie, *New Witness*, 454–57; Pratt, *Voice of Warning*, 122–24; Shipps, *Mormonism*, 29; Davies, "Mormon Canon," 50; D&C 27:5.

together.[21] In 1981, the Mormon church published the Bible together with the BoM (along with the D&C and the PGP). To celebrate this event, Elder Boyd Packer proclaimed that the two sticks were "indeed one in our hands," and that "Ezekiel's prophecy now stands fulfilled."[22]

However, what is the historical referent of the two "sticks" of Ezek 37? Contextually, the two sticks refer to the divided nation of Israel. Ezekiel was referring to exiled Israel being reunited with those of Israel still in the land (Ezek 37:21–22).[23] This contextual reading highlights an *ancient* historical referent. Interestingly, one LDS source admits to this singular interpretation of the reunification between the exiled and non-exiled Israel.[24] However, most LDS thinkers believe the passage has a secondary, "deeper" meaning—implicitly acknowledging an allegorization that highlights the modern union of the Bible with the BoM.

To defend their hermeneutical conclusions, i.e., positing a modern historical referent in the passage of Ezekiel alongside an ancient historical referent, LDS author David Wright points out the dual interpretation of other biblical passages. For example, the so-called "Immanuel Prophecy" in Isa 7:14 originally referred to events in the eighth century BC, although Matthew applied the passage to Jesus at his birth.[25] The voice calling out to prepare the way in Isa 40:3 is viewed as part of the "exodus-from-Babylon motif," that is "secondarily applied to John the Baptist (Matt. 3:3)."[26] In consequence, the LDS concludes that the meaning in Ezek 37 is the unification of Israel, *as well as* the joining together of the Bible and the BoM.

Several allegorizations also appear in LDS interpretations of Isa 29. For example, the BoM is allegedly mentioned in v. 4: "And thou shalt be brought down, *and* shalt speak out of the ground" (Isa 29:4a). As a young man, Joseph Smith had received a revelation and was told that the BoM

---

21. LDS, *Old Testament Seminary*.

22. Packer, "Scriptures"; cf. Givens, *By the Hand of Mormon*, 194. What Packer claims as prophecy, I label as allegorization.

23. See Zimmerli, *Ezekiel*, 275; Greenberg, *Ezekiel*, 755, 758.

24. Early LDS authority Heber Snell, who received a PhD in Biblical Studies from the University of Chicago in 1941, insisted on only one meaning for the passage. He argued, "the text plainly prophesied of the reuniting of Israel." Instead of using Ezek 37 to defend the legitimacy of the "stick" of the BoM, Snell argued that other evidence should be used (see Sherlock, "Faith and History," 32–33).

25. Wright, "Joseph Smith's Interpretation," 204.

26. Wright, "Joseph Smith's Interpretation," 204.

was buried in the ground. He needed to dig it "out of the ground" so that it could "speak."[27] The end result of this process, including its translation, was viewed as a "direct fulfillment of Isa 29:4."[28] Early LDS leader W. W. Phelps commented:

> If the present generation had had faith . . . [in the BoM], every honest man would have searched the scriptures daily to see if the glorious news it contained, was so . . . With but little discernment, they might have discovered that Isaiah had his eyes on the last days, when he spoke of what should happen at a future period.[29]

Isaiah 29:11 is also cited: "And the vision of all is become unto you as the words of a *book that is sealed*, Which men deliver to one that is learned, Saying, Read this, I pray thee: And he saith, *I cannot; for it is sealed*" (KJV, emphasis added). An event early in the LDS movement illustrates this verse as an allegorization. Martin Harris was one of the early scribes for the translation of the BoM (that was claimed to be originally written in "Reformed Egyptian" on metal plates). Harris had doubts concerning Joseph Smith's ability to translate, so he carried part of the translated manuscript to Charles Anthon, a well-known classical scholar in New York. After a brief discussion, Anthon asked to see the plates from which the manuscript was translated. Harris declined this request since the plates were "sealed." To this Anthon replied, "I cannot read a sealed book." This was taken as an exact echo of the words of Isa 29:11. Thus, according to Richard Bushman, "Harris and Anthon had inadvertently fulfilled a prophecy in Isaiah."[30]

Other phrases from Isa 29 exhibit allegorization. In v. 4, the words "brought down" are interpreted as a reference to the defeat in warfare of the Nephites centuries later on the American continent: "And thou shalt be brought down, and shalt speak out of the ground" (Isa 29:4a).[31] Since Joseph Smith did not receive a thorough education, a phrase taken

27. See Bushman, *Rough Stone*, 64–66; McConkie, *New Witness*, 435–50; Wright, "Joseph Smith's Interpretation," 199; Barlow, "Before Mormonism," 751–52.

28. Davies, "Mormon Canon," 50.

29. Phelps, "Letter No. 8."

30. Bushman, *Rough Stone*, 65–66; cf. McConkie, *New Witness*, 448; Barlow, *Mormons and the Bible*, 20. Again, what Bushman labels as prophecy, I label as allegorization.

31. See Crowther, *Prophecies of Joseph Smith*, 175. The Nephites are one of the people groups in the BoM. This is advanced, despite the second phrase ("and shall speak out of the ground"), referring to the BoM, as mentioned above.

from the KJV of Isa 29:12 purportedly describes this lack of an academic background: "And the book is delivered to him that is *not learned*, Saying, Read this, I pray thee: And he saith, I am *not learned*" (Isa 29:12, emphasis added).[32] According to Philip Barlow, with these interpretations of Isa 29, Smith "did more" than just feel "keenly the relevance of scripture," as did many nineteenth-century contemporaries. Rather, he "placed himself *inside* the biblical story."[33] This placing of himself inside the biblical story is an implicit acknowledgement of allegorization—the imposition of a modern historical referent.

In sum, these interpretations of Ezek 37 and Isa 29 are allegorizations. They are not legitimate biblical allegories, like the parables of Jesus, which reference ancient historical referents. These passages are quoted to emphasize modern historical referents, such as the joining together of the BoM with the Bible, the BoM speaking out of the ground, or Smith being unlearned. Reflections on this are given below.

4.2.2. *The LDS as the New Israel*

The LDS views itself as "the house of Israel and a covenant people."[34] The initial clause of Article of Faith #10 reads: "We believe in the literal gathering of Israel and in the restoration of the Ten Tribes."[35] They see themselves as "physically a rediscovered, restored, and reinterpreted 'Israel.'"[36] Some LDS members insist that "the Saints are literally adopted into Israel and are thereupon brought into the covenant by virtue of their membership in the tribes of Israel."[37] Not only does a Mormon convert "experience a spiritual

---

32. See Palmer, *Insider's View*, 44.

33. Barlow, "Before Mormonism," 752, emphasis by author; cf. Brodie, *No Man Knows*, 52. These LDS conclusions on Isa 29 are a significant departure from traditional interpretations. In actuality, the chapter is a "woe" that addresses "Ariel." This name has different meanings, although in the context, it refers to Jerusalem. Motyer states: "Zion is veiled behind Ariel—though its identity is no secret" (Motyer, *Isaiah*, 213; cf. Tucker, *Book of Isaiah*, 242; Watts, *Isaiah*, 450).

34. LDS, *New Testament Seminary*, 167; cf. Davies, "Mormon Canon," 66; Arrington and Bitton, *Mormon Experience*, 242; Johnson and Leffler, *Jews and Mormons*, 148.

35. We note here the language of literality. As Cummings notes, "Although the other articles imply literal belief, this is the only one of the thirteen which explicitly includes the term *literal*" (Cummings, "Quintessential Mormonism," 95).

36. Davies, "Mormon Canon," 44; cf. Shepherd and Shepherd, "Doctrinal and Commitment Functions," 733.

37. Shipps, *Mormonism*, 75.

transformation, but he or she also undergoes a miraculous physical change whereby his or her blood is literally transmuted from gentile blood to the blood of Israel."[38] Additionally, young LDS members receive a "patriarchal blessing" that allows them to identify with "a genealogical line back to one of the tribes of Israel."[39] However, others in the LDS concede the "new Israel" to be figurative.[40] Nonetheless, an LDS manual encourages members to "know that they are of the house of Israel."[41]

Jeremiah 23:3 speaks of the gathering of Israel: "I will gather the remnant of my flock out of all countries whither I have driven them." This gathering supposedly occurred within the organization of the LDS:

> The power and authority to direct the work of gathering the house of Israel was given to Joseph Smith by the prophet Moses, who appeared in 1836 in the Kirtland Temple (see D&C 110:11). Since that time, each prophet has held the keys for the gathering of the house of Israel, and this gathering has been an important part of the Church's work.[42]

Other biblical references are cited to sustain their perspective on being the "new Israel." A foundational event, after the death of Joseph Smith, was the trek from Nauvoo, Illinois to Salt Lake City, Utah. In this journey west, the Mormons replicated the Exodus.[43] In fact, they were "sociologically reenacting the Exodus."[44] Indeed, the "great company" that "walk[ed] by the rivers of waters"—phrases from Jer 31:8, 9—referenced this trek to Salt Lake City.[45] Brigham Young, who led the trip westward, was seen as a modern Moses,[46] and the arrival in the Rocky

38. Cummings, "Quintessential Mormonism," 96; cf. Smith, *Teachings of the Prophet Joseph Smith*, 150.

39. Ludlow, "Bible," 105; cf. Abanes, *One Nation*, 109; Davies, *Mormon Culture*, 205–7.

40. See Givens, *Wrestling the Angel*, 169–70.

41. LDS, *New Testament Seminary*, 167.

42. LDS, *Gospel Principles*, 248.

43. See Barlow, *Mormons and the Bible*, 81–83; Arrington and Bitton, *Mormon Experience*, 96; Bowman, *Mormon People*, xix.

44. Givens, in Eliason, *Mormons & Mormonism*, 107. They were re-enacting "much of the Gospels and Acts besides" (Givens, in Eliason, *Mormons & Mormonism*, 107).

45. McConkie, *New Witness*, 546–47. Nauvoo was located on the eastern side of the Mississippi River. Thus, the Mississippi was one of the "rivers of waters" from the passage of Jeremiah.

46. Cummings, "Quintessential Mormonism," 101; cf. Arrington, *Brigham Young: American Moses*.

Mountains in Utah was seen as a fulfillment of Isa 2:2 that speaks of "the top of the mountains."[47] To summarize, the deeper meanings imposed on several biblical texts to sustain this "new Israel" perspective assumes insider information that is predicated upon modern historical referents.

Nonetheless, the notion of the re-gathering of Israel, or of remnant language, is not particularly novel to the LDS. It is, in fact, not far removed from mainstream thinkers. For example, Gerhard Lohfink argues that the NT contends neither for the reformation of Israel, nor for the formation of the church, but for the restoration and re-gathering of Israel.[48] Wright also posits, "Jesus' mighty works . . . had the effect of gathering the community of 'all Israel', in accordance with ancient prophecy,"[49] and that Jesus intended for "those who responded to him to see themselves as the true, restored Israel."[50] Jesus "thought of his followers as the true people of Israel."[51] Biblical examples of a re-gathering include Jesus and his desire to gather the people of Jerusalem like a hen gathers her chicks (Matt 23:37), and John the Baptist inviting his listeners to bypass the temple, and "redo" the Exodus through baptism in the Jordan (Matt 3:5–12).[52]

However, the LDS allegorizations of the "new Israel" and the Exodus represent problematic notions. While authors such as Lohfink and Wright note the re-gathering motif with *ancient* historical referents in the NT,[53] the LDS sees it with *modern* historical referents of nineteenth-century events in the United States. Lohfink and Wright maintain a strong focus on ancient referentiality. The NT texts referred to a re-gathering of Israel as the people of God in the first century. The LDS goes beyond the mainstream view, by importing deeper meanings that only reflect modern-day realities.

---

47. Barlow, *Mormons and the Bible*, 83. However, McConkie sees the "top of the mountains" as a "specific reference to the Salt Lake temple and to the other temples built in the top of the Rocky Mountains, and it has a general reference to the temple yet to be built in the New Jerusalem in Jackson County, Missouri" (McConkie, *New Witness*, 539).

48. See Lohfink, *Jesus and Community*, xi, 7–29; Fuller, *Restoration of Israel*, 13–24, 197–273.

49. Wright, *Jesus and the Victory*, 193.

50. Wright, *Jesus and the Victory*, 316.

51. Wright, *Jesus and the Victory*, 321.

52. See Wright, *Jesus and the Victory*, 160–61, 257.

53. Lohfink, *Jesus and Community*, 75–81; Wright, *Jesus and the Victory*, 193, 316, 321.

4.2.3. *The LDS as the NT Church*

Many characteristics of the New Testament church are imported into the modern LDS organization. The NT church is viewed as a "model and prototype" for the Mormon church.[54] Although some nineteenth-century Christians believed that miracles had ceased, the early LDS movement concluded that they were living in "sacred time," and were witnesses of another age of miracles.[55] Joseph Smith even "included the resumption of New Testament charismata as one of the Church's thirteen basic Articles of Faith."[56] In addition, the actual organization of the early LDS was alleged to be consistent with the NT pattern,[57] with the earnest claim that the LDS "organization matched every feature of the NT church."[58] Specifically, "the ecclesiastical structure" of the NT church had been replicated with "a church headed by a prophet and twelve apostles."[59] In McConkie's words, "How is it that the churches of Christendom do not have apostles, prophets, high priests, seventies, and all of the New Testament offices and callings?"[60] Joseph Smith saw himself as Peter, a church founder, as well as Paul, the apostle to the Gentiles.[61] He was also proclaimed as Prophet, Priest and King on April 11, 1844.[62] He confidently testified to the restoration of "the ancient New Testament faith—the principles, practices, and doctrine originally taught by Jesus Christ and his apostles in the first century (Articles of Faith 1, 3, 4, 5, 6, and 13)."[63] Therefore, the LDS claimed to be in consonance with the NT church. To support this claim, however, insider information must be introduced into the text. They effectively import their modern perspective into the text, attempting to argue that they match every feature of the NT church.

---

54. Hutchinson, "LDS Approaches," 114.

55. Barlow, *Mormons and the Bible*, 127; cf. D&C 46:17–26.

56. Paulsen, "Are Christians Mormon?," 41; "We believe in the gift of tongues, prophecy, revelation, visions, healing, interpretation of tongues, and so forth" (AoF #7).

57. Givens, *Wrestling the Angel*, 11.

58. Barlow, *Mormons and the Bible*, 95.

59. Siebach, "Dialogue on Theology," 464.

60. McConkie, *New Witness*, 409.

61. Barlow, *Mormons and the Bible*, 75. The use of the word "Gentiles" refers to non-Mormons.

62. Bushman, *Rough Stone*, 523.

63. See Holzapfel and Wayment, *Making Sense*, 522.

4.2.4. *The Narratival Self-Understanding of the LDS*

By claiming to be the new Israel as well as the duplication of the NT church, the LDS assumes that the story of the Bible is continued in their church. Various descriptions further highlight this narratival self-understanding. The LDS community is described as a "replication"[64] or recapitulation of the story of the Bible,[65] as well as "a restoration and re-cuperation not just of New Testament Christianity but also of Old Testament priesthoods and principles."[66] For Joseph Smith, "the whole biblical narrative had come to life again, as endings were put on stories that had their beginnings in the scriptural text."[67] The early LDS members believed their lives were evidence of a work from God.[68] As we have referenced, Smith "put himself inside the Bible story," seeing "episodes in his own life as direct fulfillments of biblical prophecy."[69] Grant Underwood writes in reference to the early LDS: "*they* were the fulfillment of much of what they read about in Isaiah, Jeremiah, and Ezekiel."[70]

This narratival self-understanding is witnessed in other sources. LDS teaching is "less a set of doctrines than a collection of stories."[71] In fact, "Joseph Smith, the founder of Mormonism, wrote stories,"[72] so that their doctrine is not so much propositionally driven, but narratively driven.[73] They "are deeply invested in historical narratives."[74] The "core

---

64. Shipps, *Mormonism*, 39.

65. Barlow, *Mormons and the Bible*, 75, 103.

66. Givens, *Wrestling the Angel*, 294.

67. Barlow, "Before Mormonism," 752; cf. Abanes, *One Nation*, 84; Bowman, *Mormon People*, xvii–xviii.

68. For the narrative connection between Scripture and the United States of America, according to LDS sources, see Wright, "Joseph Smith's Interpretation," 192–93; Arrington and Bitton, *Mormon Experience*, 34; Smith, "Hermeneutical Crisis," 97; Pratt, *Voice of Warning*, 125–26; Hughes, in Eliason, *Mormons & Mormonism*, 37; Moses 7:21, 23, 62–65; D&C 57:1–3; HC 6:318–19.

69. Barlow, "Before Mormonism," 741; cf. Flake, "Translating Time," 508–9. Thus, the early Mormons "would act out Biblical narratives in their own lives" (Underwood, *Millenarian World*, 59).

70. Underwood, *Millenarian World*, 58.

71. Richard Bushman, in Oman, "Living Oracles," 2.

72. Flake, "Translating Time," 497.

73. Flake warns that "reducing Smith's event-driven narratives to propositional statements is alien to the religious system he created" (Flake, "Translating Time," 500).

74. Wilcox and Young, *Standing Apart*, 11.

religious beliefs" of the LDS are "expressed in narrative terms."[75] Benjamin Huff believes their theological discourse is "a kind of hermeneutic theology based on narrative."[76] In fact, "All of Mormonism, even its most unfamiliar tenets, rests in some element on the biblical narrative."[77] Kathleen Flake even downplays the theological acumen of her fellow Mormons: "Mormons are not theologians or even particularly doctrinaire; they are primarily narrativists. They inhabit the world of the book. They read themselves into the salvation history it tells and orient themselves to the horizon created by its promises."[78] Douglas Davies suggests that "the tradition of seeing the truth in and through stories about persons continues to lie at the heart of Mormon self-understanding."[79] The narratival impulse is manifested in their views concerning the continuation of the narrative of the Bible. However, ancient historical referents are not considered. Rather, the import of these LDS conclusions emphasizes the modern LDS Church.

4.3. The Hermeneutical Effect of LDS Allegorization

These examples of allegorization are tendentious. Even *allegory* has come under significant scrutiny and suspicion. Grondin has concluded that allegorical interpretation fell into discredit even in antiquity. This was due to its inherent subjectivity, as well as a randomness that "open[ed] the door to interpretive arbitrariness."[80] LDS scholarship shows little, if any, interest in these developments.

Supported in part by Ezek 37, Isa 29, and Jer 31, the LDS views itself in congruence with and as a recapitulation of the biblical narrative.

75. Olsen, "Theology of Memory," 27.

76. Huff, "Theology in the Light," 482.

77. Flake, "Four Books," 28. Flake continues: "Academics would explain this in terms of intertextuality, noting that the meanings of Mormonism, even its unique scriptures, are achieved within the larger context of the Christian canon" (Flake, "Four Books," 28).

78. Flake, "Four Books," 31. Relatedly, the LDS Church is well known for their genealogical work, for they "take seriously their individual and family history" (Gaustad, "History and Theology," 48). The LDS Church keeps the largest genealogical record in the world (Ostling and Ostling, *Mormon America*, 167). See the genealogical site provided by the LDS Church for members and non-members alike, with ten million hits per day, at https://familysearch.org/.

79. Davies, *Mormon Culture*, 184.

80. Grondin, *Philosophical Hermeneutics*, 28.

This is a rereading of the past with allegorization. There appears to be an invalidation of the historical moorings of the biblical text as the church assumes that ancient Scripture refers to their modern-day movement. There does not exist a specific referent in these texts that justifies their distinct uses of the texts. For example, questionable hidden meanings are advanced, such as Isa 2:2 referring to the Rocky Mountains in Utah, or Isa 29 referring to a book buried millennia later in New York. LDS author Anthony Hutchinson quotes Mark Leone, who admits to "the collapsing of the present into the past by an ever-renewed and ever-changing rereading of the past in light of the present and a constant packing of the past with anachronistic meaning and value from the present."[81] This implicit acknowledgement of allegorization makes it difficult to conclude that LDS interpretation is hermeneutically sound.

Another hermeneutical effect of these allegorizations is the implicit claim that locutionary content can be taken at face value. We saw specifically in the use of Ezek 37 and Isa 29 that these texts were not one of the passages that were corrupt or incorrectly translated. Therefore, it seems that when a text aligns with "systemic parameters," the LDS takes it at face value. When it doesn't suit them, they correct it, or at least claim corruption or incorrect translation. In addition, there is a disparity between their literal interpretations and their allegorizations. Numerous examples were given above on the "entrenched literalism"[82] of their biblical interpretations. Yet, with LDS allegorizations, a hidden meaning is found behind biblical passages. This does not coincide with a "straightforward," "plain," and "literal" meaning. One of our stated objectives was to discover the most significant sociological factors that account for the apparent inconsistencies in the interpretive methods deployed in LDS uses of the Bible. We have noted a significant sociological factor concerning Bible believers in the nineteenth-century context—they "looked to a common-sense reading of the KJV for their spiritual understanding."[83] Thus, the early LDS championed a "literal," "plain," "common-sense" reading of the Bible. At the same time, however, as a significant sociological factor, they sought contemporary relevance with their allegorizations.

Given the idea of a "new Israel," one could postulate a typology—that Smith is fitting into a pattern. Just as God acted in certain ways in

81. See Hutchinson, "LDS Approaches," 114.

82. Shepherd and Shepherd, *Kingdom Transformed*, 5; cf. Arrington and Bitton, *Mormon Experience*, 30; White, *Mormon Neo-orthodoxy*, 58.

83. Givens and Barlow, *Oxford Handbook on Mormonism*, 130.

the past, Smith, and by extension the current LDS prophet, were (and are) used by God.[84] Others might postulate similarities with replacement theology,[85] or with the concept of promise and fulfillment in salvation history.[86] Although there are similarities with these interpretive categories relating the OT with the NT, it seems more reasonable to label the aforementioned uses of the Bible by the LDS as allegorizations, especially in view of the modern aspect of the historical referent, as well as the insider information needed for these interpretations.

However, what of the views of LDS author David Wright above—on the "secondary meanings" of selected biblical passages (Isa 7:14; 40:3)?[87] Are there categories or suggestions for dealing with "secondary" meanings? It is possible that LDS thinkers could espouse a type of *sensus plenior* approach.[88] In other words, the LDS may posit that God had something more to communicate than what the human author of Scripture intended.[89] Specifically, "the *sensus plenior* of a biblical text is not a fully conscious product of its human author(s) but, rather, expresses the intentions of its divine author."[90] In addition, a *sensus plenior* reading "recognizes that the inspired meaning of a text in the canon is that which God intended or may divinely reveal through the authority of the church. This fuller sense of the text may extend beyond that which is perceived as the author's intention."[91]

Those that advocate a *sensus plenior* approach focus on the contemporary significance of biblical passages. This is similar to our subject under consideration—LDS allegorizations as a self-identification with the biblical narrative. The "literal" or "plain" meaning of the text recedes into the background in favor of what the event means today. Therefore, a

---

84. A typological understanding, however, displays repeated patterns of events, concepts or people, and describes how God has acted in the past—throughout the two Testaments—and not as regards modern-day events (see especially Goppelt, *Typos*).

85. "The church so fulfills the promises to Israel that the promises to ethnic Israel are rendered obsolete" (McKnight, "Israel," 345).

86. While "the church and Israel are two related but still individually distinguishable entities," there still exists a "continuity of salvation history" (Campbell, "Church as Israel," 211–12).

87. Wright, "Joseph Smith's Interpretation," 204.

88. For the initial discussion of this concept, see Brown, "History and Development," 143; Brown, "*Sensus Plenior* in the Last Ten Years," 268–69.

89. For this perspective of *sensus plenior*, see Barker, "Speech Act Theory," 228–30.

90. Patton and Cook, "Introduction," 37.

91. Stamps, "Use of the Old Testament," 22.

version of *sensus plenior* might be an appropriate way to label LDS methodological activity here. However, the hermeneutical legitimacy of *sensus plenior* is a matter of debate.[92] Simply put, "problematic for the *sensus plenior* view as applied to contemporary 'fuller meaning' is the lack of any adequate controls for what might be part of this new, fuller sense."[93] It is difficult to tell the difference between *sensus plenior* and "the projection on to the text of a theological idea or belief acquired by some other means."[94] Since the "meaning is not contained in the text itself," it may be more appropriate to "speak of a fuller understanding on the part of the exegete rather than of a fuller sense of the text."[95] Any random interpretation, LDS or otherwise, could be claimed as the "fuller understanding" of the *interpreter*.

These conclusions argue against the use of *sensus plenior* and can be applied to the views of LDS author David Wright. The "secondary meanings" of Wright are LDS allegorizations that advance modern meanings of an ancient text. The "fuller meaning" of the allegorization of Ezek 37, for example, is the purported uniting of the Bible and the BoM. LDS author W. W. Phelps specifically mentioned the modern referent (quoted above in reference to Isa 29): "Isaiah had his eyes on the last days, when he spoke of what should happen at a future period."[96] According to Phelps, Isa 29 refers to the "last days." This is debatable. The LDS interpretation also neglects to "listen" to what the book of Isaiah meant to the original recipients of the book. There are problems inherent in a *sensus plenior* hermeneutic, then, with a projection of modern meanings onto an ancient text. Likewise, there are problems with LDS claims of secondary or fuller meaning that focus only on contemporary significance.

Finally, an important concept to be introduced here (and more fully developed in chapter 8) centers on the implied audience of a text. As McLean writes, the ancient biblical text had numerous facets of ancient beliefs, whether of sacrifice, patriarchy, dualism, etc., that encompassed the "virtual 'unsaid' of every text."[97] Modern readers do not always rec-

---

92. In fact, "one of the most heated debates in hermeneutics has been the issue of whether Scripture has a fuller sense than that intended by the human author" (Muthengi, "Critical Analysis," 63–64).

93. Brown, *Scripture as Communication*, 115.

94. Wright, *People of God*, 58–59.

95. Muthengi, "Critical Analysis," 69.

96. Phelps, "Letter No. 8."

97. McLean, *Biblical Interpretation*, 191.

ognize these unsaid characteristics of the text—that would have been obvious to the implied audience of the text. In fact, when we approach the text with our own realities that are "unsaid," we may inadvertently ignore the ancient "unsaid" aspects of the text. This occurs in numerous LDS allegorizations. Biblical texts are used as references to their church. Yet, to "enter the story of the Bible," an identification with the implied audience of the biblical texts is the only possible avenue. A major characteristic of these allegorizations is, typically, the *neglect* of the implied audience. Rarely, if ever, do the ancient texts under consideration offer any indication of being open to modern referentialities. Instead, the hermeneutical filter of "systemic parameters" is used to perceive current LDS realities inside the ancient text itself. It is an example of hermeneutical neglect that notions of implied audience are not entertained by LDS authors.

I have argued that these interpretations, while appearing to be allegorical, are, in fact, allegorizations. In other words, only with the insider information afforded by the "systemic parameters" of the LDS system would an interpreter understand the deeper, hidden meanings of these passages. These deeper meanings reflect *modern* issues and perspectives and neglect *ancient* historical referents—thus failing to exhibit sound hermeneutical methodology. The LDS allegorizations outlined are designed to advance institutional needs. These institutional needs will continue to appear in our investigation, even more so as we turn to another hermeneutical category, that of sociological approach to interpretation.

5

A Sociological Approach

HAVING SEEN LITERALISTIC INTERPRETATIONS and allegorizations, I now want to focus on a sociological approach to the biblical text. This will highlight the perceived institutional needs of the LDS. After a brief study of the parameters of a sociological approach, followed by an investigation into specific sociological interpretations of the LDS, I will present a case study of Acts 3:21. A phrase from this passage, "the times of restitution," is interpreted not only as a validation of the LDS institution, but more specifically as a reference to the LDS Restoration.[1] As we will see, this reflects a sociological approach to the Bible by the LDS.

5.1. The Sociological Realities of the Biblical Texts

Recent decades have seen the emergence of sociological approaches to biblical interpretation. This perspective focuses on the social realities and motivations that underlie the context of the biblical texts.[2] It is helpful epistemologically, since knowledge "is social in nature and oriented within a community [that shares] convictions and assumptions."[3] Just as the ancient church evinced a social and communal reality, so also the

1. As an additional example of the overlap between my five categories, this interpretation could also be considered an allegorization. Nonetheless, I have labeled it as a sociological approach, with the reasons given below.

2. Watson, *Sociological Approach*, 19; cf. Thiessen, *Social Setting*.

3. Kee, *Knowing the Truth*, 6.

modern church as "a social institution . . . exists in an actual and concrete world."[4] Given that "human beings are essentially social," the meanings of texts, ancient or modern, are "rooted in people's enculturation, socialization, interrelationships, and interactions."[5] A sociological approach asks "a different set of questions" to highlight aspects of the text that traditional methods of interpretation often neglect.[6] In fact, "since biblical interpretation involves *readers* as well as texts—the reading of Scripture by reading communities in time and over time," this approach may draw attention to significant features of biblical dynamics that might otherwise go unnoticed.[7] While this approach to biblical interpretation primarily focuses on the *ancient* social reality that the biblical texts reflect, the approach can, nonetheless, be appropriated for the sociological interpretation by the *modern* church, as we will see.

Francis Watson proposed "two sociological models" to shed light on Paul's discussions of Gentile Christianity in the context of Judaism.[8] The first model was "the transformation of a reform-movement into a sect." Watson labeled Gentile Christianity as the "new reform-movement" and Judaism as the "parent community." This model posits that the transformation into "a sect" is often the result of opposition, with "a closely-knit group" setting up "rigid and clearly-defined barriers between itself and the parent community."[9] Watson was following the insights of Ernst Troeltsch. For Troeltsch, in order to "gain a conclusive insight into the sociological character of Christianity," the study of "development of the sects" was essential.[10] While on the one hand, the parent community is "overwhelmingly conservative" and "dominates the masses," the "sects, on the other hand, are comparatively small groups; they aspire after personal inward perfection" and are "forced to organize themselves into small groups."[11] To reiterate, the first sociological model was "the transformation of a reform-movement into a sect."[12] Watson's second model also has direct bearing on biblical interpretation by the LDS, for "if a sectarian

4. Tidball, *Social Context of the New Testament*, 15.

5. Malina, "Rhetorical Criticism," 6.

6. Barton, "Social-Scientific Criticism," 753.

7. Barton, "Social-Scientific Criticism," 753–54.

8. Watson, *Sociological Approach*, 19.

9. Watson, *Sociological Approach*, 19–20.

10. Troeltsch, *Social Teaching*, 1:330.

11. Troeltsch, *Social Teaching*, 1:331.

12. Watson, *Sociological Approach*, 19.

group is to establish and maintain separation from the religious body from which it originated, it will require *an ideology legitimating its state of separation*—i.e., a theoretical justification for its separate existence, which is shared by all the group's members and which helps to give it its cohesion."[13] What follows, then, are sociological approaches to interpretation by the LDS that attempt to legitimize a separation from the "parent community"—the Christian church that was unduly influenced by the Great Apostasy.

5.1.1. *Continuing Revelation and Sociological Interpretation*

We observed in chapter 2 numerous theological arguments by the LDS to sustain the doctrine of continuing revelation. The Bible specifically describes and upholds this doctrine, according to the LDS. After Peter confessed that Jesus was "the Christ, the Son of the living God," he was told that "flesh and blood hath not revealed *it* unto thee, but my Father which is in heaven" (Matt 16:16–17). This type of revelation is similar to what the LDS Church claims to experience today.[14] Continuing revelation is also explicated earlier in Matthew: "For whosoever hath, to him shall be given, and he shall have more abundance: but whosoever hath not, from him shall be taken away even that he hath" (Matt 13:12). According to Dallin Oaks, this verse "capsulizes the Latter-day Saint belief in the importance of continuing revelation as we read and interpret the scriptures."[15] Paul also received the gospel "by revelation from Jesus Christ" (Gal 1:12). He likewise was the recipient of "visions and revelations from the Lord" (2 Cor 12:1). Thus, believers today can also receive revelation.[16] A passage from the book of Numbers is frequently cited: "And Moses said unto him, 'Enviest thou for my sake? Would God that all the Lord's people were prophets, *and* that the Lord would put his spirit upon them!'" (Num 11:29). This passage is used to encourage LDS members, since Moses desired for all of God's people to be prophets: "through divine revelation every child of Christ may, and should, become a prophet or a prophetess to his or her own divinely appointed stewardship."[17]

13. Watson, *Sociological Approach*, 19–20.
14. LDS, *New Testament Seminary*, 41; cf. Riddle, "Revelation," 1225–28.
15. Oaks, "Scripture Reading."
16. McConkie, *New Witness*, 489.
17. Riddle, "Revelation," 1227.

The highlighting of later biblical events that supplant earlier ones also sustains the doctrine of continuing revelation. For instance, the earlier command to Abraham to sacrifice his son Isaac as "a burnt offering" (Gen 22:2), was superseded by a later injunction: "Lay not thine hand upon the lad" (Gen 22:12).[18] The law of Moses was superseded "by later revelation."[19] Indeed, the law of Moses was a "schoolmaster to bring us unto Christ" (Gal 3:24), for Jesus introduced a "new logic of justice and salvation."[20] Surprisingly, even what Jesus taught will be superseded, as explained by Paul in 1 Cor 13, for "we have reason to expect that these concepts [of Jesus] too will fail and be superseded by a fuller understanding: 'For we know in part and we prophesy in part, but when perfection comes, the imperfect disappears' (1 Cor 13:9–10)."[21] Similar to the early Christians who "took Jewish religious traditions" and "reconfigured them," the LDS, like other religious groups, develops concepts "in new directions."[22] They further assert a repeatable pattern from the first century: "The early Christians simply believed that although God had spoken once upon Sinai and had given them scriptures, he now spoke to them again and had given new revelations that superseded the old ones."[23] The reconfigured revelations update what had previously been revealed. This purported "update" established a separation from the religious group that preceded it. Previously we noted how the presupposition of continuing revelation placed the LDS in a "unique position," since they do not "limit divine revelation to the past," but believe that God "will yet reveal many great and important things."[24] Therefore, the perspective on continuing revelation, coming from a sociological approach, legitimizes the institutional existence of the LDS, and serves as a catalyst to separate themselves from the parent church that purportedly fell into apostasy.

---

18. See Robinson, *Are Mormons Christians?*, 28.

19. Robinson, *Are Mormons Christians?*, 28; cf. Gal 3:24–29; Heb 8:7–13; 10:8.

20. Huff, "Theology in the Light," 486; cf. Talmage, *Great Apostasy*, 5.

21. See Huff, "Theology in the Light," 486.

22. Davies, *Introduction to Mormonism*, 35. "Mormonism developed many pre-existing ideas into a new pattern" (Davies, *Introduction to Mormonism*, 35).

23. Robinson, *Are Mormons Christians?*, 28.

24. LDS, "Divine Revelation."

5.1.2. The "Dispensation of the Fulness of Times" as a Sociological Interpretation

An important LDS perspective concerns differing time periods, referred to as "dispensations," that have existed throughout the history of the church.[25] This word comes from the KJV: "dispensation of the fulness of times" (Eph 1:10).[26] According to Philip Barlow, this phrase has "a very specific Restorationist meaning for most Latter-day Saints," as well as indicating a "proof-text" for LDS doctrine.[27] Joseph Smith "brought the restored dispensation of the fulness of time anticipated by Paul in Eph 1:9, 10."[28] The LDS believe that the "modern dispensation of the fulness of times enjoys the unique position of gathering in aspects of previous dispensations so that in a way it is like every other dispensation, but no previous dispensation is exactly like it."[29] Neal Maxwell further explains: "Paul . . . wrote of the 'dispensation of the fulness of times' (Rom 11:25; Eph 1:10), a particular time of times, which would 'gather together in one all things in Christ' . . . Everything would be restored."[30] Because of Paul's words of "dispensation of the fulness of times," and "gathering together in one all things in Christ" (Eph 1:10), the LDS emphasizes the advantageous position of the present dispensation.

The final age embraces "all the others, tying together with cords of infinity the perfection of all previous sacred times."[31] LDS authors speak vividly of the advantage of this modern dispensation: "In our day, all the streams and rivers of the past flow into the grand ocean of revealed truth

---

25. See Wilcox and Young, *Standing Apart*, 3.

26. "Having made known unto us the mystery of his will, according to his good pleasure which he hath purposed in himself: That in the dispensation of the fulness of times he might gather together in one all things in Christ" (Eph 1:9–10).

27. Barlow, *Mormons and the Bible*, 193. In addition, the term "Latter-day" in the title of the LDS Church designates "the present age as the final dispensation" (Bitton, *Historical Dictionary of Mormonism*, 115).

28. See Davies, "Mormon Canon," 50.

29. Holzapfel and Wayment, *Making Sense*, 430. Also, the verses of Mal 4:5–6 "serve as a charter for the new dispensation of Mormonism: they herald the Restoration," for Elijah and Joseph Smith were both "prophets who bring the divine message to humanity" (Davies, *Mormon Culture*, 144–45; cf. 96; D&C 128:17).

30. Maxwell, "From the Beginning."

31. Hughes, in Eliason, *Mormons & Mormonism*, 36; cf. Smith, in Smith, *History of the Church*, 4:437.

that is the dispensation of the fulness of times."[32] Because of a God who acts with "extraordinary immediacy," the LDS has "a sense that the age they are living in is of particular cosmic relevance, to be understood as the last dispensation."[33] Thus, Joseph Smith "insisted that his role was to usher in a new dispensation, a full restoration of Christianity in its pristine purity . . . a reinauguration, not merely a reformation."[34] The particular sociological approach by the LDS to Eph 1:10 allows them to emphasize the advantageous position of the modern LDS Church, and gives justification for, as well as fuels the separation of, the "new reform-movement" (LDS) from the "parent community" (the early church overcome by the Great Apostasy).

5.1.3. Additional Examples of Sociological Approaches by the LDS

The doctrine of premortal existence has been labeled the most distinctive of all LDS doctrines.[35] Several biblical phrases are used to support this doctrine. Faulconer implies that being chosen "before the foundation of the world" (Eph 1:4), supports "the teaching of preexistence."[36] John's words of "we love him because he first loved us" (1 John 4:19), teach that God loved us "deep in the primeval past when [God] found himself in the midst of numerous spirit intelligences."[37] The question to Job of "where were you when I laid the foundation of the earth?" (Job 38:4) is "proof of [the] pre-existence of humans," since it implies that Job was existing "*somewhere* at the earth's creation."[38] The prospect of gaining a mortal body, "caused God's spirit children to shout with joy (Job 38:7)."[39] Other relevant verses include Jer 1:5: "Before I formed thee in the belly I knew thee"; Acts 17:29: "we are the offspring of God"; Rom 8:16: "we

32. Millet et al., *LDS Beliefs*, 243. Because of this emphasis on its privileged position, it is no accident that the early LDS matched Americans' "self-perceived originality, vitality, optimism, and divinely sanctioned position on the center stage of God's unfolding drama on earth" (Eliason, *Mormons & Mormonism*, 14).

33. Bowman, "History Thrown into Divinity," 82.

34. Givens, *Viper on the Hearth*, 61.

35. Terry, "Source of God's Authority," 110.

36. Faulconer, *New Testament Made Harder*, 422.

37. Givens, *Wrestling the Angel*, 238.

38. Barlow, *Mormons and the Bible*, 71.

39. Camille S. Williams, in Paulsen and Musser, *Mormonism in Dialogue*, 279. The phrase "spirit children" is another way to describe premortal human beings.

are the children of God"; and John 9:2: "Master, who did sin, this man, or his parents, that he was born blind?" A short phrase from Jude 6, "first estate," also purportedly describes premortal existence. In sum, biblical phrases are cited to promote and explicate LDS belief in premortal existence.[40] Therefore, as the most distinctive of all the LDS doctrines,[41] the promotion of the doctrine of premortal existence is a validation of a separate institution, and a fomenting of internal cohesion.

LDS sources also illuminate the meaning of the debated phrase "baptism for the dead" (1 Cor 15:29). The phrase describes proxy baptism—i.e., living LDS members performing baptisms "in behalf of the dead."[42] LDS authors declare that this "ordinance . . . is solidly based on scripture,"[43] although they admit that the doctrine "grows out of but one sentence in the New Testament, 1 Corinthians 15:29, and even that reference is in passing."[44] To illustrate the overlap with my five proposed categories, LDS authors advocate a literal interpretation of the phrase. They claim other traditions have "alternate explanations [that] force an interpretation on the Greek phrase . . . differently than its clear meaning. The phrase reads literally 'those baptized on behalf of the dead people.'"[45] According to the LDS, this rite of proxy baptism was "fairly widespread in early Christianity,"[46] although it has "not [been] practiced by major Christian groups since the fourth century AD."[47] Since "many people have died" in the past without receiving the ordinance of baptism, LDS members are baptized in Mormon temples in their place.[48] Joseph Smith

---

40. However, Givens writes that "the biblical allusions to preexistence" are "at best cryptic and scattered" (Givens, *Wrestling the Angel*, 147–48; cf. Ostler, "Idea of Preexistence," 59–78; Keller, "Latter-day Saint," 189–98). Nonetheless, Givens and others speak confidently of the doctrine of premortal existence in the Bible.

41. Terry, "Source of God's Authority," 110.

42. LDS, *Gospel Principles*, 91, 239; cf. LDS, *New Testament Seminary*, 184.

43. Draper and Rhodes, *Paul's First Epistle*, 788. It is "clearly named in the Bible" (LDS, *New Testament Seminary*, 185).

44. Draper and Rhodes, *Paul's First Epistle*, 788.

45. Draper and Rhodes, *Paul's First Epistle*, 789.

46. Arrington and Bitton, *Mormon Experience*, 35.

47. Givens and Barlow, *Oxford Handbook on Mormonism*, 125. Since Paul "does not explicitly condemn" proxy baptism, this suggests "it was among the accepted Christian practices . . . [and] it does not make sense for Paul to use a practice that he would consider heretical in order to support sound doctrine" (Draper and Rhodes, *Paul's First Epistle*, 789).

48. LDS, *Gospel Principles*, 265.

posed a poignant question in the nineteenth century: "How are all the millions who lived and died between Jesus [and himself] to be saved?" The answer was through the doctrine of "baptism for the dead."[49] Even a phrase from Rev 20:12 is used to support LDS proxy baptism, since it mentions "books being opened" at the end of the eschaton. These books are explained as the proxy baptism records kept by the LDS.[50] An isolated phrase in Zechariah is also quoted: "As for thee also, by the blood of thy covenant I have sent forth thy prisoners out of the pit wherein *is* no water" (Zech 9:11). It is unclear how the words "prisoners" and "water" constitute an explanation of baptism for the dead. Nonetheless, LDS authors believe this verse may "foreshadow the practice."[51] Thus, the sociological approach to the biblical phrase "baptism for the dead" justifies the separation of the LDS from "major Christian groups"[52] that no longer practice the rite.

The biblical names of Aaron and Melchizedek sustain a system that organizes men into one of two priesthoods—an Aaronic priesthood and a Melchizedek priesthood.[53] According to Bushman, one of the gifts and abilities of Joseph Smith "was to sense the power in biblical passages that others had long overlooked."[54] The result was the restoration of the priesthood "to the central position it had occupied in ancient Hebrew religion."[55] The "priesthood" is extremely important in the LDS system,[56] and every worthy male above twelve years old is a "member of one of the

---

49. See Bloom, *American Religion*, 121; cf. D&C 124:28–29; 127:5–12; 128:1–21.

50. See Davies, *Mormon Culture*, 96.

51. Holzapfel and Wayment, *Making Sense*, 364.

52. Givens and Barlow, *Oxford Handbook on Mormonism*, 125.

53. Early in the translation process of the Book of Mormon, the LDS claims that Smith and his scribe, Oliver Cowdery, were ordained into the Aaronic Priesthood by John the Baptist who then promised a later ordination into a higher priesthood—the Melchizedek (see LDS, *Joseph Smith*, 1:69; cf. Quinn, *Origins of Power*, 27–32).

54. Bushman, *Rough Stone*, 159.

55. Bushman, *Rough Stone*, 159. It is unclear how the reading of the names of Aaron or Melchizedek to designate a modern organizational model could hermeneutically illustrate the sensing of power in biblical passages.

56. "If a man does not have the priesthood, even though he may be sincere, the Lord does not recognize the ordinances that he performs (Matthew 7:21–23; Articles of Faith 1:5)" (LDS, *Gospel Principles*, 67); "Without the priesthood, even routine forms of church participation are beyond reach, such as distribution of the sacrament" (Ostling and Ostling, *Mormon America*, 96; cf. Flake, "Four Books," 29).

quorums of either the Aaronic or the Melchizedek priesthood."[57] Three brief verses on Melchizedek in Gen 14 are among those that Joseph Smith "embellished most elaborately" for this doctrine.[58] In addition, Acts 6 is cited, as the work designated for the seven elected men "fell within the realm of those temporal matters normally handled by the Aaronic Priesthood, thus leaving the apostles free to handle the more difficult matters of their Melchizedek ministry."[59] The lack of any reference in Acts 6 to an Aaronic or Melchizedek Priesthood does not preclude LDS authors from quoting the passage as an example of the responsibilities of the two priesthoods.[60] The sociological approach to these passages undergirds the important organizational pattern of the Aaronic and Melchizedek priesthoods, and creates cohesion as a supposedly lost biblical reality is restored—the priesthood that once held a central position in the ancient Hebrew religion.

A sociological approach also gives credence to the LDS doctrine of the Great Apostasy. For the LDS, "apostasy" is an "important New Testament theme" and its importance continues today.[61] In fact, an impending apostasy is "taught in the New Testament."[62] However, the LDS do not view Scripture as describing the totality of the Great Apostasy. Passages simply refer to an incipient apostasy that would come upon the church with the death of the apostles. The account in the book of Revelation of an angel bringing the "everlasting gospel" to earth is frequently quoted. The verse states: "And I saw another angel fly in the midst of heaven, having

57. Shipps, *Mormonism*, 134; cf. Smith, *Essentials in Church History*, 148–52.

58. Bushman, *Rough Stone*, 160.

59. McConkie, in LDS, *New Testament Seminary*, 141.

60. In addition, even LDS authors note a discrepancy between the "modern Mormon conception of priesthood" and "scriptural" clues (see Terry, "Authority and Priesthood," 2). In fact, "in LDS usage, priesthood is a word that has been wrenched from its historical and linguistic roots and given a meaning not present in any other context, even in ancient LDS scripture" (Terry, "Authority and Priesthood," 13).

61. See Faulconer, *New Testament Made Harder*, 452. Joseph Fielding Smith believed that the OT also spoke of the Great Apostasy, when Isaiah spoke of a "deep sleep" coming over prophets and rulers (Isa 29:10) and Amos spoke of a famine of "hearing the words of the Lord" (Amos 8:11) (Smith, *Essentials in Church History*, 26).

62. Robinson, *Are Mormons Christians?*, 34. For the *warnings* concerning apostasy, according to Robinson, see 2 Thess 2:1–5; Acts 20:29–31; 1 Tim 4:1–3, 2 Tim 3:1–7; Jude 17–18. According to Robinson, the passages of 2 Thess 2:7–11, 1 Tim 1:15, and 3 John 9–10 "offer a contemporary witness that the predicted rebellion (apostasy) was taking place already" (Robinson, *Are Mormons Christians?*, 116n1; cf. Jackson, "New Testament Prophecies," 394–406).

the everlasting gospel to preach unto them that dwell on the earth, and to every nation, and kindred, and tongue, and people" (Rev 14:6). The angel is Moroni, who brought the "fulness of the Gospel" to Joseph Smith by telling him of the buried plates, from which he eventually translated the BoM.[63] A reference to the Great Apostasy is claimed in this verse, for it "is illogical to assume that the gospel was to be brought to earth by a heavenly messenger if that gospel was still extant upon the earth."[64] In other words, "the gospel must have been taken from the earth."[65] Therefore, through a sociological approach to the interpretation of NT passages that speak of an impending apostasy, the LDS legitimizes their institutional existence and separates from the "parent community"—the Christian church that was unduly influenced by this apostasy.

5.2. The Hermeneutical Effect of Sociological Interpretation

The dynamics of sociological interpretation have been studied for decades, and in the process have illuminated the complex process of biblical interpretation. Ever since the early period of discussion on sociological interpretation in mainstream scholarship (Troeltsch), and more recently (Watson), the social effect of culture has been highlighted, as well as the associated commitment to perceived institutional needs as significant drivers in biblical interpretation. Francis Watson writes,

> Speech-acts require an institutional context if they are to achieve their intended effect; to make a promise or to issue a command presupposes a complex set of prior conditions and relationships. If speech-acts are embodied in written texts, their intended illocutionary and perlocutionary force as communicative actions requires institutional continuities extended through the space and time that they traverse.[66]

63. See Talmage, *Jesus the Christ*, 770; Smith, *Essentials in Church History*, 61–62; Barlow, *Mormons and the Bible*, 27; cf. McConkie, *New Witness*, 139–40; Shipps, *Mormonism*, 30. The angel Moroni is placed on top of LDS temples today with a trumpet to announce a message to the world. This is a reminder of Rev 14 (LDS, *New Testament Seminary*, 258).

64. Talmage, *Great Apostasy*, 31.

65. Talmage, *Great Apostasy*, 31; cf. McConkie, *New Witness*, 628.

66. Watson, *Text and Truth*, 117. Watson illustrates this cogently: "A Canaanite text expressing a longing for communion with Baal could no longer achieve its

Numerous biblical passages are interpreted by the LDS as communicative actions with an intended illocutionary force—justification for the separation of the "new reform-movement" from the "parent community." The sociological interpretation of the "dispensation of the fulness of times" emphasizes its modern-day relevance, and highlights perceived institutional needs.[67] Yet, because of these sociological interpretations, the individual biblical book's right to self-determination is obliterated because of modern-day priorities. That is, by reducing the sum of biblical documents to a single repository of locutions, such locutions seem to be adjusted—and their referentiality ignored. Specifically, the reading of a passage (Eph 1:10), especially the two phrases "dispensation of the fullness of times" and "gathering together in one all things in Christ," validates a belief operative in the contemporary LDS, irrespective of any contextual meaning of the ancient passage itself. The intended sense of the two phrases is not considered. The novelty of the modern obscures the legitimacy of the ancient.

The Greek phrase from which the KJV translates "dispensation of the fulness of times," does not elucidate differing time periods in church history. The word οἰκονομίαν (*oikonomían*) "refers to God's plan of salvation realized in Christ."[68] Therefore, it should not be translated "dispensation" (KJV). Again, the word "refers to the *plan of salvation* which God is bringing to reality through Christ."[69] It signals that "God's purposes and law . . . [were] fulfilled."[70] It is not referring to different time periods in church history. Concerning the KJV translation of "gather together in one," Markus Barth asserts that its meaning "is to be derived exclusively from the context of Eph 1:10," and therefore, translates it as "to make [Christ] the head."[71] Precisely because the "headship" of Christ is repeatedly emphasized in Ephesians, and is the focus of 1:10 itself, "it is likely that the readers would have read this term in light of those statements" in the book that focus

---

communicative intention, however attractive and moving it might be as a poem" (Watson, *Text and Truth*, 118).

67. Again, many of these sociological interpretations could be labeled as allegorizations since they exhibit modern historical referents.

68. Best, *Ephesians*, 24.

69. Arndt et al., *Greek-English Lexicon*, 698, emphasis in original.

70. Barth, *Ephesians*, 88.

71. Barth, *Ephesians*, 91; cf. the views of Arnold: "bring everything under the headship of [Christ]" (Arnold, *Ephesians*, 89).

on the headship of Christ (e.g., 1:22; 4:15; 5:23).[72] The original, intended sense of Eph 1:10 is a focus on Christ—not on a Mormon Restoration over 1,800 years later: "The completion of God's purpose is anticipated and the unifying of the cosmos and restoration of its harmony is seen as achieved in Christ (1:10)."[73]

Concerning the "baptism for the dead," the LDS is inclined to see implicit references to the doctrine even in unlikely places. What Paul was describing in the letter to the Corinthians, or what Zechariah was communicating to his readers, appears not to interest LDS authors—only that these passages purportedly allude to a later LDS doctrine. There is an interpretive implication here—the Bible was written, in part, to elucidate later doctrine. The investigation into sociological interpretation assists us in articulating this reality. The citation of a phrase from 1 Cor 15:29, as well as the other biblical passages we have discussed, suggests the possibility that biblical texts are seen mainly as confirmation and explanation of a later doctrine. In sum, we have learned that sociological approaches by the LDS foment cohesion of a "new reform-movement" that has separated from the "parent community." I now turn to a case study of Acts 3:19–21, to observe how this interpretive method is utilized by LDS authors as they interpret a sermon by Peter in the book of Acts. Along with this sociological approach of the LDS, I will investigate the conclusions of authors from other traditions.

5.3. Case Study: An LDS Sociological Approach to Acts 3:19–21

In Acts 3:1–10, Peter and John healed a beggar, crippled from birth. Peter then spoke to the astonished onlookers (Acts 3:11–26). He called his listeners to repent, so that "times of refreshing" would come, and mentioned soon thereafter "times of restoration." The precise identification of the "times of refreshing" and the "times of restoration" is a matter of some debate.

> Repent and turn, therefore, for the blotting out of your sins, in order that times of refreshing may come from the face of the Lord, that he may send to you the appointed Christ—(who is) Jesus, who must remain in heaven until the times of restoration

72. Barth, *Ephesians*, 91.

73. Lincoln and Wedderburn, *Theology of the Later Pauline Letters*, 96.

of all things which God spoke of through the mouth of his holy
prophets from ancient times. (Acts 3:19–21, my translation)

5.3.1. *LDS Authors and Acts 3:19–21*

LDS sources interpret the "times of restoration" ("times of restitution" in
the KJV), as the appearance of the Father and the Son to Joseph Smith in
1820. Specifically, this appearance "was the commencement of 'the times
of restitution' of which Peter spoke."[74] Other LDS authors comment: "God
had foreseen the Apostasy and prepared for the gospel to be restored. The
Apostle Peter spoke of this [in] Acts 3:20–21."[75] Other American restorationists "borrowed" the language of Acts 3:21 to speak of the "restoration
of all things," but according to Barlow, "Joseph Smith intended the phrase
quite literally."[76] Relatedly, "the times of restitution of all things" describe
"the restoration of the gospel through the Prophet Joseph Smith and the
fulfillment of all the signs of the times."[77] From the LDS perspective, "the
times of restitution of all things" is a "prominent theme of both ancient
and latter-day scripture."[78] This theme is also linked with the previously
mentioned "dispensation of the fulness of times":

> All previous dispensations were open-ended and will flow into
> this final dispensation like rivers into the seas. This dispensation
> is known as the time of 'restitution of all things,' when the cov-
> enants, promises, knowledge, doctrines, priesthood, and divine
> governing powers that were had by ancient prophets and seers
> will be established and organized again upon the earth.[79]

In 1855, Parley Pratt lamented that previous reforms were in vain, "until
the full time should arrive—'the times of restitution of all things.'"[80] A
century later, Duane Crowther wrote that the "restitution of all things"
had "now begun," and was "commenced in 1830 with the restoration of

---

74. McConkie, *New Witness*, 627; cf. McConkie, *Mormon Doctrine*, 635.

75. LDS, *Gospel Principles*, 92–93.

76. Barlow, *Mormons and the Bible*, xxxvi.

77. Ridges, *New Testament Made Easier Part 2*, 9.

78. Matthews, "Restoration of All Things," 68.

79. Matthews, "Restoration of All Things," 68; cf. Hughes, in Eliason, *Mormons & Mormonism*, 28, 31.

80. Pratt, *Key to the Science*, 18–19.

the Church through the instrumentality of Joseph Smith."[81] Finally, LDS authors elaborate on the Mormon understanding of "Restoration":

> The most common use of the term refers to the series of events and divine revelations whereby the fulness of gospel principles, ordinances, priesthood authority, and the true Church of Jesus Christ were restored to the earth. These events, beginning with Joseph Smith's First Vision in 1820, the translation and publication of the Book of Mormon, and the organization of the Church in 1830, are all part of what Latter-day Saints refer to as the Restoration—the fulfillment of Peter's prophecy of "the times of restitution" that will precede the second coming of Christ (Acts 3:21).[82]

To summarize, LDS authors claim that Peter, after the healing of the beggar outside of the temple, spoke of the Mormon restoration nearly two millennia later.

5.3.2. Mainstream Voices and Acts 3:19–21

A challenging aspect of the passage is, indeed, the exact timing of the "times of restoration." In fact, "there is no consensus as regards the precise reference of this phrase."[83] The three verses cited above constitute a "difficult passage."[84] In addition, the connection between καιροὶ ἀναψύξεως (*kairoi anapsyxeōs*) "times of refreshing" and χρόνων ἀποκαταστάσεως (*cronōn apokatastaseōs*) "times of restoration" is disputed. They may be synonymous, or sequential.[85] An additional challenge is the sending of the Christ (v. 20) that appears to precede Christ's remaining in heaven (v. 21). The word "all" adds to the dilemma, although it is a possible clue to the extent and timing of the "restoration." Furthermore, after our passage, Peter claimed that "all the prophets from Samuel on . . . foretold these days" (Acts 3:24). The import of "these days" becomes an added difficulty.

---

81. Crowther, *Prophecies of Joseph Smith*, 196.

82. Millet et al., *LDS Beliefs*, 529–30.

83. Schnabel, *Acts*, 216.

84. Pao, *Acts and the Isaianic New Exodus*, 132.

85. See, e.g., Allison, "Eschatology," 208. Both phrases are without parallel in the NT (Longenecker, *Acts of the Apostles*, 297).

It is important to keep the preceding context in mind: Acts 2:17 speaks of the initiation of the eschaton.[86] The "last days" had commenced, and this holds significant impact for our passage in Acts 3. Parallel phrases between Acts 2:38 and 3:19 are also important, for in both verses Peter calls for repentance and mentions the forgiveness of sins.[87] Acts 2:38 describes the reception of the "gift of the Holy Spirit." This appears to be echoed with the "times of refreshing" in Acts 3:19. In other words, it seems that καιροὶ ἀναψύξεως (*kairoi anapsyxeōs*) "times of refreshing" refers to the "spiritual refreshment that comes from the Holy Spirit."[88] It was the result of repentance by Peter's hearers.[89] To reiterate, Peter's hearers, upon repenting, would receive the Spirit, or in other words, "times of refreshing."

Many authors conclude that the "times of refreshing" are synonymous with the "times of restoration." Joseph Fitzmyer writes that the "times of restoration" "must be another way of saying" the "times of refreshing." The phrases "mutually explain each other" with "καιροὶ (*kairoi*) indicating the beginning of the period, and χρόνων (*cronōn*) the duration of it."[90] Others see the "times of refreshing" and "times of restoration" as "form[ing] a hendiadys reflecting the sovereign activity of God."[91] For Micheal Parsons, the two phrases are connected, based on a similarity to a rhetorical device in the writings of Cicero. Using *expolitio*, or "refining," a speaker could "dwell on a topic by expressing an idea once and then by 'repeating it once again or oftener in other, equivalent terms.'"[92] Going forward, I will assume that these two phrases are synonymous. However, their precise temporal reference remains under dispute. There are three possibilities: a first-century reference, a future event that describes the Mormon Restoration, or a future event that describes the coming of the Messiah.

---

86. Peter added the phrase "in the last days" to the passage from Joel. This is a significant assertion concerning the initiation of the eschaton (see Himes, "Peter and the Prophetic Word," 242; cf. Beale, *New Testament Biblical Theology*, 138, where the "fulfillment of other latter-day OT prophecies . . . was also an indication that the last times had begun [Acts 3:18; 22–26; 4:25–28]").

87. See Pervo, *Acts*, 108.

88. Kurz, *Acts of the Apostles*, 74; cf. Twelftree, *People of the Spirit*, 179.

89. Bruce, *Book of Acts*, 84.

90. Fitzmyer, *Acts of the Apostles*, 288.

91. Toussaint and Quine, "No, Not Yet," 143.

92. Cicero, *Rhetorica ad Herennium*, 4.42.54–55, in Parsons, *Acts*, 61.

5.3.3. *Restoration as a Future Reality*

Many maintain that the "times of refreshment/restoration" refer to the Second Coming of Christ.[93] These authors link the "times of refreshing" with what immediately follows—"that he may send to you the appointed Christ—(who is) Jesus."[94] This "sending of the appointed Christ" would refer to the Parousia (Second Coming).[95] For F. F. Bruce, these phrases are mutually confirming, with the passage implying that "Jesus is absent for a limited time, until the fulfillment of prophetic scripture."[96] George Stevens summarizes:

> The reference [to refreshment] is hardly to the resurrection, but to the *Parousia*. To the hope of this event, always viewed as imminent, all the expressions: "times of refreshing," "times of restitution" and "these days" (vv. 19–24) undoubtedly refer. So Olshansen, Meyer, Alford, Hackett, Gloag, Lechler and most recent critics.[97]

The citation of Deut 18:15 in Acts 3:22[98] is important for this interpretation. For Austin Busch, the "prophet like Moses" whom God will raise up (3:22) is the Christ of the eschaton.[99] This prophet is understood "as a figure associated with the eschatological consummation and the universal judgment."[100] This "not only makes good sense in the context of Peter's sermon," but is "thoroughly conventional in ancient Jewish literature," and therefore, it is "surprising that commentators rarely understand Acts 3:22–23's prophet like Moses as a reference to Christ's coming judgment of the world, instead preferring to interpret his raising up with historical reference to Jesus' first coming."[101] In sum, for Busch, "Context demands

---

93. See Polhill, *Acts*, 134; Alford, *Alford's Greek Testament*, 2:38; cf. Beale, "Eschatology," 333–34.

94. See Toussaint and Quine, "No, Not Yet," 143.

95. See Conzelmann, *Acts of the Apostles*, 29; Link, "Reconciliation," 3:148.

96. Bruce, *Acts of the Apostles*, 144.

97. Stevens, *Saint Chrysostom*, 11:59n1. See also Haenchen, *Die Apostelgeschichte*, 168.

98. "For Moses said, 'The Lord your God will raise up for you a prophet like me from among your own people; you must listen to everything he tells you'" (Acts 3:22).

99. Busch, "Presence Deferred," 541n45.

100. Busch, "Presence Deferred," 546.

101. Busch, "Presence Deferred," 546. As we will see, however, I believe it *is* referring to Christ's first coming.

equation of the prophet like Moses whom God will raise up (3:22–23) with the Christ whose second coming Acts 3:20–21 prophesied: his Parousia will initiate a final judgment."[102] Although Dennis Johnson, like many observers, admits to an already-not yet dynamic in the passage, he nonetheless concurs: "the fullness of the messianic restoration has not arrived. The seasons of refreshing and the times of restoration of all things still await the sending of Jesus, the appointed Messiah, from heaven."[103] Others repeat the future aspect of the restoration, for Jesus "will come at some future point to act as judge of the living and the dead and to inaugurate the 'universal restoration' (Acts 3:20–21; 10:42)."[104] Therefore, many thinkers argue that the "times of refreshment/restoration" refer to a future reality. I do not believe, however, that this is the correct temporal reference for the debated phrases.

5.3.4. Restoration as a Present Reality Begun in First Century

A crucial contextual issue is that "all the prophets from Samuel on . . . foretold *these days*" (Acts 3:24, emphasis added). Regarding the implied audience, it is important to note the relevance of the close contextual connection between "these days" and the "times of refreshment/restoration." If the "times of refreshment/restoration" were in the future, this would, in fact, appear to ignore the implied audience. It would also render Peter's mention of "these days" superfluous. For the implied audience, Christ's *first* coming was the impetus behind the call to repentance. Peter's listeners were called to listen to Jesus (and by extension, his apostles).[105] Notwithstanding Busch's views, the "prophet like Moses" that Peter references should be construed as referring to Christ's *first* coming—who with his death and resurrection initiated the restoration.[106] In addition, what is the implied *vantage point*? The passage does not refer to the future from the perspective of Jesus, but from the future of the ancient prophets.

102. Busch, "Presence Deferred," 544; cf. Munck, *Acts of the Apostles*, 29.

103. Johnson, *Message of Acts*, 65; cf. Pervo, *Acts*, 108, who states that v. 20 refers to the Second Coming of Jesus.

104. Marshall, *Acts of the Apostles*, 58; cf. Soards, *Speeches in Acts*, 39, 42; Keener, *Acts*, 2:1109n674; Marshall, *New Testament Theology*, 203; Barrett, *Acts of the Apostles*, 1:206; Goppelt, *Typos*, 123.

105. See Haenchen, *Acts of the Apostles*, 209; cf. Soards, *Speeches in Acts*, 43.

106. In other places in the NT, Deut 18:15, 18 is understood as referring to Christ's first coming (see John 6:14; cf. Matt 11:3; 21:11; Luke 7:16; 24:19; Acts 7:37).

From that perspective, the *time of the Prophet* was in the future. The future of the past, then, seems to be the "now" of the implied audience. The prophets had foretold of the days in the future—and Luke, through Peter's sermon, emphasizes the first century as the time of fulfillment. The text under consideration, then, connects the "times of refreshment/restoration," with the time period of Peter and his listeners ("these days").

Furthermore, Peter's call to repentance was expected to result in an immediate "refreshment/restoration," just as Acts 2 assumed the immediate coming of the Spirit upon repentance. Again, from Peter's vantage point, the "last days" had begun (Acts 2:17). Precisely on account of God's raising of Jesus, Peter and John healed the beggar,[107] and the "underlying theological message" was that *this is a time of life, of restoration, of resurrection.*[108] There was no need to wait for refreshment or restoration, for if one repented, "then 'times of refreshment' could come from the very presence of the Lord himself, a kind of advance anticipation of the full and final 'refreshment' that we can expect when God completes the work at last."[109] Our passage, then, advocates a first-century reality of restoration. The "reference to 'these days' in v. 24 as the time of the fulfillment of God's promises confirms that the 'times' . . . are not a future event but the present reality of God's restoration of Israel through Jesus, the Messiah."[110] David Peterson adds that "the restoration of all things has begun and will continue until it is consummated at Christ's return . . . [Luke] proclaims the realization of end-time blessings in the present through the preaching of the gospel."[111] The message to the implied audience of the first century was full of hope with the inauguration of the "times of refreshment/restoration."

What can be concluded regarding the "times of restoration *of all things*"? Is Peter claiming that God will restore "all" people regarding personal salvation, or that God will restore "all" the cosmos, or "all" Israel? The meaning of "all things" has bearing on the timing of the restoration. The church father Origen interpreted Acts 3:21 as a universalistic theory

---

107. "By faith in the name of Jesus, this man whom you see and know was made strong. It is Jesus' name and the faith that comes through him that has given this complete healing to him, as you can all see" (Acts 3:16 NIV).

108. See Wright, *Resurrection of the Son of God*, 454, emphasis added.

109. Wright, *Acts for Everyone*, 58.

110. Schnabel, *Acts*, 215; cf. Johnson, *Acts of the Apostles*, 74; Jervell, *Die Apostelgeschichte*, 171–73.

111. Peterson, *Acts of the Apostles*, 182–83.

of "the restoration of all created things." This is not likely however.[112] Others surmise that it refers to "all" Israel. According to Ben Witherington, the restoration of "all Israel" is especially strong "in view of the use of the cognate term in [Acts] 1:6." The passage in Acts 1 speaks "not of some sort of generic universal restoration of 'everything' or all persons." Rather, it speaks specifically of Israel.[113] Jaroslav Pelikan concurs with the "universal restoration" and its link to Acts 1:6, for it "seems to refer to restoration of the kingdom to Israel."[114] J. T. Carroll maintains that since "the holy prophets" spoke of this "restoration," it logically refers to Israel's restoration.[115] However, according to Graham Twelftree, although "all things" may *include* Israel, it "more likely refers to the whole of creation being returned to its former glory."[116] It probably is, indeed, more inclusive, since Luke "anticipates the restoration of all things (Acts 3:19–21) and the inclusive participation of all peoples in the more comprehensive epoch of salvation, which includes Israel's restoration, but also the inclusion of Gentiles."[117] The most important aspect, for our purposes, is that the "times of refreshment/restoration" had indeed begun—in the first century—and the "restoration *of all things*," had commenced, and would include not only the whole of creation, but also the Gentiles with Israel. Before concluding, it is important to point out that, although the times of restoration had *already* commenced in the first century, at some future point a *final* restoration will occur, with

> God summing up all things in Christ (Eph 1:10), reconciling all things to himself (Col 1:20), making new heaven and earth (Rev 21:1) . . . [yet] what has happened now is that the final restoration has already happened to Jesus himself: what God is going to do to the whole of creation, he has done for Jesus in raising him from the dead.[118]

112. See Link, "Reconciliation," 3:148; cf. Dodd, "Universalism," 1188; Witherington, *Acts of the Apostles*, 187n92; Gundry-Volf, "Paul and Universalism," 956; Kittel and Friedrich, *TDNT*, 1:391.

113. Witherington, *Acts of the Apostles*, 187; cf. Rom 11:26.

114. Pelikan, *Acts*, 68.

115. See the views of Carroll, in Busch, "Presence Deferred," 542n45.

116. Twelftree, *People of the Spirit*, 179.

117. Fuller, *Restoration of Israel*, 269. Despite Pelikan's views above, he also sees the possibility of "broadening the hope to include *all* Jews and *all* Gentiles, even all of the cosmos" (Pelikan, *Acts*, 68); cf. the "worldwide, ethnically inclusive community" mentioned by Walton (Walton, "Acts," 79).

118. Wright, *Acts for Everyone*, 58. This "final" restoration also seems to answer

5.3.5. The Hermeneutical Effect of Acts 3:19–21

As an example of a sociological approach to interpretation, the LDS claims that Peter referred to the Mormon restoration in Acts 3:19–21. However, it is not possible that Peter was speaking proleptically of the coming of Joseph Smith. Our passage refers to the reality of first-century refreshment and restoration brought on by the Holy Spirit in response to human repentance, precisely because the process of final restoration had already been inaugurated in the life and ministry of Jesus. This interpretation does not permit any LDS nuance of meaning. In this example, the LDS does not allow for the ontological realism of the biblical passage, and the resultant LDS interpretation does not occur in accordance with its intended sense.

The LDS is not taking seriously the implied realities of the biblical text. They are supplanting the implied audience with themselves in their interpretation of Acts 3:19–21. This occurs because of a sociological approach, that is fueled by a commitment to a perceived institutional need. Consideration of the implied audience is an interpretive matter. By replacing the implied audience with themselves, the LDS is leaving the interpretive realm—despite their insistence on their specific interpretation of Acts 3:19–21. One of their institutional needs is separation from the church affected by the Great Apostasy. The interpretation of Peter's speech in Acts 3 as a reference to the Mormon restoration solidifies group cohesion. The "new reform-movement" utilizes the biblical phrase of "the restitution of all things" to justify its separation from the "parent community." We continue to attempt an answer to the question of the validity, applicability and legitimacy of biblical interpretations by the LDS. Thus far, many interpretations can be questioned on hermeneutical grounds. Additional conclusions will be given after discussing the two remaining uses of the Bible by the LDS, emendatory and re-authoring, while final conclusions will be detailed in chapter 8.

---

the challenged posed by the sending of the Christ (v. 20) appearing to precede Christ's remaining in heaven (v. 21). Although the "sending" refers to "the times of restoration" that began in the first century (see also v. 26), in some sense Christ remains in heaven until the *final* restoration. The emphasis in the book of Acts concerning Christ *in heaven* (Acts 1:11; 7:55–56; 9:3, 5) corroborates this idea.

——— 6 ———

Emendatory Practices

THUS FAR, WE HAVE explored three interpretive practices under the broad categories of literal, allegorical and sociological. The fourth category, emendatory, is present in two ways in LDS sources. First, LDS authors clarify the King James Version. Second, modern LDS scriptures clarify *and* restore passages from the Bible. Such restoration is needed because of the purportedly corrupted biblical text. Restoration made to the ancient text by modern LDS scriptures uses the building blocks of biblical locutions. For our purposes, we will need to explore the extent to which this restorative practice remains in the interpretive realm. In fact, is it appropriate to discuss any type of emendation in a *hermeneutical* investigation? This question must be asked given that the normal usage of the term "emendation" assumes text-critical improvements. Going forward, however, I propose that these modern LDS scriptures do, in fact, *initially* interpret the biblical text. From this perspective, the emendatory practice is hermeneutical, for they are correcting, clarifying and emending the ancient text—to restore it to its supposed original state.

For millennia, those who have considered themselves to be God's people have approached the biblical text in a variety of ways. Paraphrastic targumim and midrashic explanations are two examples. The targumim can be characterized "as simple glosses or additional words and phrases added to the text for explanation."[1] The targumim also evinced a tendency

1. Brady, "Targum," 780.

"to update the text, answer questions raised by the text, [and] even correct the text."[2] This is similar to LDS emendation. There is also correlation between LDS emendation and the Midrashim, which endeavored to find "meanings that went beyond the obvious and got at the true thrust of a text."[3] Relatedly, "in searching the sacred text the rabbis attempted to update scriptural teaching to make it relevant to new circumstances and issues."[4] In the following pages, I will note a correspondence between LDS emendatory practice and these ancient approaches. Nevertheless, I will also note that the level of hermeneutical reflection that informs LDS emendatory practice is rudimentary.

6.1. Emendatory Clarification of the KJV by LDS Authors

The LDS uses the phrase "uniformity of the gospel" to describe the consistent presentation of the gospel throughout history. In other words, they believe that the gospel has been proclaimed in an identical manner for centuries. For instance, Joseph Fielding Smith wrote that "the Gospel is much older than the law of Moses; it existed before the foundation of the world. Its principles are eternal."[5] Since the LDS was "convinced of the truth and plainness of the Bible," they "expected the plan of salvation to be uniform."[6] They concluded that both the Old and New Testaments "ought to present the same message."[7] Indeed, the OT was said to contain the gospel of apostolic times.[8] It was the "same gospel and plan of salvation that was received by Old Testament patriarchs and taught and testified of by prophets in all dispensations."[9] Adam was said to have been baptized.[10] In addition, since God was "no respecter of persons," it was

2. Evans, "Jewish Exegesis," 380.

3. Osborne, *Hermeneutical Spiral*, 325.

4. Evans, "Midrash," 544.

5. Smith, *Essentials in Church History*, 15; cf. Millet, "Joseph Smith's Translation," 49.

6. Irving, "Mormons and the Bible," 475–76.

7. Irving, "Mormons and the Bible," 476.

8. Lassetter, "Dispensations of the Gospel," 389; cf. Underwood, "The 'Same' Organization," 167–86.

9. Millet et al., *LDS Beliefs*, 449. This could also be called a "Christianization of the Old Testament" (Smith, "Hermeneutical Crisis," 99).

10. See Räisänen, "Creative Interpreter," 74–75. Also, the "gospel of Jesus Christ was taught to Adam" (see Matthews, *Plainer Translation*, 323; Gen 4:4–9; 6:67–71 JST;

assumed that God had given the same "gospel scheme of salvation" to all who were willing to listen.[11] The LDS "worked hard to establish the concept of the unchangeability of the gospel."[12] In these examples, LDS authors are attempting to clarify the general content of both OT and NT scriptures concerning the message of salvation.

A specific interpretive clarification is witnessed with a phrase from Galatians: "And the scripture, foreseeing that God would justify the heathen through faith, *preached before the gospel unto Abraham,* saying, 'In thee shall all nations be blessed'" (Gal 3:8, emphasis added). This phrase from the KJV is clarified when it is assumed that Abraham knew the gospel mentioned by Paul.[13] We observe here a specific hermeneutical posture—an explanatory reading of Gal 3:8, along the lines of a midrashic explanation, or a targumic commentary.

The concept of "uniformity of the gospel" also helped answer a difficult question in the early years of the LDS movement. A serious concern of the nineteenth century, considering thousands of indigenous people in the Americas, was the possibility of salvation for all earnest seekers, past and present. The explanatory power of the "uniformity of the Gospel" appeared to answer this conundrum—giving all seekers a chance to be saved. Joseph Smith struggled as he read John 5:29, wondering how "God could divide people into stark categories of saved and damned."[14] Yet Smith, as well as numerous LDS thinkers, concluded that the "uniformity of the gospel" from the past to the present allowed for the salvation of those who had never heard the gospel, including the indigenous people of the Americas.[15] According to the LDS, this concept of the "uniformity of the Gospel" was even endorsed by early church fathers, for "it was post-apostolic Christianity that fully articulated the view that the gospel was literally on the earth from the time of the Fall."[16] This clarifica-

---

cf. Book of Moses 5:4–9, PGP).

11. Irving, "Mormons and the Bible," 474. The phrase that God is "no respecter of persons" comes from the KJV of Acts 10:34 and will be covered in more detail in the following chapter.

12. Irving, "Mormons and the Bible," 474.

13. See McConkie, *New Witness,* 136–37.

14. See Bushman, *Rough Stone,* 196. "Those who have done good will rise to live, and those who have done evil will rise to be condemned" (John 5:29 NIV).

15. See Craig J. Hazen, in Beckwith et al., *New Mormon Challenge,* 43–48; cf. McConkie, *New Witness,* 137.

16. Harrell, *"This Is My Doctrine,"* 294. Here, as elsewhere, there is little, if any,

tory practice of the LDS resembles rabbinic midrash, as midrash was an "updat[ing] [of] scriptural teaching to make it relevant to new circumstances and issues."[17]

The LDS teaching of "uniformity of the gospel" has been proclaimed since the beginning of their movement. However, the clarifications presented here are conjectural emendations. When the LDS cite the passage of God preaching "the gospel unto Abraham" (Gal 3:8), they intend to invoke the doctrine of the "uniformity of the gospel." However, regardless of the contextual meaning that Paul intended to convey to the church of Galatia, the LDS asserts modern significance that clarifies the ancient biblical text. Because of this, although it purports to clarify, it is not hermeneutically helpful, as it does not consider the contextual meaning of the biblical locutions contained therein. Rather, it simply imports a modern, LDS perspective. Furthermore, because of the death, resurrection, and ascension of Jesus, it is not possible that "Old Testament patriarchs" received the "same gospel and plan of salvation"[18] as those in NT times. The LDS Church is ignoring important passages such as the opening lines of Hebrews: "In the past God spoke to our forefathers through the prophets at many times and in various ways, but *in these last days he has spoken to us by his Son*" (Heb 1:1–2 NIV, emphasis added). While there are various examples of continuity between the OT and the NT, there is also discontinuity.[19] The LDS does not seem to be concerned about these realities.

---

interaction by LDS authors on the discrepancy between their views on the Great Apostasy and their use of early church fathers to substantiate LDS perspectives. See, for example, Stephen Robinson, who states that the LDS "reject the authority of traditional Christianity after the death of the New Testament Apostles" (Robinson, *Are Mormons Christians?*, 34). Yet, later in the same book, Robinson quotes no less than five church fathers: Irenaeus, Clement of Alexandria, Justin Martyr, Augustine, Athanasius. He states, "all five believed in the doctrine of deification" (Robinson, *Are Mormons Christians?*, 61). Yet, Robinson does not discuss his justification for the citation of these fathers, given that they were part of the Great Apostasy. Their authority should have been rejected.

17. Evans, "Midrash," 544.

18. Millet et al., *LDS Beliefs*, 449.

19. Important examples of discontinuity include the following: Jesus is the final sacrifice—no more daily sacrifice is needed (Heb 7:27; 9:26); Jesus is the "great high priest" who accomplished what no earthly priest could accomplish (Heb 4:14—5:10; 9:11–15). Further examples of continuity *and* discontinuity are found in Rom 3:21, as well as between these passages: Isa 45:23 and Phil 2:10–11; Joel 2:32 and Rom 10:9, 13; Deut 6:4 and 1 Cor 8:6.

6.2. Restoration of the Bible by Modern LDS Scriptures

From the standpoint of the LDS, modern scriptures are imperative for biblical interpretation. "Modern revelation and restored scripture offer indispensable interpretations of the Bible."[20] LDS members "read the Bible through the lens of Restoration scriptures."[21] The "real key" to understanding the message of Christ in the NT is through "expanding that knowledge by adding what inspired men have known of him in the Old Testament, the Pearl of Great Price, the Book of Mormon, and the Doctrine and Covenants."[22] These books herald the arrival of the "fullness of the scriptures" as well as shedding "great light on the New Testament" and "illuminat[ing] its doctrines and teachings."[23] Restored scripture and modern revelation "reestablished the lost key of knowledge."[24] For the First Presidency, the "most reliable way to measure the accuracy of any biblical passage is not by comparing different texts, but by comparison with the Book of Mormon and modern-day revelation."[25] LDS author Mauro Properzi believes that "the LDS hermeneutical background is uniquely shaped"[26] by their modern scriptures.

Partially owing to their relativizing, even oscillating view of the Bible, the LDS is convinced of the superior clarity of modern scripture: "Many of the clearest explanations of doctrines arise from modern revelations or restored scripture."[27] LDS authors use the analogy of being lost and in need of the most recent map to locate oneself and then compare this to the advantage that modern scripture has over the Bible. They ask: "Which map would you rather have? . . . Which of these is most accurate? Which block of scripture would you rather study from?"[28] The answer,

20. Thomas, "Scripture," 1284; The three LDS scriptures, BoM, D&C, and the PGP all "interpret the Bible" (Thomas, "Scripture," 1283; cf. also Joseph Smith—History 1:11–20, PGP).

21. Millet, *Getting at the Truth*, 94.

22. Carmack, *New Testament*, 10.

23. Carmack, *New Testament*, 20.

24. Thomas, "Scripture," 1284; cf. Matthews, *Plainer Translation*, 372–73. See Luke 11:52: "Woe unto you, lawyers! for ye have taken away the key to knowledge."

25. See Millet et al., *LDS Beliefs*, 69; cf. Hopkins, *Biblical Mormonism*, 40; Holzapfel and Wayment, *Making Sense*, 522–23.

26. Properzi, *Mormonism and the Emotions*, 119.

27. Thomas, "Scripture," 1283; cf. Givens, *Wrestling the Angel*, 83; Black, *Expressions of Faith*, 125.

28. LDS, *New Testament Seminary*, 51.

of course, is their modern scriptural collection. The following sections describe significant examples of restorations of the Bible by the three LDS modern scriptures, the BoM, the D&C, and the PGP. I will also explore the emendatory practice of the JST (Joseph Smith Translation). I will note the similarity between these LDS emendations and the targumim and the Midrashim and will also point out the rudimentary level of hermeneutical reflection evinced in their interpretations.

6.2.1. The Book of Mormon and the Restoration of the Bible

According to the LDS, the Book of Mormon contains the "fullness of the gospel."[29] This "fullness" implies a deficiency in ancient revelation, and the need for restoration. The BoM also clarifies biblical content. Specifically, McConkie expressed, "without question, that in ninety-five of the one hundred cases, the Book of Mormon teaching is clearer, plainer, more expansive, and better than the biblical word."[30] For Kent Jackson, the BoM contains theology that "far excels in clarity and direction than the doctrines preserved in the New Testament."[31] The BoM prophets Lehi and Jacob "excel Paul in teaching the atonement" and "Nephi makes a better exposition of the scattering and gathering of Israel than do Isaiah, Jeremiah, and Ezekiel combined."[32] The BoM is viewed as the "key" to "unlock the true meaning of the Old and New Testaments."[33] The "Book of Mormon clarifies many of the writings of Old Testament prophets," and even "explains the Bible."[34] Since the "words of Isaiah are not plain," the BoM translates its message in "plain" language.[35] Faulconer states that the BoM "sheds light" on Bible passages.[36]

---

29. Davies, "Mormon Canon," 49; D&C 19:26; 42:12.

30. McConkie, New Witness, 467.

31. Jackson, "Latter-day Saints," 73. Particular areas where the BoM is purportedly clearer are the nature of Jesus and his atoning sacrifice, the purpose of humankind, the fall of Adam, and the concept of revelation (Jackson, "Latter-day Saints," 74; cf. Holzapfel and Wayment, Making Sense, 522).

32. McConkie, "What Think Ye."

33. Fielding McConkie, "The 'How' of Scriptural Study," 63.

34. Thomas, "Scripture," 1283; cf. Phelps, in Smith, "Hermeneutical Crisis," 97; Wright, "Joseph Smith's Interpretation," 206; Stark, Rise of Mormonism, 116.

35. Smith, "Hermeneutical Crisis," 98.

36. E.g., Mosiah 27:24–26 explains John 3 and the story of Jesus and Nicodemus (Faulconer, New Testament Made Harder, 61).

Paradoxically, the vital importance of the Book of Mormon was the fact that it *appeared*, as opposed to its subject matter. Grant Hardy wrote that the "actual contents" of the BoM "could often seem of secondary importance when compared to the sheer fact of its existence."[37] Givens even speaks of the "unblushing indifference to the book's *content*."[38] This indifference would seem to call into question the ardent endorsements of its clarity and explanatory power just referenced. Yet such issues do not concern these LDS authors. An emphasis remains—the appearance of the BoM that signified the God of the Bible was again communicating with the people of God. Such communication helped clarify and restore ancient revelation.

To cite a repeated LDS refrain, the BoM is "the most correct book on earth."[39] Jeffrey Holland claims that "in an effort to give the world back its Bible and a correct view of Deity with it, what we have in the Book of Mormon is a uniform view of God."[40] With this in mind, the following examples from the BoM illustrate LDS emendatory practice. The BoM text of Alma 13:7 explains the enigmatic phrase "without father or mother" of Heb 7:3. This refers not to Melchizedek, but to "the high priesthood."[41] Third Nephi 18:7 is a "corrective lens" as it counters the doctrine of transubstantiation and advocates the Lord's Supper as a simple remembrance of Jesus.[42] The identification of the "other sheep" of John 10:16 is an example of a "problematical passage in the Bible."[43] Therefore, the BoM identifies the "other sheep" as the Nephites that were visited by Jesus on the American continent after his resurrection (see 3 Nephi 15:21). Concerning the passage of Rev 17:5–6, LDS authors state that "the Lord has given inspired commentary on this passage of Revelation. Nephi saw a similar vision and recorded what he saw."[44] Two examples of clarificatory expansion include Ether 13:3–11 with the KJV

37. Hardy, *Understanding the Book of Mormon*, 268.

38. Givens, in Eliason, *Mormons & Mormonism*, 110, emphasis by author.

39. Millet, "Most Correct Book," 55–71.

40. Holland, in Millet et al., *LDS Beliefs*, 79.

41. Dennis L. Largey, in Carmack, *New Testament*, 140.

42. See also 3 Nephi 20:3; cf. Largey, in Carmack, *New Testament*, 140; Arrington and Bitton, *Mormon Experience*, 33.

43. Arrington and Bitton, *Mormon Experience*, 33; cf. Talmage, *Jesus the Christ*, 419.

44. LDS, *New Testament Seminary*, 261. See 1 Nephi 14:9–12.

of Rev 21:1–17, and Moroni 7:42–46 with the KJV of 1 Cor 13.[45] Concerning the latter example, Moroni 7:46 states: "Wherefore, my beloved brethren, if ye have not charity, ye are nothing, for charity never faileth. Wherefore, cleave unto charity, which is the greatest of all, for all things must fail." These are examples similar to a paraphrastic Targum, or a midrashic explanation.

The clarificatory expansion of a biblical text is, in fact, the biblical pattern, according to LDS thinking. Heikki Räisänen, a historical-critical scholar with significant empathy for the LDS, writes that just as there is a "retelling" of the stories of Samuel and Kings in the books of Chronicles, so also the BoM displays a parallel phenomenon. The Apostle Paul expands on the OT scriptures, according to Räisänen. Furthermore, just as Matthew spiritualizes Luke in the Sermon on the Mount, or as Jesus speaks in a manner quite different in John when compared with the Synoptic Gospels, so also the BoM expands on ancient scripture.[46] Krister Stendahl holds similar views and is "one of the few non-Mormon academics to look closely at LDS Scripture."[47] Stendahl concludes that

> the Book of Mormon belongs to and shows many of the signs of the Targums and the pseudepigraphic recasting of biblical material. The targumic tendencies are those of clarifying and actualizing translations, usually by expansion and more specific application to the need and situation of the community. The pseudepigraphic, both apocalyptic and didactic, tend to fill out the gaps in our knowledge about sacred events, truths, and predictions . . . It is obvious to me that the Book of Mormon stands within both of these traditions if considered as a phenomenon of religious texts.[48]

Stendahl also writes, "the laws of creative interpretation by which we analyze materials from the first and second Christian centuries operate on and are significantly elucidated by works like the Book of Mormon and by other writings of revelatory character."[49] He insists that "such authentic writing should not be confused with spurious gospel forgeries."[50] Sten-

45. See Barlow, "Before Mormonism," 757; cf. Barlow, *Mormons and the Bible*, 29.

46. See Räisänen, "Creative Interpreter," 66–67.

47. Givens, *By the Hand of Mormon*, 138.

48. Stendahl, "Sermon on the Mount," 152.

49. See Stendahl, *Meanings*, 99.

50. Stendahl, *Meanings*, 99. However, non-LDS scholar W. D. Davies calls for these strong views of Stendahl to be scrutinized, and claims Stendahl's views are, in reality,

dahl views 3 Nephi in the BoM, "as a nineteenth-century expansion and application of ancient material."[51] Reflections on the views of Räisänen and Stendahl will be given in the conclusion of the chapter.

Many critics of the LDS claim that the BoM "plagiarizes" the Bible.[52] One response to this criticism is that the BoM is an expansion and clarification—with similar vocabulary and concepts used.[53] For Alan Goff, the intertextuality between the BoM and the Bible is proof of the legitimacy of both.[54] Also, "Mormons believe that God simply delivered the same basic message twice."[55] The message was clarified in the later version. Furthermore, LDS thinkers assert that Joseph Smith operated under "the editorial conventions" of his day, and that what we consider plagiarism today was all-too frequent (and accepted) in his day.[56] Since the "culture of Smith's day was immersed in biblical literacy," it is natural for the BoM to reflect the diction that came from Joseph Smith that, it turn, reflected his knowledge of the Bible.[57] In sum, similar to the ancient targumim, the *Book of Mormon* attempts to clarify and explain ancient Scripture.

6.2.2. *The Doctrine and Covenants and the Restoration of the Bible*

The D&C is "a collection of divine revelations and inspired declarations"; is of "modern origin"; and is not "a translation of an ancient document."[58] The collection describes "ordinances and performances that pertain to

---

"more provocative than convincing" (Davies, "Mormon Canon," 48n9).

51. See Givens, *By the Hand of Mormon*, 138. Also, LDS author Daniel Peterson writes of Stendahl and his "strikingly affirmative remarks" concerning the LDS doctrine of "baptism for the dead" (Peterson, "Defending the Faith").

52. See the responses of LDS authors in Givens, *By the Hand of Mormon*, 135–38; Barlow, *Mormons and the Bible*, 26–33.

53. E.g., the "Book of Mormon quotes extensively and directly from the King James Version: Exod 20:2–4, 3–17; Isa 2–14; 48:1—49:26; 52:7–15; 53:1–12; 54:1–17; Mic 4:12–13; 5:8–11; Mal 3, 4; and Matt 5–7. In some cases, the wording has been altered slightly" (Forsberg, *Equal Rites*, 101).

54. Goff, "How Should We Then Read?," 146.

55. Leone, *Roots of Mormonism*, 12; cf. Palmer, *Insider's View*, 55.

56. Barlow, "Joseph Smith's Revision," 62; cf. Barlow, "Before Mormonism," 758n16, for the view that the incredible speed with which the BoM was produced ("most of it was dictated in 60–90 days"), seems to preclude the possibility of Smith borrowing from the King James Version.

57. Ostling and Ostling, *Mormon America*, 294.

58. *Doctrine and Covenants*; cf. Doxey, "Doctrine and Covenants," 405.

salvation," is "of great value to the human family."[59] It contains teachings
central to the LDS faith.[60] The LDS believes the collection is "less obscure, more current, and less marred in transmission" than the Bible.[61] As
a consequence, the D&C clarify and restore the content of the Bible. For
example, in view of the conundrum of Adam and Eve "not dying" on the
day they ate of the fruit, in spite of God's warning in Gen 2:17, the D&C
explain they "spiritually died" (see D&C 29:41). The D&C also give an
"explication on several obscure points in the book of Revelation."[62] The
identification and location of the new Jerusalem of Rev 21:2 is given as
Independence, Missouri.[63] The meanings of the white stone and the new
name in Rev 2:17 are explained.[64] In response to the challenging passage
in Matt 12:31–32 concerning "blasphemy against the Holy Ghost," D&C
132:27 states that it is murder of innocent blood.[65] For LDS authors, in
view of the question of the survival of the Apostle John in John 21, "it
is fortunate that latter-day revelation offers clarification on this matter."[66]
D&C 7:1–4 explains that John "shalt tarry" upon the earth until the Lord
comes in his glory. The verse of 1 Pet 3:19, that possibly describes the
descent of Jesus into hell, is clarified in D&C 138, where the gospel is
preached among the dead, and all are given the opportunity to repent and
receive the gospel.[67] Joseph Smith, along with early LDS leader Sidney
Rigdon, received a vision about the correct interpretation of John 5:28–29.

59. See the introduction to *Doctrine and Covenants* (as well as the introduction to
D&C 70). See also Jackson, "Latter-day Saints," 75; Givens, *Wrestling the Angel*, 9–10.
The D&C was published in 1835 (although previously published in 1833 under the
title "Book of Commandments").

60. See Ostling and Ostling, *Mormon America*, 293.

61. Barlow, "Before Mormonism," 752n11.

62. Thomas, "Scripture," 1283. See, for example, the exact identification of the "sea
of glass" and the "four beasts" of Rev 4:6 in D&C 77:1–4; for the "four angels" in Rev
7:1, see D&C 77:8; for the "144,000" of Rev 7:4, see D&C 77:11.

63. "This land, which is the land of Missouri . . . this is the land of promise, and the
place for the city of Zion . . . the place which is now called Independence is the center
place" (D&C 57:1–3; cf. D&C 90:37, 101:17; Arbaugh, *Revelation*, 72–73).

64. See D&C 130:10–11; cf. Faulconer, *New Testament Made Harder*, 500.

65. Other possible meanings of the phrase are discussed in LDS, *New Testament
Seminary*, 37–38; see also D&C 76:31–36.

66. Holzapfel and Wayment, *Making Sense*, 270.

67. LDS, *New Testament Seminary*, 236; cf. Esplin, "Wondering at His Words,"
296–312; Ridges, *New Testament Made Easier Part 1*, 386.

This vision defended a universalist outlook,[68] and was later recorded as D&C 76:15–24. The modern book of *Doctrine and Covenants* claims to illuminate and explain numerous biblical texts.

6.2.3. *The Pearl of Great Price and the Restoration of the Bible*

The PGP "clarifies doctrines and teachings that were lost from the Bible and gives added information concerning the Creation of the earth."[69] The PGP also mentions "mysterious" biblical passages that needed clarification. Early in his ministry, along with a colleague, Smith received a visit from John the Baptist, and they subsequently understood the "true meaning" of the "more mysterious passages."[70] According to LDS authors, the PGP elucidates numerous biblical ideas: "the premortal Council in Heaven, the nature of God, the reality of Satan, the Creation and the Fall, the rise of the kingdom of Satan, the revelation of the gospel to Adam, the ministry and translation of Enoch and his city, the early life of the family of Noah, Abraham and the covenant Jehovah made with him."[71] For Daniel Peterson, the Book of Abraham helps explain the "gods" of Psalm 82, who were the "intelligences that were organized before the world was" (Abraham 3:22–23 PGP).[72] Another example is found in the "revised form" of Matt 23:39 and Matt 24, that illustrates "some points reworded and . . . some verses expanded, by Joseph Smith."[73]

The Book of Moses in the PGP contains several examples of emendatory practices. It originally consisted of revelations given to Joseph Smith as he was "revising the Bible under inspiration."[74] In order to

68. See Bowman, *Mormon People*, 33.

69. LDS, *Gospel Principles*, 48; The PGP is composed of five sections. Two of the sections deal with the topic of creation: the Book of Moses and the Book of Abraham. The other three sections are "Joseph Smith—Matthew," an extract from the JST (Joseph Smith's translation work on the book of Matthew), as well as "Joseph Smith—History," which contains excerpts from LDS history, and the 13 Articles of Faith. See "Pearl of Great Price"; cf. Palmer, *Insider's View*, 12–25.

70. Joseph Smith—History 1:74, PGP. See also Bushman, *Rough Stone*, 75–76. In this event, the Scriptures were "laid open" as never before (Barlow, *Mormons and the Bible*, 26; cf. Matthews, *Plainer Translation*, 24).

71. Millet et al., *LDS Beliefs*, 486–87.

72. See Daniel Peterson, in Beckwith et al., *New Mormon Challenge*, 311–12. This is another reference to premortal existence.

73. Davies, "Mormon Canon," 50; cf. "Joseph Smith—Matthew," PGP.

74. Baldridge, "Pearl of Great Price," 1071.

resolve "apparently contradictory accounts of the Creation in Genesis 1 and Genesis 2, the Book of Moses explained that there were, in fact, two creations. The first was spiritual, the second physical."[75] In addition, Moses 5:1–5 is "a lengthy expansion dealing with the cultic and family life of Adam and Eve after their expulsion from the garden."[76] The passage helps answer questions such as how Cain and Abel found wives. Finally, the fifth chapter of Moses "provides a plausible dramatic background for the seemingly inexplicable rejection of Cain's sacrifice and his subsequent murder of Abel."[77] Similar to midrashic writings, the *Pearl of Great Price* updated, clarified, and restored the biblical text.

6.2.4. *The Joseph Smith Translation*

Through the revision of the Bible, now known as the Joseph Smith Translation (JST), "the Lord has expanded our understanding of some passages in the Bible."[78] Although the JST is not the official Bible of the LDS, it "offers many interesting insights and is an invaluable aid to biblical interpretation and understanding."[79] The purpose of the JST is "to provide knowledge not found in other Bibles."[80] It also provides "*a plainer translation* of the Bible."[81] It can "correct false doctrine."[82] The JST was formed because "the Lord inspired the Prophet Joseph to restore truths to the Bible text that had been lost or changed since the original words were

---

75. Quinn, *Early Mormonism*, 169; cf. Hutchinson, "Mormon Midrash," 37, 69; Rees, "Midrashic Imagination," 52.

76. Hutchinson, "Mormon Midrash," 59.

77. Hutchinson, "Mormon Midrash," 59. Specifically, see Moses 5:18, 21–31, PGP.

78. LDS, *Gospel Principles*, 46.

79. LDS, "Joseph Smith Translation"; cf. Millet, "Joseph Smith's Translation," 43–53. The JST is a "revision or translation of the King James Version of the Bible begun by the Prophet Joseph Smith in June 1830" (LDS, "Joseph Smith Translation"). For the full text of the JST, see Smith, "Inspired Version." The amount of attention given to the JST by the Utah-based LDS Church is closely "interlinked" with its complex relationship with the Independence, Missouri-based Community of Christ (formerly known as the Reorganized Church of Jesus Christ of Latter-day Saints and organized under Joseph Smith's oldest son) who have always held the copyright and ownership of the JST (see Properzi, *Mormonism and the Emotions*, 113). The Community of Christ refers to the translation as the "Inspired Version" while Utah-based LDS labels it the "Joseph Smith Translation" (see Davies, *Mormon Culture*, 65–66).

80. Matthews, "Joseph Smith Translation," 767.

81. Matthews, *Plainer Translation*, 391.

82. Smith, "She Hath Wrought a Good Work," 44.

written."[83] In 1830, by revising the Bible, Smith was "straightening out contradictions, correcting errors, and adding lost portions."[84]

For example, the LDS considers that marriage is a crucial aspect of salvation.[85] However, the apparent singleness of the Apostle Paul in 1 Cor 7:7–8 presented a problem. McConkie proposed that while "uninspired men" were translating 1 Cor 7, they "changed Paul's words" to make it "appear as though even Paul himself was unmarried."[86] Therefore, Joseph Smith corrected this passage to reflect the supposed original wording that elevated the state of marriage. The KJV states in 1 Cor 7:38: "So then he that giveth *her* in marriage doeth well." However, the JST changes this to, "So then he that giveth *himself* in marriage doeth well."[87] Referring to this passage in 1 Cor 7, an LDS manual mentions the "blessing it is to have prophetic help to understand difficult passages of scripture."[88]

Further instructive examples include the following. The apparent discrepancy of the number of angels at the tomb of Jesus was harmonized in the JST (Mark 16:3, 4; John 20:12), as was the supposed contradiction with the number of demoniacs healed (Matt 8:28, 29; Mark 5:2).[89] The enigmatic idea of God "repenting" was corrected: "And it repented Noah, and his heart was pained that the Lord had made man on the earth" (Gen 8:13 JST).[90] The "interpretive" piece in these examples seems to be

83. LDS, *Gospel Principles*, 46; Matthews, *Plainer Translation*, 12. However, for a dissenting view, David Wright sees the JST as "not a restoration of original material, but a commentary on the KJV" (Wright, in Greaves, "Education of a Bible Scholar," 65). In addition, LDS author Russell Nelson viewed many of the changes in the JST as clarifications, and not "textual restorations" (see Nelson, *Accomplishing the Impossible*, 18–19, 46).

84. Bushman, *Rough Stone*, 132.

85. Marriage is eternal and "essential for exaltation" (LDS, *Gospel Principles*, 219; cf. D&C 132; LDS, "Marriage").

86. McConkie, *New Witness*, 404–5.

87. Smith, "Inspired Version," emphasis added; cf. Matthews, *Plainer Translation*, 355–58.

88. LDS, *New Testament Seminary*, 179.

89. See Smith, "Inspired Version." To agree with the two angels in John 20:12, "two angels in white sitting" (KJV), the JST was changed in Mark 16:3: "two angels sitting thereon" (JST); although the supposedly erroneous KJV of Mark 16:5 states: "a young man sitting on the right side" (Mark 16:3 in the JST is equivalent to Mark 16:5 in the KJV). Similarly, to agree with one man healed in Mark 5:2, "a man with an unclean spirit" (KJV), the JST was changed in Matt 8:29: "a man possessed of devils" (JST). See the (supposedly erroneous) KJV of Matt 8:28: "two possessed with devils."

90. The KJV has this passage as Gen 6:6. See also the JST of Gen 8:15.

straightforward—the Prophet recognized a problem with the biblical text, and reconstructed it via prophetic authority. The issue, however, is how this recognition took place. It appears that, at times, translation adjustments are made to prevent unwelcome interpretation—and introduce straightforward interpretation or "plainness." As an additional example, Smith considered a verse in Acts 13 as theologically biased. The KJV of Acts 13:48 reads: "And when the Gentiles heard this, they were glad, and glorified the word of the Lord: and as many as were ordained to eternal life believed." However, given Smith's rejection of Calvinism that he felt endorsed an unmoving God "without body, parts or passions," he updated Acts 13:48 to read, "and as many as *believed* were *ordained* unto eternal life."[91]

A different explanatory attempt by Smith centered on word meanings. In Heb 6:1, the KJV translators rendered τῆς ἀρχῆς (*tēs archēs*) as "the principles": "Therefore leaving the principles [τῆς ἀρχῆς (*tēs archēs*)] of the doctrine of Christ, let us go on unto perfection" (KJV). Because of a lack of understanding of the underlying Greek, Smith responded: "If a man leaves the principles of the doctrine of Christ, how can he be saved in the principles? This is a contradiction. I don't believe it. I will render it as it should be—'Therefore *not* leaving the principles of the doctrine of Christ, let us go on to perfection.'"[92] If Smith had investigated the preceding context—only three verses earlier—he would have noticed τῆς ἀρχῆς (*tēs archēs*) in Heb 5:12. There the words τῆς ἀρχῆς (*tēs archēs*) carry the meaning of "first principles" or "elementary teaching."[93] Thus, the writer of Hebrews was, in truth, calling for a leaving behind of the *elementary truths* of the faith—so as to progress toward a more mature faith. The contextual content of this "elementary teaching" about Christ "could include a number of elements, such as Christ's role as high priest after the order of Melchizedek, a discussion that surrounds the paraenesis in

91. Acts 13:48 JST, emphasis added; see Räisänen, "Creative Interpreter," 73.

92. Smith, in Smith, *History of the Church*, 6:57–58, emphasis added. See also Smith "Inspired Version."

93. "For when for the time ye ought to be teachers, ye have need that one teach you again which *be* the first principles of the oracles of God" (Heb 5:12 KJV). See Müller, "Beginning," 1:166. For other authors, τῆς ἀρχῆς (*tēs archēs*) denotes "elementary principles" in Heb 5:12 and "elementary Christian teaching" in Heb 6:1 (see Arndt et al., *Greek-English Lexicon*, 138).

5:11—6:20."[94] However, Smith sought to clarify and restore the text by adding the word "not."[95]

There are additional passages from the JST that illustrate corrections and clarifications. On the identification of the mysterious "naked youth" mentioned in Mark 14:51–52, the JST establishes the young man as a disciple.[96] In Matt 7:1 of the JST, we are told to "judge not *unrighteously*,"[97] to avoid the appearance of unfair judgment. LDS authors contend the Greek of John 1:21 is "rather cumbersome"; therefore, the JST "makes it clear."[98] During the nineteenth century, apparently on account of an "American sensitivity about the demonic reputation of snakes," the JST was changed to "be ye therefore wise *servants*, and as harmless as doves" (Matt 10:14 JST, emphasis added).[99] In order to avoid an unwelcome interpretation (becoming like snakes)—and to introduce straightforward interpretation or "plainness"—the text was revised to better cohere with what appears to be a more mature spirituality. In John 1:31, 33, John the Baptist does not appear to know Jesus by sight—despite their filial relation. Thus, the JST "makes it clear that the Baptist *did* know Jesus when he saw him (JST, John 1:29–33)."[100] In the parable of the lost sheep, the JST suggests that Jesus wouldn't irresponsibly leave 99 sheep "in the wilderness," so he went "*into* the wilderness"—presumably leaving the 99 in a safe place.[101] Dallin Oaks emphasizes that "the scriptures can be comprehended only by the

---

94. Hurst, in Easter, *Faith and the Faithfulness*, 188–89.

95. See Barlow, *Mormons and the Bible*, 59; Bowman, "Book of Hebrews."

96. See Mark 14:57 (Smith, "Inspired Version"). LDS authors further clarify: "It is likely that it was Mark himself" (LDS, *New Testament Seminary*, 70).

97. Emphasis added. "Judge not unrighteously, that ye be not judged; but judge righteous judgment" (Matt 7:2 JST). Note the difference with the KJV: "Judge not, that ye be not judged" (Matt 7:1).

98. Holzapfel and Wayment, *Making Sense*, 27. For LDS readers, the cumbersome Greek translation is evident in the back-and-forth dialogue of the KJV: "And they asked him, 'What then? Art thou Elias?' And he saith, 'I am not.' 'Art thou that prophet?' And he answered, 'No' (John 1:21 KJV). This is in contrast to the JST: "And he confessed, and denied not that he was Elias; but confessed, saying; 'I am not the Christ'" (John 1:21 JST).

99. See Hutchinson, "LDS Approaches," 109–10. Again, in various passages, the JST has numbered the verses differently. The KJV states "be ye therefore wise as *serpents*, and harmless as doves" (Matt 10:16, emphasis added).

100. Holzapfel and Wayment, *Making Sense*, 29.

101. Matthews, *Plainer Translation*, 352.

inspiration of the Holy Ghost."[102] He cites the JST of 1 Cor 2:11 and the subtle change from the KJV: "The things of God knoweth no man, except *he has the Spirit of God*" (1 Cor 2:11 JST); "The things of God knoweth no man, but *the Spirit of God*" (1 Cor 2:11 KJV).[103] In sum, because of the Joseph Smith Translation, "many plain and precious things were revealed which throw great light upon many subjects."[104]

6.3. The Hermeneutical Effect of LDS Emendatory Practice

LDS author Anthony Hutchinson writes that, just as there was a midrashic re-working of texts in biblical history, so also "much of Restoration Scripture could be so categorized."[105] Hutchinson continues: "one could argue that much of the New Testament consists of midrashic readings of the Old Testament."[106] In addition, throughout the Judeo-Christian tradition, clarification and restoration were deployed in the targumim and the Midrashim. Could this give justification for the emendatory practice of the LDS?

We have noted the foundational event of the FV in 1820, where Joseph Smith sought wisdom from God because of the mutually contradictory interpretations of the Bible. Because of these readings, "it was impossible to resolve religious questions by an appeal to the existing Bible."[107] In his handling of the Bible, then, Smith made "interpretive additions,"[108] theological as well as "common sense" changes, harmonizations, and additions with no biblical parallel.[109] Obviously, interpretation occurs when

102. Oaks, "Scripture Reading."

103. See Smith, "Inspired Version." For other changes in the JST, see Barlow, "Revision of the Bible," 55–57.

104. Smith, *Essentials in Church History*, 116–17.

105. Hutchinson, "Mormon Midrash," 52.

106. Hutchinson, "Mormon Midrash," 48. Surprisingly, Hutchinson calls for a recasting of modern scripture, "including the creation of a body of midrashic readings" of LDS scripture (Hutchinson, "Mormon Midrash," 62).

107. Millet et al., *LDS Beliefs*, 347; cf. Joseph Smith–History 1:12, PGP.

108. Barlow, "Revision of the Bible," 55.

109. See Barlow, "Revision of the Bible," 55–58. Interestingly, Joseph Smith also revised the BoM two times after its initial appearance in 1830 (Gutjahr, *Book of Mormon*, 148). The rationale given was that a "living prophet made it a living book, capable of change" (Gutjahr, *Book of Mormon*, 63). The *Doctrine and Covenants* were also revised

scriptural passages are determined to be mutually contradictory, or when additions and harmonizations are purportedly needed. However, the reference to contradictory passages may be an exercise in safeguarding doctrinal parameters. Therefore, the interpretation of the ancient text is abandoned because of its inability to be resolved on its own. The novelty of the modern is leveraged to trump the ancient.

The implied realities of the biblical text are not taken seriously with LDS emendatory practice. Instead of accounting for "the textually embodied intentionality of the author"[110] arrived at through implied realities, the LDS is supplanting the implied audience with themselves—and revising, correcting or clarifying—because of perceived institutional needs. They are making contemporary adjustments to ancient texts.

Conceivably, however, the views of non-LDS scholars Räisänen and Stendahl could hermeneutically justify LDS emendatory practice. Yet, for modern LDS scriptures to claim the ability to update Scripture, one would expect to see better evidence than simple changes applied to the text. What we are seeing is an adjustment of the ancient text to conform to the perceived institutional needs of the current body of believers. Stendahl asserts the "revelatory character"[111] of the BoM. Nevertheless, this stance is difficult to accept for those outside of the "systemic parameters" of the church—or for those not as sympathetic to the LDS as is Stendahl. Although the BoM, for example, *purports* to explain and clarify ancient Scripture, Stendahl, along with Räisänen, are overly optimistic about its explanatory power.

I claimed earlier that the level of hermeneutical reflection that informs LDS emendatory practice is rudimentary. In other words, there is a simple adjustment of biblical locutions, and there is no concern for illocutionary matters. At a rudimentary level, LDS emendatory practice is hermeneutical, to the extent that they are dealing with locutions. Yet, it is not consciously hermeneutical in the fuller sense of considering authorial intention, or the narratival dynamics of the text, or whether they are violating the intended sense of the text. Simply put, these restorations and clarifications are doctrinal in nature. They are using the building blocks of biblical locutions to conform to modern-day LDS perspectives.

---

twice—in 1835 and in 1844 (Gutjahr, *Book of Mormon*, 62, 218–19n3).

   110. Moritz, "Critical Realism," 149.

   111. Stendahl, *Meanings*, 99.

In chapter 1, I mentioned the acceptance of the *Book of Mormon*, the *Doctrine and Covenants*, and the *Pearl of Great Price* as additional scriptures alongside the Bible. We have now seen that all three books attempt to clarify and/or restore the Bible. In conclusion, however, the commitment of the LDS to its perceived institutional needs, and the apparent utilization of "systemic parameters" to emend the ancient text by locutionary clarification or restoration, ends up displacing hermeneutical accountability.

7

Re-Authoring

Locutionary Reassignment

IT IS THE CONTENTION of this chapter that some hermeneutical activity by the LDS is a "re-authoring" of the biblical text. A "re-authoring" occurs when a phrase or word is lifted from its original context and re-used with a new meaning. In other words, it is locutionary reassignment.[1] Ostensibly, the use of the text is presented as interpretation, although, this is not the case. An important consideration follows: LDS re-authoring appears under the guise of interpretation, and is utilized for the purpose of exhibiting an "air" or "mantle" of authority. In other words, with the examples explored below, the implied author of a re-authoring hermeneutic aims for legitimacy by citing biblical locutions, so that implied readers will recognize the provenance of the locutions. In what follows, we will witness three outcomes of LDS re-authoring of biblical phrases and words: (1) Elevation of Joseph Smith as the founder; (2) Advancement of distinct doctrines; (3) Promotion of the institution.[2] All three of these outcomes actively privilege the modern LDS Church.

---

1. I am using this concept of "re-authoring" as it is used by Moritz (see Moritz, "Scripture and Theological Exegesis," 133).

2. At the end of the chapter, I will present a case study of Isa 28:7–11. The LDS cites this passage to champion their views on continuing revelation. Therefore, it is a re-authoring that attempts to advance a distinct doctrine.

7.1. Re-Authoring Practices

7.1.1. Re-Authored Phrases by the LDS

A frequently cited text in LDS circles is from the book of Hebrews: "Jesus Christ the same yesterday, and today, and forever" (Heb 13:8). Since God revealed himself in the past, and often did so by means of the prophets, they conclude: "Knowing as we do that God is the same yesterday, to-day, and forever, that he spoke to [the prophets], however poorly they preserved it, witnesses that he can speak to us."[3] David Seely comments on God's prerogative to *send* prophets "at his discretion," since he is "the same yesterday, today, and forever."[4] The doctrine of salvation was proclaimed not only *during* the life and ministry of Jesus, but also *before* and *after*, for the Spirit "is the same yesterday, today and forever."[5] What the author of Hebrews intended to communicate concerning Jesus Christ is not considered in these examples of locutionary reassignment. One prominent outcome of this re-authoring is a promotion of the institution, as seen in prophetic priority.

Joseph Smith separated biblical locutions and re-used them in a new context. In one instance, he alluded to Phil 2:12: "I saw the Father work out His kingdom with fear and trembling and I am doing the same, too."[6] However, in the book to the Philippians, the Apostle Paul was calling his readers to work out their *salvation* "with fear and trembling"—yet Smith re-authored the phrase for a new meaning. Whether he was aware of Paul's motivation in writing this exhortation to the Philippians is impossible to say. What seems clear, however, is that for Smith, this kind of re-authoring opened the door to an elevation of his status in the community.

A particularly instructive example is the re-authoring of the Isaianic "Here am I, send me." In the distant past, the Father needed a Redeemer to send to earth. There were two volunteers, Jesus and Satan, both of whom responded with "Here am I, send me."[7] The Book of Moses in the PGP recounts the scene:

3. Millet, *Getting at the Truth*, 104.

4. Seely, "Prophecy in Biblical Times," 1163; cf. 2 Nephi 29:9.

5. See Millet et al., *LDS Beliefs*, 289–90.

6. Smith, "King Follett"; cf. Givens, *Wrestling the Angel*, 102.

7. See Restoration Branches, *Times and Seasons*, 3.10. *Times and Seasons* was an early LDS newspaper. See also Abraham 3:27; Givens, *Wrestling the Angel*, 122–23; LDS, *Gospel Principles*, 13.

> And I, the Lord God, spake unto Moses, saying: "That Satan, whom thou hast commanded in the name of mine Only Begotten, is the same which was from the beginning, and he came before me, saying—'Behold, here am I, send me, I will be thy son, and I will redeem all mankind, that one soul shall not be lost, and surely I will do it; wherefore give me thine honor.'"
> (Moses 4:1)

God did not choose Satan, however, as the Redeemer. The phrase of "Here am I, send me" comes from Isa 6:8. The contextual meaning of the phrase deals with "the decision of the prophet to deliver Yahweh's message to His people."[8] Far from a formulaic resolution to be repeated in one's life, the phrase is a "personal account by the prophet of a momentous event in *his* life, the defining vision."[9] The message for Isaiah, "could hardly be more incompatible with his prophetic sensibility . . . [He] is now told to tell his neighbors, who so far have been deaf to his pleas, not to see or hear."[10] Yet, the LDS ignores the original context of the biblical locutions in the Isaianic context, and instead re-authors the phrase.

This heavenly "volunteering" scene is also described in the Book of Abraham. When Satan was rejected, he "was angry, and kept not his first estate; and, at that day, many followed after him" (Abraham 3:28 PGP). The "first estate" reference is from Jude 6. It is a phrase separated from its context and used to refer to Satan's apparent withdrawal (voluntarily?) from heaven. This example of re-authoring by locutionary reassignment advances the legitimacy of modern LDS scripture. Since the Book of Abraham uses biblical language, it appears with a "mantle of authority."

An additional example from the book of Isaiah is the complex relationship between the BoM prophet Nephi and his "interpretation" of the book of Isaiah. According to LDS author Grant Hardy, Nephi does not deny "the validity of the original, historic meaning of Isaiah," although he "virtually ignores the original setting in favor of reinterpreting the words so that they apply to his own predictions of the distant future."[11] It appears that Hardy believes that Nephi is updating the book of Isaiah. Although this may seem to be another example of emendation, it is, more accurately, a re-authoring. Hardy's mention of "reinterpreting" is important. I quote 2 Nephi 26:16:

8. Gray, *Book of Isaiah*, 1:101.

9. Tucker, *Book of Isaiah*, 102, emphasis added.

10. Tull, *Isaiah*, 145.

11. Hardy, *Understanding the Book of Mormon*, 61.

> For those who shall be destroyed shall speak unto them out of
> the ground, and their speech shall be low out of the dust, and
> their voice shall be as one that hath a familiar spirit; for the Lord
> God will give unto him power, that he may whisper concerning
> them, even as it were out of the ground; and their speech shall
> whisper out of the dust.

In this passage, numerous phrases from Isa 29 are repeated—"speak unto
them out of the ground," "familiar spirit," "speech shall whisper out of the
dust," etc.[12] However, there is no consideration of any Isaianic meaning.
Rather, Nephi is prophesying the destruction of his own people on the
continent of the Americas. The term used by Hardy of "reinterpreting"
should be considered synonymous with re-authoring. Both create new
meanings from locutions that are lifted from their original contexts. In
one sense, Hardy should be applauded for correctly describing Nephi's
use of the Isaianic speech-act ("he virtually ignores the original setting").
However, in doing so, he casually refers to Nephi's reinterpretation of
Isaiah. Hardy uncritically assumes the legitimacy of a "reinterpretation."
Furthermore, what is occurring is a reassignment of locutions (i.e., re-
authoring). To sustain the authority of the LDS institution, and the legitimacy of their modern scriptures, Hardy argues for the hermeneutical
viability of a locutionary reassignment by Nephi, a BoM prophet.

Returning to the book of Jude, the re-authoring of "first estate" from
Jude 6 (KJV) is designed to teach that humankind had a spiritual premortal existence. However, Jude 6 states that *angels* did not keep their
"first estate" (ἴδιον οἰκητήριον (*idion oikētērion*) NASB: "proper abode";
NIV: "own home"; KJV: "first estate"). In spite of this, Millet writes that
humans came to earth to take a physical body, to gain experiences that
were not possible "in the premortal life, our 'first estate.'"[13] The earthly life
is referred to as a "second estate."[14] The phrase, "first estate," then, entirely
independent of what Jude intended to communicate, is re-authored to
advance the doctrine of premortal existence.[15] Mainstream scholars, on

12. "And thou shalt be brought down, and shalt speak out of the ground, and thy
speech shall be low out of the dust, and thy voice shall be, as of one that hath a familiar
spirit, out of the ground, and thy speech shall whisper out of the dust" (Isa 29:4 KJV).
We noted this passage in chapter 4 as an example of allegorization.

13. Millet, *Getting at the Truth*, 113.

14. LDS, *New Testament Seminary*, 280; cf. Hutchinson, "Mormon Midrash," 51.
See also Abraham 3:26: "They who keep their second estate shall have glory added
upon their heads for ever and ever."

15. As we saw in chapter 5, it could also be categorized as a sociological

the other hand, are agreed that Jude 6 does not speak of human premortal existence. Contrary to the translation of the phrase ἴδιον οἰκητήριον (*ídion oikētēríon*) as "first estate," Daniel Harrington views it as "domain" or "proper dwelling place."[16] It refers to where the angels "were assigned by God in the heavenly court." The passage echoes Gen 6:1–4, where the angels left their "proper place" and introduced "sinful behavior to people on earth." Instead of a human premortal existence, then, Jude 6 mentions "rebellious angels [who] failed to keep to their own heavenly domain [and] were consigned to be chained in the underworld."[17] Given the importance of this teaching for the LDS, this locutionary reassignment serves the dual purpose of advancing an important doctrine as well as promoting the institution.

That God is "no respecter of persons" is another phrase that is commonly re-authored for doctrinal purposes. The phrase originates in the KJV of Acts 10:34, where contextually, Peter describes God's acceptance of Gentiles.[18] We have seen this concept with the aforementioned "uniformity of the gospel," since God "has given and will continue to give the gospel scheme of salvation to all those willing to be instructed."[19] The phrase is also used in reference to those who have died: "Jesus explained that he is God of both the living and the dead ... both living and dead must be saved by the same gospel principles. The Lord is no respecter of persons."[20] It is used as a counter example to those who showed "preferential treatment of the rich" in Jas 2:1–13. Since God is "no respecter of persons," neither should LDS members show preferential treatment.[21] LDS authors use this KJV phrase in creative ways to buttress their doctrines, yet these uses have no connection to the contextual meaning of Acts 10:34.

---

interpretation, as it legitimizes a separation from the parent community that no longer maintains human premortal existence.

16. Harrington, *1 Peter, Jude and 2 Peter*, 196.

17. Harrington, *1 Peter, Jude and 2 Peter*, 204; cf. Watson, *Second Letter*, 488.

18. "The impartiality Peter is speaking about refers specifically to God's justice or fairness in judging human beings in regard to what they have done" (Witherington, *Acts of the Apostles*, 356).

19. Irving, "Mormons and the Bible," 474.

20. Mark E. Petersen, in LDS, *New Testament Seminary*, 236.

21. Holzapfel and Wayment, *Making Sense*, 462.

7.1.2. Re-Authored Words by the LDS

LDS thinkers re-author biblical *words* to bolster their claims. For instance, "seventy" is used to buttress their bureaucracy-heavy organization.[22] According to D. Michael Quinn, although Joseph Smith claimed to have received visions and revelations authorizing the use of the word "seventy," it is more probable that "biblical precedents influenced Smith's thinking on this matter."[23] Indeed, Richard Bushman writes that the word "seventy" is taken from "several obscure biblical references."[24] Exodus 24:1 mentions Moses taking "seventy of the elders of Israel," while Luke 10:1 reports that Jesus "appointed other seventy also, and sent them two and two before his face into every city and place." In the modern church, the "seventy" are leaders who are called by the twelve apostles.[25] The biblical word "seventy" is taken from different contexts and re-authored to promote a modern, organizational pattern in the LDS.

A complicated example of advancing a distinct LDS doctrine by ostensibly drawing on biblical texts is found in the use of 1 Cor 15 and 2 Cor 12. From these passages, the LDS arrive at their perspective on the "three levels in heaven." Although these three levels are not explicitly detailed in the Bible, they are purportedly "alluded to" in these chapters.[26] This example of re-authoring is more nuanced, and involves several steps. First, it is noted that the words "celestial" and "terrestrial" refer to bodies in the KJV of 1 Cor 15:40. These words are re-authored to describe two of the three levels of heaven. Then, "Joseph Smith added a reference to telestial glory alongside the references to celestial and terrestrial glory."[27] This word comes from a revelation that Joseph Smith received.[28] As a result, the three levels of heaven are denominated "celestial," "terrestrial," and "telestial." Additionally, the threefold mention in the same chapter of

---

22. See LDS "Global Leadership."

23. Quinn, *Origins of Power*, 67.

24. Bushman, *Rough Stone*, 255; cf. Millet et al., *LDS Beliefs*, 584–86.

25. See D&C 107:25: "The Seventy are also called to preach the gospel, and to be especial witnesses unto the Gentiles and in all the world"; cf. Davies, *Mormon Culture*, 199.

26. See Robinson, in Blomberg and Robinson, *How Wide?*, 153–54; cf. *History of the Church*, 5:402, in Paulsen and Musser, *Mormonism in Dialogue*, 54n127.

27. Holzapfel and Wayment, *Making Sense*, 365.

28. Brodie explains, "painstaking study of the Bible served . . . to stimulate some of his best revelations" (Brodie, *No Man Knows*, 117; cf. Quinn, *Early Mormonism*, 172–73).

the glory of the sun, the moon, and the stars (1 Cor 15:41), is speculated to be a "threefold distinction that seems to have impressed itself upon Joseph Smith," who then took this threefold concept back "into the duality of verse 40" (that, again, refers only to "celestial" and "terrestrial").[29] LDS thinkers also use 2 Cor 12:2 to corroborate the doctrine, which states that Paul was caught up to the third heaven.[30] The LDS re-authors individual words ("bodies," "third heaven," "sun," "moon," "stars," etc.), to form the distinctive doctrine of "three levels in heaven." This doctrine, in turn, holds significant value for the institution.[31]

The biblical word "sealing" is also re-authored. The word appears in various biblical contexts (e.g., 1 Kgs 21:8; John 3:33; Rom 4:11; 1 Cor 9:2; Eph 1:13 KJV). An LDS sealing is "(a)n ordinance performed in the temple eternally uniting a husband and wife, or children and their parents."[32] To be sealed in the temple is a "necessary saving ordinance,"[33] where the Lord "seals [believers] up unto eternal life."[34] In Mormon parlance, to "seal" a blessing or relationship "signifies making a promised result legitimate and permanent, both in this life and in the life to come."[35] The word "sealed" is used in other contexts as well. The BoM refers to itself more than twenty times as a sealed book.[36] The LDS look forward to a "sealed" portion of the BoM to be opened in the future.[37] In fact, LDS scriptures refer to writings that are sealed until God deems humankind ready to receive them.[38]

Promotion of the institution occurs with the biblical word "keys." We noted in the previous chapter that modern scripture "reestablished

---

29. See Davies, *Mormon Culture*, 66; cf. D&C 76:70–109; 131.

30. See LDS, *Gospel Principles*, 275; Robinson, *Are Mormons Christians?*, 97.

31. See e.g., Ballard, *Three Degrees of Glory*, 6–10.

32. LDS, "Sealing"; cf. Arrington and Bitton, *Mormon Experience*, 69.

33. See LDS, *New Testament Seminary*, 240; cf. Davies, *Mormon Culture*, 154.

34. Millet in Baker, *Mormonism at the Crossroads*, 265.

35. Shepherd and Shepherd, "Doctrinal and Commitment Functions," 723n5.

36. Quinn, *Early Mormonism*, 153. E.g., 2 Nephi 27:7–8, 10–11, 15, 17, 21–22; Ether 4:5; 5:1; Moroni 10:2. It is also paralleled with the "sealed book" in Rev 5:1 (Quinn, *Early Mormonism*, 153).

37. See Rees, "Midrashic Imagination," 60.

38. See Mould, *Still*, 409n44; cf. "Until the fullness of time, and the law and the testimony shall be sealed " (Luke 3:8 JST). An emendation also occurs with "sealing": "Whatsoever thou shalt bind on earth shall be bound in heaven" (Matt 16:19). The meaning of "bind" is explained as sealing (see LDS, *Gospel Principles*, 235).

the lost key of knowledge."[39] This refers to Luke 11:52: "Woe unto you, lawyers! for ye have taken away the key to knowledge." Keys are also used to validate the LDS authority structure: "The keys of the priesthood refer to the right to exercise power in the name of Jesus Christ or to preside over a priesthood function, quorum, or organizational division of the Church."[40] The book of *Doctrine and Covenants* contains similar references. Keys are utilized by the institution for translation (D&C 6:28); for ministry (D&C 7:7); for "turning the hearts of the fathers to the children" (D&C 27:9); for the "mysteries of the kingdom" (D&C 64:5); for the "Presidency of the High Priesthood" (D&C 81:2); for blessing (D&C 124:92); for the "key of the knowledge of God" (D&C 84:19); and even as "keys of the kingdom and a dispensation of the gospel for the last times" (D&C 27:5–13).[41]

Additionally, Joseph Smith used this word to defend his prophetic ministry. For example, he used the physical instruments of "seerstones," also known as "keys," to translate the BoM.[42] The LDS defend this activity by observing that just as the *biblical* Joseph used a cup in divination (Gen 44:5), so also the modern Joseph used seerstones to practice divination.[43] These stones enabled him to see things "invisible to the natural eye."[44] The seerstones eventually were called the "Urim and Thummim," ostensibly providing "an explicitly biblical framework for their use."[45] The Urim and

---

39. Thomas, "Scripture," 1284; cf. Matthews, *Plainer Translation*, 372–73.

40. Parrish, "Keys of the Priesthood," 780; cf. Wilcox and Young, *Standing Apart*, 3.

41. Parrish, "Keys of the Priesthood," 781; cf. Davies, *Introduction to Mormonism*, 41–42.

42. To translate the BoM, Joseph Smith sat with the seerstones in a hat, and bending over with his face looking into the hat, dictated to various scribes (see Bushman, *Rough Stone*, 71–72; Shipps, *Mormonism*, 14; Palmer, *Insider's View*, 2–3; Jackson, "Latter-day Saints," 77).

43. See Smith, "Hermeneutical Crisis," 94. LDS authors highlight other biblical examples of physical objects used by God to accomplish his work: blood on a doorpost (Exod 12:7); the staff of Moses (Exod 4:3; 7:20; Num 20:11); a snake on a pole (Num 21:8); the coat of Elijah (2 Kgs 2:8, 14); the corpse coming to life when touched by Elisha's bones (2 Kgs 13:21); mud on blind eyes (Matt 9:6); and Paul's handkerchief (Acts 19:12) (see Quinn, *Early Mormonism*, 2–4; cf. MacKay and Frederick, *Joseph Smith's Seer Stones*).

44. Bushman, *Rough Stone*, 48; cf. Arrington and Bitton, *Mormon Experience*, 11.

45. Givens, in Fluhman, "*A Peculiar People*," 42; cf. Millet et al., *LDS Beliefs*, 647–50; Givens, *By the Hand of Mormon*, 22–24 (see Exod 28:30; Lev 8:8; Num 27:21; Deut 33:8; Ezra 2:63; Neh 7:65).

Thummin were used to read and understand the Bible.[46] While many others in Smith's time claimed the "keys" to biblical interpretation, the seerstones were "uniquely tangible,"[47] and allegedly enabled him to arrive at the correct interpretation. Significantly, however, Smith's understanding underwent a subtle transformation. As he matured, these physical instruments of revelation became unnecessary, and the terminology of "keys" was transferred to the Melchizedek priesthood.[48] He began to refer to this Priesthood as the "key of the mysteries of the kingdom, even the key of the knowledge of God."[49] He also added, "I have a key by which I understand the scriptures."[50] During his life and ministry, Smith "did not believe he was reading anything new into the book, but instead was simply drawing the true meaning out of the Bible."[51] Thus, an important pattern emerged in the foundational years of the LDS—the Prophet claimed the "key" to biblical interpretation—first through seerstones and then through the Melchizedek priesthood.

To understand the LDS perspective here, it is important to emphasize a distinction that we have previously discussed. Re-authoring effectively entails the creation of a new text out of the locutionary components of a prior text. It is a severing of any connection between the ancient contextual meaning and the modern interpreter. Yet, reader recognition of these locutions is crucial. In other words, to reinforce and shore up the institution and its doctrines, or to elevate the authority of Smith, it is vital that readers recognize the provenance of the locutions. From their perspective, therefore, when biblical phrases/words are used to describe modern LDS realities, irrespective of being contextually faithful or not, their institution and doctrines are validated. Therefore, in one sense, the Mormon church is very much concerned with the ancient text, for it repeatedly quotes its locutions for contemporary validation. However, despite this, the ancient text is relativized and neglected because of modern institutional needs. The presuppositional matters of asymmetry of the

46. See Matthews, *Plainer Translation*, 25–26.

47. Smith, "Hermeneutical Crisis," 94; cf. Shipps, *Mormonism*, 14.

48. See Smith, "Hermeneutical Crisis," 95.

49. D&C 84:19; cf. D&C 35:18, 20. Again, these keys enabled him to "understand the Bible" (Matthews, *Plainer Translation*, 28). Brigham Young proclaimed that after the death of his predecessor "Smith holds the keys of this last dispensation, and is now engaged behind the veil in the great work of the last days" (Young, "Intelligence").

50. Smith, in Faulconer, *New Testament Made Harder*, 102.

51. Holzapfel and Wayment, *Making Sense*, 523.

Bible as well as continuing revelation again come to the forefront, as does our notion of perceived institutional needs driving biblical interpretation.

7.1.3. Possible LDS Responses to the Concept of Re-Authoring

According to Philip Barlow, Joseph Smith used the Bible like a poet, subject to refinement and improvement. For Smith, "scripture was not the static, final, untouchable, once-and-for-all Word of God that it was for many antebellum Christians."[52] Barlow even concedes that Smith's objective was rarely to interpret the Bible. Rather, he used the Bible to express new revelation or proclaim restored truth.[53] This is puzzling, for if LDS claims some validation from the ancient text, there must be some interpretive component to it. Yet, Barlow here minimizes the impact that the Bible may have, while at the same time uncritically assuming that re-authoring of biblical locutions is legitimate. Interestingly, other authors claim that the "New Testament was a *springboard* for Joseph Smith."[54] For Smith, the "Bible was a gate, not a fence."[55] Smith admitted a year before his death: "There are many things in the Bible which do not, as they now stand, accord with the revelations of the Holy Ghost to me."[56] Smith, then, initiated an interpretive model that was "profoundly adaptive of historic Christianity's theological traditions."[57] Taking into account these views, we again note the elevation of Smith as the founder of the LDS. We also note a re-authoring hermeneutic that is implicitly acknowledged, as Smith "adapted" Christian traditions. He pronounced new revelation and restored truth by using biblical locutions. On one hand, the LDS authors are correct—Smith used the Bible (read: "re-authored by locutionary reassignment") to establish a claim to authority. On the other hand, the hermeneutical legitimacy of this re-authoring is debatable.

---

52. Barlow, *Mormons and the Bible*, 46, 47, 79.

53. See Barlow, *Mormons and the Bible*, xxxii–xxxiii. These views by Barlow are in direct contradiction to the words just cited, that Smith was "drawing the true meaning out of the Bible" (Holzapfel and Wayment, *Making Sense*, 523).

54. Holzapfel and Wayment, *Making Sense*, 523, emphasis added.

55. Bushman, *Rough Stone*, 274. Translating and interpreting the Bible held a "trove of possibilities" (Bushman, *Rough Stone*, 560).

56. Quoted in Matthews, "Role," 40; cf. Ostling and Ostling, *Mormon America*, 428–29.

57. Flake, "Four Books," 29.

However, a re-authoring hermeneutic might be theologically legiti-
mized based on biblical examples of an apparently similar interpretive
practice. There are passages from the NT where selected texts from the
OT appear to be re-authored. For example, Paul seems to re-author the
phrase "the righteous will live by his faith" from Hab 2:4 (see Rom 1:17
and Gal 3:11). In the original context of Habakkuk, the phrase is God's
answer to the prophet's complaint about the judgment of Israel through
the wicked Chaldeans.[58] Nevertheless, Paul uses it in Rom 1:17 and Gal
3:11 to defend his views on salvation. Thus, we note an apparent change
in meaning, as an OT phrase appears to be re-authored, and used to defend a later doctrine. Could this legitimize LDS hermeneutical practice?

One possible answer to Paul's usage of the phrase is given by Steve
Moyise. The use of an underlying Greek grammatical feature (a subjective genitive) by Paul in Rom 1:17 is for the purpose of focusing "on
Christ's own faithfulness," and not on the individual's faith in Christ. This
connects with "the revelation of God's righteousness" in the Habakkuk
passage.[59] Moyise continues by quoting the preceding context in Habakkuk: "the revelation awaits an appointed time" (Hab 2:3). Although Paul
does, in fact,

> go beyond what the prophet understood . . . Habakkuk is told
> that there is a vision to be made plain now and a vision for the
> future. In other words, Habakkuk envisages a fuller revelation
> in the end time, and Paul sees himself as providing it. Paul goes
> beyond what Habakkuk wrote, but it falls within Habakkuk's
> "speech-act," which envisages an interpreter such as Paul speak-
> ing from the standpoint of its fulfillment.[60]

The fulfillment is not a re-authoring, but a continuation of the foundational
concept of "the righteousness of God," first seen by Habakkuk, then reiterated by Paul. Francis Watson also quotes the important Pauline phrase
in Rom 1:17 "it is written," to validate Paul's use of Habakkuk: "That the
righteousness of which the prophet speaks is 'of God' is already implied in
the claim to normativity entailed by 'it is written.'" Therefore, this "righteousness is asserted by the normative prophetic text—from which indeed
Paul's claim derives . . . Paul's gloss remains faithful to the text it interprets:
the revelation of God's righteousness in the gospel corresponds exactly to

58. See Moo, "Problem of Sensus Plenior," 208.

59. Moyise, "Quotations," 20–21.

60. Moyise, "Quotations," 21; cf. Watson, *Paul and the Hermeneutics of Faith*, 48.

the identification of true righteousness in the prophetic text."[61] Paul's use of "the righteous will live by his faith" is not a locutionary reassignment, but a plausible rendering of a concept from Habakkuk.

Nonetheless, LDS interpreters seem to think they are justified with their instances of re-authoring. Charles Harrell discusses examples from the NT where OT passages are altered to fit a different context, with the conclusion that "LDS scripture and authoritative commentary seem to follow this same tradition of reinterpretation and reformulation to accommodate new times and changing paradigms."[62] For Anthony Hutchinson, "the reworking of doctrines and texts in Joseph Smith tends to ally him more with the ancient prophets of Israel and authors of the Bible than it separates him from them."[63] Thus, just as the ancient prophets supposedly re-authored passages, so also modern LDS prophets. However, the LDS is guilty here of failing to focus on hermeneutical issues. There is little effort in the LDS community to distinguish between issues of provenance, inspiration and authority on the one hand, and issues of the interpretation of the available text on the other hand. In a re-authoring hermeneutic, the emphasis is rarely on the text itself—other than a citation of biblical locutions outside of their contextual meaning for the purpose of suggesting an "air" of authority.

7.2. The Hermeneutical Effect of LDS Re-Authoring

A disparity exists as LDS interpreters, at times, ignore the original context of a passage, while at other times perceive a "plain" and "straightforward" interpretation. When a "re-authoring" of the biblical text takes place, the LDS show an unrestrained freedom in isolating words irrespective of their contextual meanings. It appears that they simply use ancient Scripture as a repository of potential words and phrases, from which to assemble various doctrines. Barlow even admits that "biblical language provides many of the vocabulary building blocks of Smith's revelations."[64] The examples given highlight the absence of a methodological investigation into the contextual meaning of the individual words in question, as well as an interpretive disruption of the text that isolates words and

61. Watson, *Paul and the Hermeneutics of Faith*, 48–49.

62. Harrell, *"This Is My Doctrine,"* 11.

63. Hutchinson, "Mormon Midrash," 70.

64. Barlow, *Mormons and the Bible*, xxxiii.

phrases. It is entirely possible that the Scriptures are simply probed and scrutinized for words or phrases to use for already-existing doctrines. LDS re-authoring is not only characterized by a supplanting of the textually implied audience with themselves, but with the advancement of the modern institution with its distinctive doctrines.

Given the numerous challenges mentioned in our five categories, one conclusion is that the LDS is not executing well hermeneutically. Because of higher doctrinal and institutional priorities, responsible hermeneutical execution is lacking. The maintenance of the system itself becomes the impetus behind their biblical interpretation. Their hermeneutics demonstrates a prioritization not to the biblical text, but to their institution. Further conclusions will be given in chapter 8 after our investigation into philosophical hermeneutics. For now, however, I will present one final example of re-authoring. A phrase from Isaiah 28, "line upon line, precept upon precept," is the most important, if not the most frequently cited, re-authored biblical phrase. The investigation of Isa 28:10 will show the extent to which biblical locutions are re-authored to further institutional needs.

7.3. Case Study: The Re-Authoring of Isaiah 28:10

Having explored several examples to demonstrate the breadth of LDS re-authoring, I now wish to investigate in more detail a re-authored phrase from Isa 28:10. Numerous LDS authors re-author this passage to defend their doctrine of continuing revelation. The passage in question is "precept *must be* upon precept, precept upon precept; Line upon line, line upon line; Here a little, *and* there a little" (Isa 28:10 KJV). From this verse, the LDS conclude that truth is apprehended "line upon line and precept upon precept."[65] In fact, "Revelation may break forth anywhere and anytime. The hard-hearted pay no heed and despise the words of God. The receptive are instructed line upon line."[66] There is a "commitment to ongoing revelation" and "truth is revealed line upon line."[67] For Grant Underwood, the "line-upon-line manner" is how "truth has been

---

65. See Millet, in Millet and Johnson, *Bridging the Divide*, 145. Millet also quotes McConkie: "We get our truth and our light line upon line" (Millet, *Getting at the Truth*, 63).

66. Bushman, *Rough Stone*, 101; cf. Barlow, *Mormons and the Bible*, 51.

67. See Ostler, *Of God and Gods*, 35.

revealed."[68] An LDS publication maintains that "gospel light does not burst upon men in full noonday splendor, but . . . arises in their hearts gradually, line upon line, precept upon precept, here a little and there a little."[69] The Book of Mormon agrees: "Wo be unto him that shall say: We have received the word of God, and we need no more of the word of God, for we have enough! For behold, thus saith the Lord God: I will give unto the children of men line upon line, precept upon precept, here a little and there a little" (2 Nephi 28:29–30).[70] Edward Brandt proposes that "the degree of gospel light that provides true perspective to gospel understanding and use comes line upon line, here a little and there a little, according to one's heed and diligence in willingly choosing to seek and follow that portion of gospel light that he has already received. (See Isaiah 28:10)."[71] Even the writing of the JST occurred since "a prophet learns line upon line" and "enlightenment comes 'line upon line' . . . and grows 'brighter and brighter.' . . . The whole of any principle of the gospel cannot be grasped by man in a single moment."[72] In sum, for the LDS, the phrase "line upon line" from Isaiah 28:10 elucidates a gradual, incremental stream of communication from God.

The passage of Isa 28:7–11 reads as follows:

> 7 But they also have erred through wine, and through strong drink are out of the way; The priest and the prophet have erred through strong drink, They are swallowed up of wine, they are out of the way through strong drink; They err in vision, they stumble *in* judgment.
> 8 For all tables are full of vomit *and* filthiness,
> *So that there is* no place *clean.*
> 9 Whom shall he teach knowledge?
> And whom shall he make to understand doctrine?
> *Them that are* weaned from the milk,
> *And* drawn from the breasts.
> 10 For precept *must be* upon precept, precept upon precept;
> Line upon line, line upon line;

68. Underwood, "More than an Index," 119.

69. McConkie in LDS, *New Testament Seminary*, 61; cf. McConkie, *Mormon Doctrine*, 648. The changing of the order of the words "precept" and "line" is seen in nearly every LDS source.

70. See also D&C 98:12: "For he will give unto the faithful line upon line, precept upon precept"; cf. D&C 128:21.

71. Brandt, in Carmack, *New Testament*, 61.

72. Matthews, *Plainer Translation*, 86, 215.

Here a little, *and* there a little:
[11] For with stammering lips and another tongue
Will he speak to this people. (Isa 28:7–11 KJV).

Several problems arise with the LDS use of the verse. First and foremost is the issue of whether the passage speaks of gradual, never-ending communication from God to his people. Additional issues include the mention of priests and prophets stumbling physically and spiritually on account of "strong drink" (v. 7), and the graphic description of foul and rank tables full of filthy vomit (v. 8). The identification of the one "teaching knowledge" (v. 9) is also important, as well as those "he" is teaching (v. 9). Another consideration is the apparent mention of infants—those "weaned from the milk" (v. 9). Finally, the precise meaning of "line upon line" is the crucial interpretive issue. Verse 10 contains a debated Hebrew phrase: צַו לָצָו צַו לָצָו קַו לָקָו קַו לָקָו (*ṣǎw laṣǎw, ṣǎw laṣǎw, qǎw laqǎw, qǎw laqǎw*). What could this repeated refrain mean?[73] For our purposes, were the King James translators justified in rendering this phrase "precept upon precept" and "line upon line"?

Isaiah 28–33 describes a series of woe oracles against the people of God.[74] The oracles are a response to the foolishness of trusting in pagan nations instead of God. The alliances with Assyria and Egypt signaled a "course of action which could only be proposed by a cynical, faithless leadership drunk on its own power and privilege."[75] Thus, the thrust of chapter 28 is an "announcement of judgment" because of "the actions and attitudes of its prophets, priests and other leaders."[76]

In v. 7, the religious leaders are depicted as staggering and wandering because of wine and strong drink. The "repetitive language (stagger-wine, wander-beer, stagger-beer, swallowed up-wine, wander-beer, stagger-reel) seems to imitate the stumblings and gigglings of the drunk."[77]

73. According to Cook, these words are "cryptic expressions" (Cook, "Hebrew Language," 307).

74. Childs, *Isaiah*, 199; Isa 28:1, 29:1, 29:15, 30:1, 31:1 and 33:1 "all begin with a woe marker" (Childs, *Isaiah*, 204–5).

75. Oswalt, *Book of Isaiah*, 504. See Isa 1:23; 7:13; 9:14–16; 19:11–15; 29:15–16; 30:1. Indeed, "the whole context of chs. 28–31 has to do with leaders who are either too stupid or too depraved to distinguish between wise and foolish counsel" (Oswalt, *Book of Isaiah*, 511n33).

76. Tucker, *Book of Isaiah*, 235.

77. Oswalt, *Book of Isaiah*, 510. My translation of Isa 28:7: "And these reel from wine and stagger because of strong drink; the priest and the prophet reel because of strong drink; they are confused by the wine and stagger by the strong drink. They reel in visions, and stumble in decisions."

Instead of obediently performing their duties in the temple, their actions are degenerate and debauched. Isaiah accuses these leaders of "drunken revelry" and this "is part of the stock-in-trade of prophetic diatribe."[78] On account of this vivid description of staggering and stumbling leaders, the passage displays a "sense of horror," as "the rot has reached even the religious leadership."[79]

The graphic depiction of filthy vomit (v. 8) adds to this sense of horror. The drunken priests have left behind rank reminders of their debauchery. What follows then, in vv. 9–10, is a contentious verbal exchange that "seems to be a genuine confrontation between Isaiah and drunken officials, prophets and priests."[80] It is fairly clear in v. 9 that the opponents of Isaiah are talking. The religious leaders mockingly challenge and question the teaching of the Prophet Isaiah: "Who does he think he is teaching—ignorant children?" (v. 9), as it were. The question of "To whom is he teaching?," implies the answer by the leaders—"Not us."[81] They "complain that Isaiah's message is simplistic and infantile, more suited to young, newly weaned children."[82] They snidely express their "indignation and contempt at the Prophet's undertaking to instruct them as if they were children."[83] Then, they respond with our debated phrase (v. 10). As we will see, it is difficult to determine conclusively the exact meaning of the debated phrase. However, one aspect of the passage seems clear: the drunken religious leaders are mocking the Prophet Isaiah with a repetitive ṣaw laṣaw, ṣaw laṣaw, qaw laqaw, qaw laqaw.

Some understand צַו ṣaw as "command," hence, the KJV version of "precept upon precept." It is the traditional rendering, and is advanced as the "most straightforward"—since it is the meaning of the word in Hos 5:11.[84] The Isaiah Targum seems to repeat this idea, translating Isa 28:10

---

78. Blenkinsopp, *Isaiah*, 388. Such diatribe "seems to go back, like so much else, to Amos (2:8; 6:4–7)" (Blenkinsopp, *Isaiah*, 388). See also Isa 5:12 for drinking and festivals as well as Isa 22:13 for drinking and sacrifices.

79. Oswalt, *Book of Isaiah*, 510.

80. Childs, *Isaiah*, 206.

81. Brueggemann, *Isaiah*, 223.

82. Roberts, *First Isaiah*, 351.

83. Alexander, *Prophecies of Isaiah*, 450.

84. "Ephraim is oppressed and crushed in judgment because he was determined to go after a (human) command (ṣaw)" (Hos 5:11, my translation). See Oswalt, *Book of Isaiah*, 512; Høgenhaven, *Gott Und Volk*, 203; Alexander, *Prophecies of Isaiah*, 452; Watts, *Isaiah*, 428; Wildberger, *Isaiah*, 17; Young, *Book of Isaiah*, 275–76.

as: "They were commanded to perform the law, and what they were commanded to do they did not wish to do."[85] The קַו *qăw*, then, in v. 10, would
mean "line," or "measuring line," as it does in v. 17 of the same chapter.[86]
Therefore, the drunken priests' mocking response would have been, as it
were, "Command after command, line after line (of commands)—does
he ever talk about anything else?!" While this remains a possible meaning
of v. 10, I do not believe it to be the most probable. The meanings of צַו
şăw and קַו *qăw* proposed here appear to be gleaned from contexts too far
removed from the *immediate* context of v. 10.[87] This is especially the case
with the use of צַו *şăw* in Hosea as determining its meaning in the book
of Isaiah. The main thrust however, remains—drunken religious leaders
mocking the Prophet. Nonetheless, it does *not* appear that the King James
translators were justified in rendering this phrase "precept upon precept"
and "line upon line."

What are the other possibilities for the meaning of the debated
phrase? Some take it as a rudimentary recitation of the alphabet. It is
surmised that the religious leaders "feel that they themselves are being
taken to task just as if they are being corrected by their first teacher in
school . . . [who] drills the alphabet . . . [and has] just gotten to tsade and
qoph."[88] The voice of a teacher "repeating the letters over and over again
to the boys who are writing them could sound ridiculous to someone
who overheard them by chance, particularly if he heard only the sounds."[89]
The phrase may be a parody on teaching the alphabet, and the sarcastic
reply of the leaders (v. 10) implied that the Prophet is "a boring repeater
of elemental, obvious claims, sounding the a-b-c's of Yahwism over and
over, when the prophets and priests are sophisticated and have moved
well beyond such elemental data."[90] The problem with this interpretation,
however, is that the letters tsade and qoph are found towards the end of

85. Chilton, *Isaiah Targum*, 11:55.

86. "And I will make justice as a measuring line (*qăw*)" (Isa 28:17a, my translation). For Oswalt, this word denotes a "measuring line, which along with a plumb line
was used to determine whether a building could be repaired or must be destroyed (2
K. 21:13; Isa. 28:17; 34:11)" (Oswalt, *Book of Isaiah*, 512; cf. Swanson, *Dictionary of
Biblical Languages*, §7742).

87. See also Blenkinsopp, *Isaiah*, 389; Kaiser, *Isaiah*, 245.

88. Wildberger, *Isaiah*, 16; Grogan, *Isaiah*, 184; tsade (צ); qoph (ק).

89. Kaiser, *Isaiah*, 246.

90. Brueggemann, *Isaiah*, 223–24.

the Hebrew alphabet.[91] This would be a strange place to begin a recitation of the alphabet.

Interestingly, some take our debated phrase to refer to the language of the Assyrians. This interpretation sees Yahweh as speaking Akkadian in v. 10, since v. 11 mentions the speaking with "a foreign tongue." The advantage of this view is that v. 13 also appears to quote the words of Yahweh—and our debated phrase in v. 10 appears again in v. 13. However, while v. 13 does, in fact, appear to cite Yahweh, it seems here the tables are turned on the rebellious leaders, and their own words (of v. 10) are used against them.[92] Nevertheless, while it is possible that Isaiah may have known some Akkadian, it is improbable that he had the "exact knowledge about details of that language as this interpretation would presume."[93] In addition, translations produced on this assumption do not suit the context well, and it is highly unlikely that the Assyrians gave orders to the inhabitants of Palestine in Akkadian.[94]

Some see the phrase as childishly repeating the words "excrement/filthiness" and "vomit" from v. 8: "For all tables are full of vomit *and* filthiness." The KJV translates the phrase as "vomit *and* filthiness,"[95] with קִיא *qî* as "vomit" and צֹאָה *ṣō·'āh* as "filthiness." These two words begin, respectively, with the same letter as our debated words in v. 10: צַו *ṣaw* and קַו *qaw*. Thus, the mocking has deteriorated to a juvenile level. The drunken leaders only repeat the first sounds of צֹאָה *ṣō·'āh* and קִיא *qî* from v. 8, with the result that our phrase in v. 10 would be "babyisms": צַו *ṣaw* and קַו *qaw*.[96] J. A. Emerton suggests that "these expressions may be baby talk" for excrement and vomit.[97] According to Roberts, the translation of v. 8, "Tables full of vomit . . . excrement until there is no more room," becomes in v. 10: "Doo-doo to doo-doo, doo-doo to doo-doo,

---

91. See Roberts, *First Isaiah*, 351; Hays, "Covenant with Mut," 235.

92. It is also possible that the phrase was spoken by the Assyrians, with both vv. 10 and 13 as "an imitation of sentences often heard in the mouths of the Assyrians" while they were driving the people of Israel into exile (Selms, "Isaiah 28:9–13," 333–34). It could also be a metaphor for the invasion (see Høgenhaven, *Gott Und Volk*, 203).

93. Wildberger, *Isaiah*, 17.

94. Hays, "Covenant with Mut," 234–35.

95. Other translations, however, have "filthy vomit" (e.g., NASB, ESV).

96. See Hays, "Covenant with Mut," 233. Roberts says the phrase is "some sort of baby talk" (Roberts, *First Isaiah*, 351).

97. Emerton, in Roberts, *First Isaiah*, 351.

Yuk-yuk to yuk-yuk, Yuk-yuk to yuk-yuk, A little here, a little there."[98]
Hays gives a similar translation for v. 10: "It is 'poo-poo, poo-poo, bleh-bleh, bleh-bleh', a little here, a little there."[99] The צַו *ṣǎw* of v. 10 would mean "doo-doo" or "poo-poo" because of the צֹאָה *ṣō·'āh* of v. 8. The leaders in their drunken state have descended to such a low level that they repeat juvenile vulgarities for the (surely) surprised Prophet. The resultant uproarious laughter among the intoxicated leaders can easily be imagined. The religious leaders, by repeating such foul words, would be "obviously picking up on Isaiah's earlier graphic portrayal of their drunkenness, and their response suggests that Isaiah, like a naughty child, is hung up on infantile bathroom language."[100] One difficulty with this interpretation, however, is that Yahweh speaks the same phrase in 13. Furthermore, not only is the order of the words different in v. 8, but it is also unclear in context whether צֹאָה *ṣō·'āh* means "filth" or "excrement"—or if it was an adjectival description of קִיא *qî'* "vomit" (so, "filthy vomit").[101] The latter seems more probable—a vivid description of vomit. Regardless, one aspect remains certain: the drunken religious leaders are repetitively mocking the Prophet Isaiah in v. 10—and it is possible that they spewed this juvenile slang.

The Septuagint does not help with the conundrum, since it carries a different idea entirely, translating the words as "tribulation" and "hope."[102] Apparently, the LXX translators did not see צַו *ṣǎw* but rather צַר *ṣār*: "trouble, distress, or enemy."[103] They also apparently took קַו *qǎw* for קָוֶה *qā·wāh*: "wait for" or "hope."[104] Therefore, a possible rendering of the LXX is that Isaiah is frustrating the priests—since he is vacillating

98. Roberts, *First Isaiah*, 348.

99. Hays, "Covenant with Mut," 214.

100. Roberts, *First Isaiah*, 351.

101. Possible literal translation of Isa 28:8: "For all the tables are full of vomit and excrement without a (single clean) place." However, it is improbable that it means "excrement," given that Isaiah uses a different word for "excrement" in 36:12: ". . . to eat their own excrement and drink their own urine with you." Thus, we note a better translation of Isa 28:8: "For all the tables are full of filthy vomit without a [single clean] place."

102. See Rahlfs and Hanhart, *Septuaginta*, 601.

103. Swanson, *Dictionary of Biblical Languages*, §7639–40; cf. Brown, *Brown-Driver-Briggs*, 862.

104. Blenkinsopp, *Isaiah*, 389; cf. Watts, *Isaiah*, 428; Brown, *Brown-Driver-Briggs*, 875; Holladay and Köhler, *Concise Hebrew and Aramaic Lexicon*, 315.

between judgment and salvation, being a prophet of doom yet also of salvation. In other words, he would be considered unreliable.[105]

Finally, the phrase may convey a sense of gibberish and nonsensical language. In v. 9, the derisive challenge by the religious leaders would be: "Who does he think we are to require his instruction? Are we merely children? All we ever hear from the prophet is the same tired old gibberish!"[106] Then they, in turn, repeat the "gibberish" back to Isaiah in v. 10. They "mimic the language of the prophet, as if it were the unintelligible babbling of infants,"[107] and they attempt "to discredit Isaiah's proclamation."[108] It is striking to note "the mockery of the despisers [that] comes to clear expression, as they utter their drunken stammering, seeking to imitate and caricature the message of Isaiah."[109] This interpretation, or some close variant, seems to be the most probable—gibberish spoken by the drunken religious leaders in v. 10 as a continuation of their mocking questions in v. 9.

Concerning the final words of v. 10: זְעֵיר שָׁם זְעֵיר שָׁם *ze'êr šām, ze'êr šām*, "a little here, a little there," it is unclear what "little" זְעֵיר *ze'êr* refers to. Watts believes it "most likely" refers to "the children of v 9b."[110] Similarly, it is seen as a comment by the teacher, so: "Little one, here! Little one, 'over' there!" The teacher would be calling on one child, then another.[111] Some think that it refers to "another little drink"—they are still calling for more.[112] It could even pick up the theme of vomit (or excrement) from v. 8—a little here and a little there, i.e., "everywhere!"[113] Or it may

---

105. Wildberger, *Isaiah*, 16, 23.

106. Childs, *Isaiah*, 207; cf. Swanson, *Dictionary of Biblical Languages*, §7744; Holladay and Köhler, *Hebrew and Aramaic Lexicon*, 245.

107. Tucker, *Book of Isaiah*, 237; cf. Grogan, *Isaiah*, 179; Ciampa and Rosner, "1 Corinthians," 740–41.

108. Even replicating a speech defect that Isaiah had (see Wildberger, *Isaiah*, 23).

109. Young, *Book of Isaiah*, 275. Another possible concept is that Isaiah was mocking the drunken leaders. They were like infants who couldn't receive the prophetic message. So, Isaiah throws back into their faces a "meaningless chant": *şāw laşāw, şāw laşāw, qāw laqāw, qāw laqāw*. The leaders were like "infants in their intellectual capacity" (Miscall, *Isaiah*, 74; cf. Alexander, *Prophecies of Isaiah*, 452). Again however, contextually it seems that v. 10 comes from the lips of the religious leaders.

110. Watts, *Isaiah*, 430.

111. Procksch, in Wildberger, *Isaiah*, 16.

112. See Driver, in Watts, *Isaiah*, 428.

113. See Roberts, *First Isaiah*, 351.

be a fitting end to the mocking gibberish of the leaders—intimating the ubiquity of the prophetic gibberish.

Our passage pictures inebriated, staggering, vomiting religious leaders (vv. 7–8), followed by juvenile, sarcastic, mocking gibberish (vv. 9–10). It is possible that their provocation has escalated to spewing vulgarities at the solitary Prophet (v. 10). Incredibly, those responsible for the interpretation of the word of God can only mutter and stammer.[114] Verse 11 brings an abrupt change—the childish dialogue has come to an end, as the Creator has come upon the scene. He "will speak to this people" in a foreign tongue—and just as Isaiah has written of the gibberish of the religious leaders in v. 10, Yahweh himself will send the Assyrian army that will speak what sounds like gibberish to the leaders: "So the word of the Lord to them will be, *ṣăw laṣăw, ṣăw laṣăw, qăw laqăw, qăw laqăw*" (v. 13). The irony of the passage is stunning. The announcement of judgment will not be brought by the Prophet—but by foreigners. The penetrating message appears, in effect: "You religious leaders [who] speak words without sense will be judged by words 'without sense,' i.e., 'with foreign lips' (v. 11)."[115] The same gibberish will be turned back upon their own heads. The babble that they used to mock the Prophet will be echoed in the strange language of the foreign invaders, who will be the instrument of judgment by Yahweh. Yahweh will confront the rebellious religious leaders with the cacophony of rapid-fire foreign words spoken by a pagan, godless invading army.

Our central concern with the passage pertains to the difficult Hebrew phrase, since the LDS authors quote it extensively. Yet, the precise identification of the words *ṣăw* and *qăw* is not as important as the obvious thrust of the passage. We have seen that the passage is concerned with the issue of teaching knowledge (v. 9) as well as the incompetency of the religious leaders.[116] Thus, the whole of the passage deals with the *lack of* understanding and knowledge. This picks up central themes throughout chapters 28–33: "comprehensibility and accessibility of the divine word and revelation" and "reception of the Lord's word."[117] Yet the message in our passage arrives through irony and sarcasm—even gibberish. In sum, the thrust of the passage is a lack of understanding on the part

---

114. See Tucker, *Book of Isaiah*, 237.

115. Childs, *Isaiah*, 202.

116. Watts, *Isaiah*, 430.

117. Mischall, *Isaiah*, 74.

of drunken religious leaders who mock the prophet Isaiah with offensive gibberish, and the announcement of judgment from Yahweh.

The LDS citation of the debated phrase from Isa 28:10 for their doctrine of continuing revelation—learning spiritual truths "line upon line"—is ironic at best, and excessive at worst. They have taken a suspect translation from the KJV ("precept upon precept, line upon line") and re-authored it to become a central doctrine. The thrust of the passage— gibberish by drunken leaders, and a lack of understanding—has been turned on its head by the LDS to speak of incremental reception, and the consequent understanding, of revelation. The intended sense of the passage is ignored—and a contemporary meaning entirely foreign to the ancient text is postulated.

LDS scholar Kevin Barney admits that the LDS take the passage out of context.[118] He views the debated phrase as "heavily influenced" by the verse in the BoM: "For behold, thus saith the Lord God: 'I will give unto the children of men line upon line, precept upon precept, here a little and there a little; and blessed are those who hearken unto my precepts, and lend an ear unto my counsel'" (2 Nephi 28:30). For Barney, the phrase "line upon line" is an incremental "increase in knowledge, understanding and revelation," and the LDS is "taught by degrees instead of all at once." Barney continues: "of course [this] meshes well with our belief in ongoing, continuing revelation and in the need for a modern prophet." He then admits "that [the LDS] understanding, as valid as it may be on its own terms, is not a contextual reading of Isaiah. I would view our conception of the phrase as deriving from Nephi. In turn, I would view Nephi's take as a *pesher*." He then proceeds through the Isaianic passage as I have done, suggesting that "the repetitive line is either baby talk ('goo goo gah gah')" or, more likely, a "portion of a child's spelling lesson." He summarizes his interpretation:

> Therefore, in what I view as the best available contextual reading of this passage of Isaiah, the emphasis is less on the incremental increase in knowledge (although it is certainly true that chil- dren learn incrementally) and more on the simplicity and basic nature of the prophet's warnings. The leaders of Israel viewed themselves as sophisticated men of the world and did not appre- ciate what they saw as Isaiah's condescending approach to them, so they mocked him by sarcastically imitating his message to them. Isaiah in turn ironically repeats their sarcastic version of

118. Barney, "Line upon Line."

his message, for it is a lesson they will have to learn one way or
the other: the easy way in Hebrew from Isaiah, or the hard way
in Assyrian from their captors and new masters.[119]

Despite claiming to give "the best available contextual reading of this passage of Isaiah" (even after admitting that the LDS take it out of context),
Barney quickly passes over the actual meaning of the passage. The emphasis is "more on the simplicity and basic nature of the prophet's warnings."
While he correctly summarizes contextual features, such as the sarcasm
and the mocking attitude of the leaders, Barney doesn't take seriously the
intended sense of Isaiah 28:10. He is aware of the numerous LDS authors
that cite the passage to champion the doctrine of continuing revelation.

7.3.1. The Hermeneutical Effect of the LDS
Re-Authoring of Isaiah 28:10

The citation of "line upon line" suggests a major focus on the text. They
are taking at face value the content of the KJV translation of Isaiah. Yet,
they deny any static notion of the meaning of the text itself—instead
only focusing on what they believe "line upon line" means. A *selective*
straightforward reading and interpretation of the Bible suits the LDS
ecclesiologically and sociologically, for it allows them to position themselves as the unique receptors of ongoing communication from God. We
have seen this hermeneutical procedure with the specific methodological
hermeneutic of *selective* literalism. They lift the locution "line upon line"
from its context, and wholly unconcerned with the textual viability of
their reading, re-author the phrase to defend their doctrine of continuing
revelation. In the end, the LDS does not appear to be concerned with the
original, intended sense of the passage. Modern significance overrides
ancient meaning. Clearly, institutional needs are allowed to take prece-
dence over contextual meaning. "Line upon line" becomes a repeated
refrain that advances a modern LDS doctrine.

We have investigated five uses of the Bible by the LDS. In the
process, we attempted to approach their core hermeneutic on its own
terms, endeavoring to give the LDS a fair hearing. Following the insights
garnered from the framework of Critical Realism, external data was collected, and with our epistemic relativity, several judgments were offered.
We noted the difficulty inherent in the investigation of an entire religious

119. Barney, "Line upon Line."

system. We proposed that LDS approaches to the Bible are varied and
diverse. Yet, we introduced the possibility of a single, stable hermeneutical framework. In one sense, "systemic parameters" is a single framework
that drives their interpretation. Yet, in another sense, LDS hermeneutics
is quite eclectic, as reflected in our five categories. Given the difficulty
encountered so far, as well as the complexity inherent in their hermeneutics, it is imperative to consider other hermeneutical voices. The field of
hermeneutics has advanced significantly over the past century, and we
need to listen to those in this field before we draw our final conclusions.
Given that it is difficult to align the interpretive tendencies of the LDS
with accepted hermeneutical conclusions, one wonders if philosophical
hermeneutics offers a better possibility of justification.

8

LDS Interpretive Practice in Light of
Philosophical Hermeneutics

Having examined numerous biblical interpretations by the LDS, I will now bring philosophical hermeneutics more fully into the discussion.[1] This evaluative phase will take advantage of the insights of Hans-Georg Gadamer, mainly because of his stature and his understanding of the issues at hand. Considering the interpretive practices of the LDS, the content of this chapter will answer the question: what potential do the concepts of philosophical hermeneutics have for our evaluation of their hermeneutics?

8.1. General Philosophical Matters

8.1.1. Inescapability of Interpretation

As self-aware individuals, we never experience the world in uninterpreted ways.[2] Existence itself presupposes a state of constant interpretation as we discern and evaluate the dialogues and events surrounding

---

1. Whereas "philosophical hermeneutics" narrowly refers to Hans-Georg Gadamer's account of the interpretive process, it can also be applied to other thinkers as well (see Weinsheimer, *Philosophical Hermeneutics*, ix; cf. Grondin, *Philosophical Hermeneutics*, 2).

2. McLean, *Biblical Interpretation*, 71.

us.[3] Indeed, Gadamer's "foundational insight" was this "universality of hermeneutics."[4] It is important in any discussion of hermeneutical practice, LDS or otherwise, to acknowledge this foundation. In fact, "all human behavior is based on making sense of things."[5] Yet, as Westphal notes, interpretation often happens without a reflected hermeneutical theory in place.[6] The hermeneutical activity by the LDS is no exception. We have seen, for example, "the majority of Mormons remain in a hermeneutical Eden, innocent of a conscious philosophy of interpretation."[7] There is significant hesitation in the LDS to articulate a hermeneutic, or to assume hermeneutical accountability. Also, LDS authors assume that Joseph Smith can "bypass" hermeneutical activity,[8] use the Bible as a poet;[9] or make "additions."[10] There is also the assumption that other churches interpret, while the LDS reads the Bible in its "literal, plain, simple meaning."[11] This, of course, runs counter to this widespread notion on the inescapability of interpretation. We have also seen the LDS claim that it is problematic "to assume that systemic philosophical thought—even the application of hermeneutical categories—ought to be employed in order to clarify the content of revelation."[12] Considering the concept of the universality of hermeneutics, this assertion is unsustainable. The LDS appear to be unaware of their hermeneutical activity. This will cast doubt on their ability to correctly interpret ancient Scripture. To continue, we now turn to two of the main architects of the concept of the inescapability of interpretation.

3. Palmer, *Hermeneutics*, 9.

4. Brown, *Scripture as Communication*, 66; cf. Gadamer, *Philosophical Hermeneutics*, 19.

5. Grondin, *Philosophical Hermeneutics*, 19.

6. See Westphal, *Whose Community?*, 149; cf. Wright, *People of God*, 103–4.

7. Barlow, *Mormons and the Bible*, 248.

8. Paulsen, "Are Christians Mormon?," 128.

9. Barlow, *Mormons and the Bible*, 79.

10. Barlow, "Revision of the Bible," 55.

11. Young, "Effects and Privileges."

12. Siebach, "Dialogue on Theology," 467.

8.1.2. Martin Heidegger: Being and Understanding

A main thrust of Martin Heidegger's perspective is that hermeneutics should be approached from an ontological orientation.[13] Instead of automatically assuming that interpretation begins (and ends) with the deciphering of the text, the significance of the interpreter's "being-ness" should be recognized. Heidegger demonstrated that "being" for every individual implied the embedment in a particular place and time.[14] There is a social locatedness of every interpreter, and this always influences understanding.[15] It is only through "being-there" that understanding of the text occurs authentically. For Heidegger, understanding was an existential endeavor—it was "mastery" and a "way of existing."[16] This ontological reality is "subjectivity in place"—for "to be" is to be *somewhere*. Consequently, the notion of interpretive postures driving interpretation is inescapable.

8.1.3. H.-G. Gadamer: Being and Fusion of Horizons

Gadamer developed this ontological focus in several ways. He considered that everything (including the interpreter) is conditioned by its place in history.[17] He agreed with Heidegger's existential structure of understanding. He also saw that historical understanding becomes viable only with an ontological foundation.[18] As readers, we are "embedded" in our context.[19] We are even "thrown" into our context.[20] Yet, while embedded, readers need to recognize the context of the text, to avoid reading into

13. See Heidegger, *Being and Time*, 10–11; cf. Selby, *Comical Doctrine*, 136; Schrijver, "Hermeneutics and Tradition," 33–34.

14. See McLean, *Biblical Interpretation*, 103.

15. Heidegger, *Being and Time*, 144–49; cf. Brown, *Scripture as Communication*, 69; Thiselton, *New Horizons*, 319.

16. See Grondin, *Philosophical Hermeneutics*, 92–98. Also, according to Heidegger, "being" is intricately related to language (see Heidegger, *On the Way to Language*, 63, 85; cf. Porter and Robinson, *Hermeneutics*, 61–64; Treier, *Theological Interpretation*, 129).

17. Gadamer, *Wahrheit und Methode*, 366, 452.

18. Gadamer, *Wahrheit und Methode*, 265.

19. See Westphal, *Whose Community?*, 132, cf. 35, 72, 141; Scott, "Gadamer's *Truth and Method*," 67; Wright, *People of God*, 138; Bartholomew, "Three Horizons," 122.

20. *Geworfenheit* is the German word. See McLean, *Biblical Interpretation*, 104–6; cf. Wachterhauser, *Hermeneutics and Modern Philosophy*, 7.

the text their own contextual assumptions. If we do not recognize our ontologically solidified, modern filters, we may be unduly predisposed to highlight (or ignore) certain aspects of the context of the text.[21] For both Heidegger and Gadamer, the very situatedness of the interpreter, far from being a limiting, negative reality, was a positive feature that became the foundation for the *possibility* of understanding.[22] Correct interpretation "fuses" ancient and modern horizons. However, this fusion is not a mere amalgamation of the two horizons,[23] but recognition of their differences.

Gadamer consistently pointed out the difficulties in using a "method" from the natural sciences and applying it to the "sociohistorical world."[24] His aim was to avoid "imposing *a priori* a preconstructed conceptual grid of 'closed' assumptions" upon the text.[25] Such utilization of a "method" reflects a Western epistemology where only scientific, repeatable investigation is valid.[26] Thus, an ontological orientation to the interpretive process prevents a "located" interpreter from mechanically utilizing a supposedly unassailable methodology to flawlessly decipher the ancient text—because his/her embeddedness would unduly distort the use of a method. We emphasize here the descriptive nature of Gadamer's hermeneutical reflections, for he avoids giving a step-by-step methodology to fuel and sustain the interpretive process. Rather, he is attempting to elucidate the complex process that is the understanding event.[27]

---

21. See Wright, *Scripture*, 129; cf. Selby, *Comical Doctrine*, 187.

22. See Selby, *Comical Doctrine*, 20.

23. The German term for the fusion of horizons is *Horizontverschmelzung*. See Gadamer in McLean, *Biblical Interpretation*, 192; cf. Thiselton, *Hermeneutics of Doctrine*, 261; Grünfeld, "Gadamer's Hermeneutics," 234; Dunn, *Jesus Remembered*, 123; Bartholomew, "Three Horizons," 125; Westphal, *Whose Community?*, 78; Schrijver, "Hermeneutics and Tradition," 44.

24. See Gadamer, *Wahrheit und Methode*, 10.

25. See Thiselton, *Hermeneutics of Doctrine*, 409; cf. Porter and Robinson, *Hermeneutics*, 87.

26. Fowl, "Effective History," 155; cf. Detweiler and Robbins, "From New Criticisms," 240.

27. See Westphal, *Whose Community?*, 69. Warnke, however, points out that although his aim is descriptive, Gadamer "sometimes uses prescriptive language" (Warnke, *Inheriting Gadamer*, 12).

8.1.4. LDS Hermeneutics: Ontology and Interpretation

The epistemological shift brought about by Heidegger and Gadamer is of paradigmatic proportions. For purposes of our study, we ask if any aspects thereof could be deployed in our evaluation of LDS hermeneutics. The LDS maintain "a hermeneutic of relations, practices, and events" in contradistinction to "a hermeneutic of texts,"[28] and "any Mormon hermeneutic is bound to be pragmatic, presentist, and performative."[29] We noted in chapter 1 that an LDS self-understanding has often been described as "concerned more with praxis than dogmatic theology."[30] Mormonism is a forward-thinking movement intensely interested in a pragmatic orientation to life and spirituality.

However, the LDS authors quoted above emphasize what a Mormon interpreter *does*, as opposed to an interpreter's "being-ness." A verse from the BoM states the following:

> And I did read many things unto them which were written in the books of Moses; but that I might more fully persuade them to believe in the Lord their Redeemer I did read unto them that which was written by the prophet Isaiah; for *I did liken all scriptures unto us*, that it might be for our profit and learning. (1 Nephi 19:23, emphasis added)

Many LDS books, both scholarly and popular, admonish the faithful to "liken the scriptures" to themselves.[31] Indeed, "Scripture requires our response in interpretation and meditation: the appropriation of scripture—in Mormon terminology, likening it to ourselves (1 Nephi 19:23)—more so than its rational exegesis."[32] In another writing, Faulconer states that LDS members "are doing textual exegesis and thinking about what the results of that exegesis mean for our own lives."[33] These statements illustrate the distance between the LDS worldview and the insights of Heidegger and Gadamer. The "locatedness" of every interpreter receives

---

28. Faulconer, "Dialogue on Theology," 476. Faulconer also states that "religion is primarily a matter of practice rather than propositional belief" (Faulconer, "Dialogue on Theology," 475).

29. The Literary Critic, "Thursday, June 26, 2003."

30. Baker, *Mormonism at the Crossroads*, xiii.

31. LDS, *New Testament Seminary*, 266; Jackson, "Latter-day Saints," 80; Nyman and Bolin Hawkins, "Book of Mormon," 143.

32. Faulconer, "Dialogue on Theology," 475.

33. Faulconer, *New Testament Made Harder*, 8.

an overemphasis in LDS thinking. An LDS interpretation gives priority to the modern horizon, as opposed to the pursuit of a fusion between the horizon of the text and their own. Faulconer's statement corroborates this, for they perform textual exegesis for what it means for their lives. Furthermore, a consequence of the "appropriation of scripture" is a promotion of the LDS community. Thus, the LDS is only interested in ontological matters if it pertains to their communal identity. A well balanced, Gadamerian ontological focus will consider more than just the actions of the interpreter.

The lack of a published hermeneutical framework by the LDS aligns with Gadamer's suspicion towards the role of methodology in the interpretive process. However, the interpretive examples I have noted throughout this investigation, whether Prophetic interpretation of scripture, restoration by modern LDS scriptures, or even "systemic parameters," demonstrate methodological instincts on the part of the LDS. This is in opposition to Gadamer's suspicion toward the role of methodology. While lacking an explicit hermeneutical methodology, the LDS, nonetheless, demonstrates numerous hermeneutical practices. At the very least, these practices confirm the "inescapability of interpretation," although at the expense of compatibility with Gadamer. However, as we have seen, the extent to which the LDS is aware of this hermeneutical activity is unclear.

8.1.5. Presuppositions; Pre-Understanding; Self-Deception and Awareness

The impossibility of presuppositionless exegesis is a widely held notion.[34] Previously, the Enlightenment had a "prejudice against prejudice" which tried to eliminate the existence of presuppositions in the understanding process.[35] There existed a goal of "presuppositionless recreation of an author's intention."[36] Yet, the "locatedness" of every interpreter includes his or her own presuppositions. True understanding is "never without presuppositions," since we are located in a specific place and time.[37] Further-

34. See Treier, *Theological Interpretation*, 34; cf. Westphal, in Porter and Stovell, *Hermeneutics*, 73; Bultmann, "Is Exegesis without Presuppositions Possible?," 289–96.

35. See Gadamer, *Truth and Method*, 239–40; cf. Gadamer, *Wahrheit und Methode*, 275.

36. See Arthur, "Gadamer and Hirsch," 183.

37. Porter and Robinson, *Hermeneutics*, 60. Indeed, presuppositional matters are pervasive, since all communication exhibits "presuppositions that never get expressed" (Gadamer, in Grondin, *Philosophical Hermeneutics*, 38).

more, a presupposition can be "a particular starting point from which understanding advances."[38]

Gadamer differentiates between legitimate and illegitimate prejudices. He laments the pejorative use of "prejudice" and famously called for "a fundamental rehabilitation of the concept of prejudice."[39] How do we distinguish between legitimate and illegitimate presuppositions? An infallible criterion is not permissible since this would "certify objectivity" and give validity to an all-encompassing methodology.[40] Yet Gadamer offers the beginning of a solution with the concept of temporal distance. He states, "It is only this temporal distance that can solve the really critical question of hermeneutics, namely of distinguishing the true prejudices, by which we understand, from the false ones by which we misunderstand."[41]

Conceptual analysis of what constitutes "legitimate prejudices" will also assist us. Also called "pre-understandings," they play an essential role in the interpretive process.[42] A "fruitful starting point" for understanding is in the realm of "pre-understanding."[43] Indeed,

> A thought that is to be conveyed to the reader by words often presupposes other conceptions without which it is not conceivable; if a reader is not already in possession of these conceptions, therefore, the words cannot effect the same result in him as in another reader who is thoroughly knowledgeable about these conceptions.[44]

38. Linge, in Gadamer, *Philosophical Hermeneutics*, xxx; Selby, *Comical Doctrine*, 20.

39. Gadamer, *Truth and Method*, 246; cf. Gadamer, *Wahrheit und Methode*, 281; Kennedy Schmidt, *Epistemology of Hans-Georg Gadamer*, 34, 61. Dunn calls his readers to notice Gadamer's "striking defense" of prejudice (Dunn, *Jesus Remembered*, 121n82). Selby writes that "pre-judgments" have a positive role (Selby, *Comical Doctrine*, 166); Malcolm even calls for "the faithful prejudice of Christian interpretation" (Malcolm, "Biblical Hermeneutics," 84).

40. Grondin, *Philosophical Hermeneutics*, 112.

41. Gadamer, *Truth and Method*, 266; The phrase "only temporal distance," was later softened by Gadamer to read "often temporal distance" (see Grondin, *Philosophical Hermeneutics*, 113).

42. See Westphal, *Whose Community?*, 85; Weinsheimer, *Philosophical Hermeneutics*, 15.

43. Thiselton, *Hermeneutics*, 12.

44. Chladenius, in Grondin, *Philosophical Hermeneutics*, 53. For example, the phrase "The horse is fast" is understandable because of our pre-understanding of "horse." In contrast, the phrase "The petuba is fast" is incomprehensible, because of the non-sensical word "petuba."

Before true understanding emerges, every interpreter will have some type of pre-understanding of the subject at hand. Reflecting the inescapability of interpretation, we see that "understanding is always interpretive. Understanding is always inextricably informed by the perspective we bring to bear in the act of understanding."[45] Indeed, there is no such thing as presuppositionless thought.[46] Interpretation "begins with foreconceptions that are replaced by more suitable ones."[47] We are not blank slates but rather complex individuals with past experiences that help us navigate and interpret every new experience.

These pre-understandings are always brought to new experiences, whether we are conscious of them or not.[48] Perhaps it is the "almost boundless human capacity for self-deception,"[49] that explains why pre-understandings often go unnoticed. The interpreter needs to be vigilant to avoid being seduced by self-interest.[50] Porter and Robinson cite Gadamer's argument that "any inquiry or investigation believed to be without prejudice or bias is in denial of its own conditioned ways of understanding."[51] With an echo from our ontological analysis, we must "turn to an understanding of ourselves."[52]

Recognizing our blind spots and avoiding self-deception can be exceedingly difficult, especially "without outside assistance."[53] The insights of philosophy and theology can help us detect our own presuppositions and pre-understandings.[54] One benefit of philosophical hermeneutics is "its constant insistence that we remember we belong to history and thus to a finite perspective."[55] A distinct yet related concept that we noted in

---

45. Mootz and Taylor, *Gadamer and Ricoeur*, 1.

46. Westphal, in Porter and Stovell, *Hermeneutics*, 72.

47. Gadamer, *Truth and Method*, 236; cf. McLean, *Biblical Interpretation*, 113–14; Thiselton, *Hermeneutics*, 208; Weinsheimer, *Philosophical Hermeneutics*, 14.

48. In many ways "we are hidden from ourselves" (see Porter and Robinson, *Hermeneutics*, 90).

49. Wright, *People of God*, 135.

50. Thiselton, *Hermeneutics*, 5; cf. McLean, *Biblical Interpretation*, 182. For the dangers of "corporate self-interest" see Porter, *Horizons in Hermeneutics*, 271.

51. See Porter and Robinson, *Hermeneutics*, 85; cf. Gadamer, *Truth and Method*, 241–45.

52. Porter and Robinson, *Hermeneutics*, 36.

53. Brown, *Scripture as Communication*, 123.

54. Bartholomew, "Three Horizons," 125, 127.

55. Westphal, in Porter and Stovell, *Hermeneutics*, 168.

chapter 1 is a consideration of the "other." Not only is it necessary to be aware of one's own presuppositions, but it is also imperative to consider the "other." Gadamer emphasized the need to keep "oneself open to what is other" and "to distance oneself from oneself and from one's private purposes."[56] In the end, awareness of ourselves, including our pre-understandings, as well as "genuine hermeneutical engagement with 'the other' may begin to erode the spell of idolatrous self-deception,"[57] and will aid us in the complexity of the interpretive process.

8.1.6. LDS Hermeneutics: Presuppositions

Somewhat surprisingly, many LDS authors write of presuppositional matters. This is surprising, for one, because of their insistence on the "plain" meaning of the biblical text. Faulconer acknowledges that "at play in every interpretation are our prejudices," and through them we "make our interpretations," even though "[they] may, unbeknownst to us, influence our understanding."[58] In fact, readers "cannot help but apply our modern biases to the texts we read because we are creatures of history as much as were the writers who produced the scriptures."[59] For Hutchinson, revelation does not occur in a vacuum.[60] In addition, "one's own theological biases and presuppositions also color the way scriptures are read, which can sometimes lead to scriptural proof-texting."[61] Ostler concedes that "one's reflection on scripture is most often guided by one's prior theological commitments that often more or less place horizons on what one is able to see."[62] Relatedly, LDS authors grant that it is naïve to deny personal involvement in interpretation.[63]

Nonetheless, in general, LDS authors point out the illegitimate prejudices of *others*. We have already seen McConkie describe "the

---

56. Gadamer, *Truth and Method*, 17.

57. Thiselton, *Hermeneutics of Doctrine*, 85.

58. Faulconer, "Recovering Truth," 3. See also his brief discussion of Gadamer, Ricoeur, and pre-understanding in Faulconer, "Scripture as Incarnation."

59. Goff, "How Should We Then Read?," 140.

60. See Hutchinson, "LDS Approaches," 107, where he discusses four groups of LDS scholars, each exhibiting different tendencies in their hermeneutical orientations.

61. See Harrell, *"This Is My Doctrine,"* 8.

62. Ostler, *Of God and Gods*, 615.

63. See Holland, "Daddy"; cf. Oaks, "Scripture Reading"; Nibley, *World and the Prophets*, 3:202; Barber, "Literalist Constraint," 21.

theological bias of the translators" in the formation of the Bible, which
"caused them to change the meaning or paraphrase texts that were either unclear or embarrassing to them."[64] LDS authors accuse others of
being tied to a "theological agenda"[65] or operating with "assumptions"
that are not "well-founded."[66] Matthew Bowman writes of the "ability"
of his fellow Mormon thinkers, especially Joseph Smith, to "shatter the
binding presuppositions of Western culture and produce ideas of great
insight and power."[67] Implicit in Bowman's view is that other Christian
traditions are unable to overcome these "binding presuppositions." In
matters of God's nature, Ostler calls into question a "key assumption"
that holds to the "view that there is necessarily a metaphysically unique
being or 'God' that is the explanation of everything else that exists." This
assumption comes from Greek philosophy and has "often controlled the
reading of the biblical texts."[68] Ostler adds that other traditions have "assumptions" that are "derived from ontological categories that are absent
from and contrary to the biblical culture and texts."[69] Thus, he believes
that the meaning of "God" in other traditions comes from a distorted
reading of the Bible, while he implicitly advances the idea that the LDS
perspective is free from prejudice. Specifically, he suspects "that the most
powerful resistance to the doctrine of robust deification arises not from
the scriptural argument but from the metaphysical assumptions that are
brought to the biblical texts which control how they are read."[70] For Benjamin Huff, early Christians assumed a "Platonic view of embodiment"
that caused them to deny that "God the Father is corporeal."[71] Similarly,
for Huff, "Platonic and Aristotelian reasoning about God led to the
traditional understanding of the Trinity in terms of one metaphysical

---

64. McConkie, *New Witness*, 403; For McConkie, the Book of Mormon should be
read "with an open mind; a mind unshackled by the prejudices of men" (McConkie,
New Witness, 465).

65. Davies, in Ostler, *Of God and Gods*, 657.

66. Faulconer, "Philosophy and Transcendence," 73.

67. Bowman, "History Thrown into Divinity," 89.

68. Ostler, *Of God and Gods*, 13–14. Concerning divine corporeality in chapter 3,
we also noted Robinson's views that other churches are influenced by Greek philosophy (Robinson, *Are Mormons Christians?*, 80–81).

69. Ostler, *Of God and Gods*, 68.

70. Ostler, *Of God and Gods*, 587.

71. Huff, "Theology in the Light," 480.

substance."[72] Early LDS leaders rejected the "central 'Christian' premise'"
that "Baconian rationalism was the only proper lens through which the
Bible should be viewed."[73] In 1871, George Cannon, an early Mormon
leader, spoke of the distorting assumption in other religious traditions
that consisted of "the soul-destroying and damnable heresy that God
cannot or will not speak to man again from the heavens."[74]

These strong perspectives by LDS authors have significant hermeneutical impact. These authors declare that other traditions exhibit illegitimate prejudices, and they implicitly claim to be free of such negative
distortions. There is little evidence of LDS authors acknowledging their
own presuppositions, or how the topic of presuppositions influences their
biblical interpretations.[75] Although LDS scholar James Faulconer does
correctly describe several Gadamerian insights in his review of *Truth
and Method*,[76] he does not explicitly relate Gadamerian insights to LDS
thinking, especially the insights on presuppositional matters. Faulconer
merely uses Gadamer to combat what he considers to be the prevailing
methodological posture of scientism.[77] One might have expected him
to utilize Gadamer for constructing a positive case for LDS hermeneutics, but, surprisingly, he does not appear to be interested in that. One
wonders if this is an indication of a wider LDS posture of disinterest in
hermeneutical matters. To reiterate, the LDS often focuses on the illegitimate presuppositions of others. In the process, they appear to disregard

72. Huff, "Theology in the Light," 480.

73. Hughes, in Eliason, *Mormons & Mormonism*, 23.

74. Cannon, "Persecution."

75. I noted two pervasive LDS presuppositions in chapter 2: asymmetry concerning the Bible and continuing revelation. In general, LDS authors do not adequately
acknowledge the effect of these presuppositions on their biblical interpretations.

76. Again, see Faulconer, "Recovering Truth," 1–7.

77. A limited amount of interaction between philosophical hermeneutics and LDS
hermeneutical perspectives can be seen in Faulconer and Wrathall, *Appropriating
Heidegger*. In another writing, Faulconer even writes that Heidegger, Gadamer, and
Ricoeur "are not among the philosophers to whom most Mormons are likely to refer,"
though "that seems to be changing" (Faulconer, "Dialogue on Theology," 477). Brian
Birch acknowledges the influence of "philosophical hermeneutics" on his thinking
(Birch in Baker, *Mormonism at the Crossroads*, 51n12). Also, LDS scholar David Bohn
references Gadamer to warn LDS history writers of the impossibility of mechanically
reporting history as simple facts. He writes of the necessary inclusion of presuppositional matters in such writing (see Bohn, "Unfounded Claims," 227–56; cf. Bohn,
"Larger Issue," 45–63; Midgley, "Challenge of Historical Consciousness," 2:502–51).
Hutchinson holds similar views in "LDS Approaches," 118n8, 119n9.

Gadamer's admonition "to distance oneself from oneself and from one's private purposes."[78] The LDS ignores the reality of their own "located-ness" and assumptions, as well as the voice of the "other."

8.1.7. Community and Tradition

All interpreters evaluate experiences within the context of their own traditions.[79] We "stand always within tradition . . . It is always a part of us."[80] These traditions, or communities, are key to understanding.[81] The tradition of an interpreter should "be raised to consciousness in order to 'monitor' the way it deals with texts or [other] traditions."[82] Gadamer's perspective calls for a "heightening of reflection."[83] Our own tradition is not just a filter that we use to see the world, but it is, in fact, who or what we are.[84] This understanding in community is in contrast to "the individual-centered rationalism of Descartes."[85] For Gadamer, the possibility of understanding is a move from private isolation "into a community or tradition of understanding."[86] The situatedness in community and its corresponding tools will help "determine the proper boundaries of interpretation."[87] Authentic interpretation even "presupposes participation . . . in community."[88] Scripture itself displays a communal focus, as

78. Gadamer, *Truth and Method*, 17.

79. See Fowl, "Effective History," 156; cf. Weinsheimer, *Philosophical Hermeneutics*, 38–39.

80. Gadamer, *Truth and Method*, 250.

81. See Thiselton, *Hermeneutics*, 18, 135; cf. Warnke, *Inheriting Gadamer*, 4; Hovey and Olsen, *Hermeneutics of Tradition*, xi; see also p. 103 above with the "Sociological Approach" to biblical interpretation.

82. Grondin, *Philosophical Hermeneutics*, 113–14.

83. See Grondin, *Philosophical Hermeneutics*, 115.

84. See Porter and Robinson, *Hermeneutics*, 88.

85. See Thiselton, *Hermeneutics of Doctrine*, xvii; in fact, "the very possibility of expressing *cogito ergo sum* depends upon the existence of, and participation in, a community of language users" (Selby, *Comical Doctrine*, 37).

86. See Adams, *Oxford Handbook of Theology*, 512.

87. Brown, *Scripture as Communication*, 68; cf. Thiselton, *Hermeneutics of Doctrine*, 91, 97; Selby, *Comical Doctrine*, 37, 39–40; Also, a community can serve as a "major checkpoint to help us prevent uncontrolled speculation" (see Carson, "Recent Developments," 18).

88. See Hays, *Conversion of the Imagination*, 49n42; cf. Marshall, *New Testament Theology*, 46.

"the New Testament leaves no doubt about the major role of community in interpretation."[89]

However, while some emphasize these positive facets of communal interpretation, others highlight the negative aspect of being in a confining location, for the interpreter in a specific community can only perceive and evaluate from that particular perspective.[90] Some lament that every interpretive community does what is right in their own eyes.[91] The reflection and monitoring concerning one's tradition can never be completely carried out, since we are inescapably situated in a tradition, and "any methodological distanciation we might undertake will itself always be situated and tradition laden."[92] Thus, a careful interpreter will need to be aware of any "ideological prejudices" that come from being a part of a tradition/community.[93]

8.1.8. LDS Hermeneutics: Community and Tradition

The Utah-based LDS community is well known for its unity and communal identity. The entire LDS "cosmology and philosophical anthropology" is "social or relational."[94] There is a "strong communal sentiment . . . reinforced by doctrines contained in [Joseph Smith's] . . . revelations and by deliberate church policy."[95] There is a "strong emphasis on communal

---

89. Moritz, "Scripture and Theological Exegesis," 130. Among the many specific NT examples of community, we note the church as the household of God and as a holy nation (1 Pet 2:4–9) (see Westphal, *Whose Community?*, 124). We also observe the vine and the branches (John 15), the sheep and the flock (John 10), the remnant (Rom 9:27), and God's field, building, and temple (1 Cor 3:9–17). Additionally, the book of Hebrews describes the pilgrim people of God (see Thiselton, *Hermeneutics of Doctrine*, 482, 497).

90. See Westphal, *Whose Community?*, 71.

91. See Vanhoozer, "Theological Interpretation," 15.

92. Mootz and Taylor, *Gadamer and Ricoeur*, 47.

93. McLean, *Biblical Interpretation*, 308. In addition, Jürgen Habermas criticized Gadamer for his overly optimistic views on tradition (see Habermas, *On the Logic*, 169; cf. Dostal, *Cambridge Companion to Gadamer*, 27). For Habermas, tradition was a "possible carrier of ideology" (see McLean, *Biblical Interpretation*, 213). For another perspective on potential problems with "community-driven interpretation" see Shannon, "His Community," 421.

94. Davies, *Mormon Culture*, 156.

95. Dean L. May, in Eliason, *Mormons & Mormonism*, 53.

solidarity."[96] LDS author Grant Underwood even recognizes "a communal quality to interpretation."[97] As a recapitulation of the biblical narrative, we have noted that the LDS itself plays a major role in interpretation.

What matters for our purposes, is a dual recognition that (1) LDS
claims an important role in the interpretive process for the modern community even while disagreeing on the legitimacy of prior generations,
and (2) whereas other Christian traditions claim to be firmly rooted in
the ancient text,[98] the concomitant mooring in the text by the LDS is at
best, much more selective. Be that as it may, it is noteworthy how LDS
considers the modern community to play a hermeneutically crucial role.

However, the hermeneutical filter of "systemic parameters" becomes
an unwieldy hegemony of privileged discourse. Institutional outlooks
actuate biblical interpretation. In addition, the sociological interpretations of the LDS result in their separation from the parent community.
The role of the "other"—i.e., a voice from outside of the community—is
diminished. Separation was deemed necessary, and, in effect, the voice
of the parent community was muffled. Furthermore, since the LDS is the
presumed continuation of the biblical narrative, this holds implications
for other Christian communities who claim the Bible as their own. Since
the perceived institutional needs of the LDS drive much of their use of
the Bible, this warrants scrutiny.

Given what we have seen about the epistemological oneness between the Prophet and God (the equation of the "mind of God" seamlessly with the LDS president), another concern is with the apparent
"'monological self-certainty' of an isolated interpreter."[99] Concomitantly,
on account of the primacy of personal and prophetic interpretation, and
notwithstanding *claims* of communal solidarity, little room is left for the
LDS community in interpretation. In addition, the "historically effected
consciousness"[100] of the LDS interpreter would be negatively influenced
by the doctrine of the Great Apostasy. In sum, the LDS speaks consistently of communal solidarity, and may even justify their hermeneutical actions and attitudes by citing similar features of other Christian

96. Jospe et al., *Covenant and Chosenness*, 12.

97. Underwood, "More than an Index," 118.

98. See Vanhoozer, "Theological Interpretation," 24; Green, *Practicing Theological
Interpretation*, 22; Treier, *Theological Interpretation*, 15, 32.

99. See McLean, *Biblical Interpretation*, 223.

100. The German phrase is *Wirkungsgeschichtliches Bewusstsein* (see Dunn, *Jesus
Remembered*, 121; cf. McLean, *Biblical Interpretation*, 181).

traditions. However, in the end, the lack of dialogue and openness with other traditions, especially other Christian communities in the past, as well as their focus on individualistic interpretation, demonstrates more of a privatizing of biblical interpretation—in harmony only with their own modern worldview and perspective.

8.1.9. Gadamer and Application as Part of Interpretation

Gadamer's concept of application is not a delayed step that follows interpretation, for he "regularly insists that application is an essential part of interpretation and not a subsequent and different activity."[101] He perceived "application to be an essential ingredient in the process of understanding."[102] True understanding implies personal involvement—"We always take ourselves along when we understand."[103] Understanding happens in the context of experience. Gadamer discusses this notion of experience as not only an immediacy of, but also the lasting result of, understanding.[104] Every interpreter can be likened to a performer in the symphony who is not mechanically reproducing the musical score, but who completely understands the score by performing it. True understanding entails not only reproduction but production as well, i.e., the performance/application by the interpreter. Thus, reading with understanding requires reproduction, performance, and application.[105] Perspectives within Critical Realism are similar, for CR is not only "intensely empirical," but also "acknowledges the primacy of performance."[106] When application is included as a part of interpretation, meaning becomes concrete, and specific weight is given to abstract language.

101. Mootz and Taylor, *Gadamer and Ricoeur*, 48.

102. See Stroup, *Narrative Theology*, 207.

103. Grondin, *Philosophical Hermeneutics*, 115; cf. 61.

104. See Gadamer, *Truth and Method*, 55–56, 60.

105. Gadamer, *Truth and Method*, 118–27; cf. Westphal, *Whose Community?*, 62, 78, 98, 110; Weinsheimer, *Philosophical Hermeneutics*, 119–20; Selby, *Comical Doctrine*, 79; Brown, *Scripture as Communication*, 26, 95, 117, 233, 250; Nathan, "Truth and Prejudice," 297; Furthermore, "we are not passive describers but engaged performers" (Zabala, "Anarchy of Hermeneutics," 76). Besides "application," the process could also be referred to as "contextualization" (Brown, *Scripture as Communication*, 117), or even "perlocutionary notion of transformation" (Moritz, "Scripture and Theological Exegesis," 136).

106. Meyer, *Critical Realism*, x.

In today's academic climate, we hesitate to concern ourselves exclusively with the ancient context of biblical texts, thereby sidelining the role of the modern, situated interpreter. An exclusive concern on the ancient context reflects an outdated historicism that simplistically objectifies textual meaning and is not an adequate interpretive tool. We recognize the need to venture beyond the "ancient meaning." This is the case especially since biblical studies over the past century have "almost exclusively concerned itself with the 'founding-sense event' of texts."[107] *Applying* the text will allow a move beyond this "founding-sense event" to a "present-sense event." When this occurs, "the interpretive act becomes complete."[108]

8.1.10. LDS Hermeneutics: Application as Part of Interpretation

In matters of application, the pragmatic focus of the LDS comes to the forefront. According to Alan Goff, the scriptures were written specifically for application purposes.[109] The "real value of scripture" is changed lives.[110] Obedience is "the first law of heaven" and is "a Mormon mantra."[111] Lowell Bennion, an early LDS leader, maintained that correct interpretation results in application to one's personal life.[112] The church has a tradition of "avoiding theological quagmires" and of "being a practical" religion, because "people are more important than dogmas."[113] Although education and the intellectual life have their merits, "when contrasted with spiritual endowments, they are of but slight and passing worth."[114] What the LDS member should strive for is "a Ph.D. in faith and righteousness."[115] Ian Barber describes this concept as "LDS doctrine represent[ing] a process rather than a single event."[116] According to Faulconer, "religion is primarily a matter of practice rather than propositional belief." These beliefs are

---

107. McLean, *Biblical Interpretation*, 2.

108. McLean, *Biblical Interpretation*, 2.

109. Goff, "How Should We Then Read?," 139.

110. Gardner, "I Do Not Think That Word Means," 50.

111. Givens, *Wrestling the Angel*, 308.

112. See Barlow, *Mormons and the Bible*, 222.

113. Bailey, "Mormons and the Omnis," 38.

114. McConkie, in Millet, *Getting at the Truth*, 42.

115. McConkie, in Millet, *Getting at the Truth*, 42.

116. Barber, "Literalist Constraint," 24; cf. Alexander, "Reconstruction," 24–33.

still "relevant and important," although "only in terms of the practices of which they are part."[117]

"Bearing a testimony" on the truthfulness of church doctrine is a specific manifestation of their emphasis on application. The verbalization of the faith illustrates their personal involvement in the understanding process. For example, "through revelation we can obtain a testimony of Jesus Christ and receive direction from God."[118] Joseph Smith modeled this "testimony-bearing" behavior in his King Follett Discourse, with the bold statement of "I know that my testimony is true."[119] Millet admits that, although the plates from which the BoM were translated are not accessible today, LDS members should still "bear testimony of verities," including the truthfulness of the BoM.[120]

In matters of application, however, a fundamental aspect for the understanding of LDS hermeneutics is a privileging of the "present-sense event" at the expense of the "founding-sense event."[121] Given their focus on "likening the scriptures," the overriding concern is to move directly from the scriptures to their own context/horizon. The ancient horizon of the scriptures is neglected. The LDS quest for application displaces textual interpretation. Interpretation should be characterized by a merging of the ancient and modern horizons. The pragmatic focus of the LDS exaggerates the importance of application as regards the biblical text.

Nonetheless, for some decades, there has been an emphasis in biblical scholarship on recognizing the "intense involvement of the reader in the process of interpreting Scripture."[122] Many mainstream Christian traditions posit a crucial role for analogy in the pursuit of application, and this is seen in the common tendency to compare the community or oneself to Bible characters. For example, an analogy is found in a biblical reference, and then applied to one's life—the tribulations of Paul,

117. Faulconer, "Dialogue on Theology," 475; cf. Faulconer, "Are Mormons Christians?"

118. LDS, *New Testament Seminary*, 72.

119. Smith, "King Follett"; cf. Ostling and Ostling, *Mormon America*, 400. We noted earlier in chapter 2 the testimony meetings that occur on the first Sunday of the month for LDS members, when they "bear a testimony": "I *know* Christ lives"; "I *know* Joseph Smith was a prophet of God"; "I *know* the church is true" (Givens, *People of Paradox*, 26).

120. Millet, *Getting at the Truth*, 36–37.

121. Again, these terms come from McLean. See McLean, *Biblical Interpretation*, 2.

122. Silva, in Kaiser and Silva, *Biblical Hermeneutics*, 289.

Abraham, or Noah are used as inspiration to persevere, and the patience of Job is used as an exemplary example. In this manner, a transfer from ancient realities to modern contexts is attempted. Ironically, despite varying commitments to the sacredness of the text, these traditions often end up locating the transfer from ancient to modern in homiletics, not hermeneutics. We saw in chapter 1 that "the overwhelming majority" of LDS publications "is homiletic and is meant to inspire and motivate its audience rather than provide them with careful conceptual analysis."[123] One wonders how the approach to application compares with such "analogizing" that merely inspires. In some Christian circles, analogizing often supplants interpretation. Therefore, as mentioned in the introduction, the LDS is not the only tradition that has tendencies to neglect the ancient horizon.

One wonders if LDS authors sufficiently reflect on the significance of the doctrines and beliefs that Faulconer deemed "relevant and important."[124] For, on the one hand, they speak of "Mormonism's freedom from the obsession in traditional theology for system building and logical completeness."[125] Yet, on the other hand, authors such as Faulconer, Webb, Millet, and others, inescapably find themselves expressing "doctrinal" claims, with a view to informing the kind of orthopraxis that the church mandates. This holds, despite Faulconer's claim that they are "more interested in orthopraxy than orthodoxy."[126] He is, in fact, more interested in "orthodoxy" than his words imply. Such interest is, however, despite the LDS focus on application concerns.

From what we have seen, application for the LDS is not a separate step that follows the act of interpretation. If anything, application is wrapped into the process of "interpretation." We recognize this serious intent in applying the text. Their use of the Bible here is potentially compatible with Gadamerian insights. It is possible that mainstream authors who agree with Gadamer's combination of application and interpretation could afford the LDS the benefit of the doubt here. However, as we have seen, the LDS shows little interest in utilizing these insights of Gadamer.

To summarize, the LDS advances directly to the "likening" of the Scriptures to themselves and tends to neglect the interpretation of the

123. Oman, "Living Oracles," 2.

124. Faulconer, "Dialogue on Theology," 475.

125. Webb, *Mormon Christianity*, 213.

126. Faulconer, "Are Mormons Christians?"

biblical text in reference to its ancient horizon. By doing so, they overgeneralize the complexity of the hermeneutical process. This raises the question whether it is possible to honor the deep concern for contemporary contextualization while at the same time respecting the textual horizons of the scriptures. Therefore, the "application hermeneutics" of the LDS does not appear to be compatible with the accepted parameters of hermeneutical scholarship, perhaps by design. It has been the contention of this study, therefore, that because of this lack of engagement with various hermeneutical insights, the LDS perspective warrants scrutiny.

8.1.11. Artistic Aspect: "Method vs. Art"

Gadamer saw the necessity of going *beyond* method to see the text as art.[127] Other authors assert that interpretation is more art than science. Schleiermacher, for instance, believed that interpretation required the skill of a loving craftsman. He argued that interpretation could not be reduced to a certain fixed technique to be "followed mechanically to achieve objective results."[128] Gadamer spoke of the transformation that art often brings to the person experiencing it, in much the same way that texts can impact an interpreter.[129] Indeed, art is "something that occurs to us as an event of being,"[130] that even "suddenly takes the person experiencing it out of the context of his life."[131] This resonates with Critical Realism's view of the apprehension of meaning through our own perspectives and experiences.[132] An artistic approach allows interpretation to develop slowly through experience and concentrated reflection, as opposed to a programmed, "scientific" methodology.

8.1.12. LDS Hermeneutics: "Method vs. Art"

The LDS would likely concur with these insights, as we intimated above in our discussion concerning ontology and interpretation. In LDS thinking,

127. See Westphal, *Whose Community?*, 82, 87.

128. See McLean, *Biblical Interpretation*, 44.

129. See Gadamer, *Truth and Method*, 119–27.

130. Porter and Robinson, *Hermeneutics*, 93.

131. Gadamer, *Truth and Method*, 63.

132. See Westphal, *Whose Community?*, 18; cf. Wright, *People of God*, 35; Moritz, "Critical Realism," 147.

reason and logical thinking tend to be rejected in favor of experiential knowledge. Their view of access to knowledge may reflect an artistic epistemology. This holds the potential for overlap between their hermeneutics and Gadamerian thinking. However, many of the hermeneutical examples we have seen exhibit more a methodological maneuvering than an artistic interpretation. For instance, we noted literalistic interpretations; allegorizations; perceived institutional needs; clarification and restoration through emendation; the elevation of Joseph Smith through re-authoring, and even "systemic parameters." These tendencies work against attempts to defend on intellectual grounds any artistic approach to interpretation by the LDS.

8.1.13. Critical Realism (CR)

Throughout our investigation, Critical Realism has been a helpful guide since we are subjectivity-located interpreters, influenced by traditions and often with unnoticed presuppositions. The "locatedness" of modern interpreters does not annul the possibility of the correct interpretation of ancient texts, and "this limitation is not a fate to be outwitted and escaped, but [it reflects] the simple fact that we are human and not divine."[133] As we saw, the grid, or lens, through which reality is viewed is not necessarily unfavorable, as the ability to be subjective affords us the opportunity to be relevant.[134] Here we note that Gadamerian concepts of ontology, application and performance merge well with a Critical Realist perspective on the existence of an empirical world, combined with its sense of the "critical" subjectivity of interpreters located in that world.

Thus far in this chapter, we have investigated the perspectives in philosophical hermeneutics on the inescapability of interpretation, awareness in the interpretation process, ontological matters, presuppositions in the interpretive process, a communal emphasis, and application notions. We have compared these to LDS distinctives and have observed *some* overlap between philosophical hermeneutics and the LDS, producing an initial, seeming correspondence between the two perspectives. However, there are significant differences as well. Insufficient attention is paid by LDS interpreters to the influence of traditions, horizons, worldviews,

---

133. Mootz and Taylor, *Gadamer and Ricoeur*, 48–49.

134. Wright, *People of God*, 44–46; cf. Moritz, "Critical Realism," 147, 149; Meyer, *Critical Realism*, xiii.

and self-understandings. This occurs because of the overriding presence of LDS assumptions and perspectives that impede the fusion between ancient and modern horizons. Examples of such LDS assumptions and perspectives include continuing revelation, pragmatism, and perceived institutional needs. Additional aspects of philosophical hermeneutics will corroborate these conclusions.

8.1.14. The Implied Author and Reader

In the course of writing a text, authors create an implied version of themselves.[135] As a careful reader studies the text, the implied author (IA) becomes a reconstructed inference from the text.[136] An IA is discernable from the text,[137] and is an "ideal, literary, created version" of the empirical author.[138] In fact, the IA is "that singular consciousness which the reader constructs from the words of the text; a consciousness which knows the story backward and forward . . . the static, overarching view of a text that a reader might develop from multiple readings."[139]

The implied reader (IR) is the textually constructed reader "presupposed" by the text.[140] The IR is being actively influenced by the IA—who insists through the content of the text that the reader take a certain point of view.[141] A serious consideration of the text will influence the reader. A conscientious reader will be open to persuasion "rather than be critically distanced."[142] As readers are affected by the text, they are inevitably involved in the production of meaning. Careful readers become "a part of the narrative as they unfold its meaning."[143] The IR "responds to the narratological movement" of the text and helps determine the meaning

---

135. Booth, *Rhetoric of Fiction*, 70. Authors are not necessarily aware of this creation.

136. Westphal, in Porter and Stovell, *Hermeneutics*, 169–70; cf. Chatman, *Story and Discourse*, 148; Powell, *Narrative Criticism*, 5.

137. Brown, *Scripture as Communication*, 42; cf. Powell, *Narrative Criticism*, 5.

138. Booth, *Rhetoric of Fiction*, 74–75.

139. Robbins, "Social Location," 311.

140. See Brown, *Scripture as Communication*, 40; cf. Powell, *Narrative Criticism*, 15; Chatman, *Story and Discourse*, 149–50.

141. Powell, *Narrative Criticism*, 23.

142. Young, "Pastoral Epistles," 111.

143. See Porter and Robinson, *Hermeneutics*, 284.

of the text by actualizing it in concrete form.[144] The meaning of the text, then, is found in the dialectic and conversation between the IA and the IR that is embodied in the text. When we, as ideal readers, focus intently on the text itself to discover the implied author's performative aims, our modern stories intertwine with the ancient stories.

8.1.15. LDS Hermeneutics: Role of the Implied Author and Reader

At the outset, these concepts such as involvement "in the production of meaning," or becoming "a part of the narrative," seem to resonate with LDS thinking. Upon closer look, however, the resonance fades. For example, a justifiably held view by many in the hermeneutical community is that the IR is a function of the text itself, and that the IR becomes a part of the narrative only to the degree that the interpretation remains tethered to the text. Yet, within much of LDS hermeneutics, this anchoring to the text is fragile and tenuous. Since the IA is discovered through an investigation of the text itself, this has little appeal for the LDS interpreter—especially if such an "academic" exercise would prevent them from pursuing their "hermeneutics of practice." Is LDS hermeneutics capable of embracing the concepts of the IA and the IR? Given their desire for a "likening the scriptures" to themselves—it appears to be so. However, instead of an interpreter focusing on the text to aid in the reconstruction of implied realities of the text, LDS interpretations tend to supplant the implied audience with their own community. We have witnessed this in numerous instances. At the outset of this chapter, I proposed that insights of philosophical hermeneutics could help explain what we have seen in this investigation. The sustained focus on the text, evinced in the concepts of the IA and the IR, is not a concern for the LDS.

8.2. Location of Meaning

8.2.1. Hermeneutical Geography

Traditionally, the interpretive process is discussed with reference to three hermeneutical ("geographical") locations: author, text, and reader.[145] We

---

144. Powell, *Narrative Criticism*, 16.

145. See Brown, *Scripture as Communication*, 14, 27; Treier, *Theological Interpretation*, 135; Porter and Stovell, in *Hermeneutics*, 12.

will briefly investigate only the latter two locations.[146] By attending to these varied locations in the geographical landscape of hermeneutics, the interpreter is better able to avoid one-sided, simplistic interpretations, and is alerted to particular vistas on the circuitous journey of the interpretive process. An interpretation has a greater likelihood of plausibility when it accounts for as many geographical components as possible. This is a highly significant notion for our evaluative investigation: any interpretation, LDS or otherwise, will be more likely to be correct if it is able to comprehensively utilize these locations of hermeneutical geography.

8.2.2. The Reader

As we have seen in the discussion of the implied reader, there is a current preoccupation with the "reemployment of the reader," for the reader is no longer irrelevant.[147] Umberto Eco speaks of "model readers," that guard against "too easily colonizing or objectifying the text."[148] Textual communication occurs as "readers play a part in the realization of meaning" since the text only possesses potentiality until the reader actualizes it.[149] Part of this actualization is the entering of the reader into the projected world of the text—experiencing the text as it was intended.[150] Such a comprehensive experience typifies "fully hooked readers."[151]

However, some postmodern strategies over-emphasize these components, by shifting the interpretive weight too far in the direction of the reader.[152] Others excessively underscore this activity when readers control the text.[153] The text, at times, is reduced to a lifeless object, like a "cadaver handed over for autopsy."[154] Wright calls this naïve real-

---

146. For important discussions surrounding the biblical *author's* context, see Brown, *Scripture as Communication*, 281–82; Wright, *Scripture*, 128–29; Hughes, "Truth of Scripture," 175.

147. Resseguie, *Narrative Criticism*, 32–33.

148. See Green, *Practicing Theological Interpretation*, 20.

149. See Thiselton, *Hermeneutics*, 97–98, 306.

150. See Brown, *Scripture as Communication*, 50–51.

151. Booth, "Resurrection of the Implied Author," 86.

152. See Moritz, "Mark," 41.

153. As can be observed in Deconstructionism (Derrida), or with dominating interpretive communities (Fish) (see Powell, *Narrative Criticism*, 16; cf. Resseguie, *Narrative Criticism*, 30).

154. See these notions of Paul Ricoeur in Porter and Stovell, *Hermeneutics*, 81.

ism, where there is no event, no author, and not even a text: the reader
interprets, and the whole process deconstructs into the feelings and
thoughts of the reader.[155]

At the same time, there are positive aspects to a focus on the reader,
since the subjectivity of the empirical interpreter is to be welcomed "as
an aspect of human creationality."[156] If the perception of truth were not a
subjective process, it would be impossible to demonstrate the relevance
of truth.[157] Gadamer sees "the structure of our experiences of understanding as an event in which we participate."[158]

8.2.3. LDS Hermeneutics: The Reader

Undoubtedly, LDS authors would agree with many of these concepts.
James McLachlan, an LDS author, writes: "the message always comes
through the filter of human understanding."[159] However, the conclusions detailed earlier hold here as well—individualistic interpretation of
"likening the Scriptures to themselves" engenders a strong possibility of
masking the ontological realism of the biblical text. The conceptuality
embodied in the text is obscured with the confined subjectivity of the individual LDS interpreter. In addition, the use of hermeneutical language
as it concerns the Prophet makes it appear as if they are dealing with
interpretive matters. However, the LDS Prophet is simply using locutions
to affirm his perspective. Often, he is announcing entirely new declarations that have no referentiality to the biblical text. The prophetic voice
is not interpretive but exhibits a re-authoring of the biblical text. I have
noted this with examples such as the "Melchizedek priesthood," or the
use of "line by line" of Isa 28:10. I have referenced a number of times the
conclusion that texts have "a *prima facie* claim on the reader, namely, to

Also note the danger of the use of the historical-critical method placing "the interpreter above Scripture" (see Gaffin, in Porter and Stovell, *Hermeneutics*, 181).

155. Wright, *People of God*, 59.

156. Moritz, "Critical Realism," 149.

157. See Treier, *Theological Interpretation*, 152.

158. Porter and Robinson, *Hermeneutics*, 86; cf. Thiselton, *New Horizons*, 316.
Also note the idea of "live encounters [in] a given reading experience" (Booth, *Company We Keep*, 169).

159. James McLachlan, in Paulsen and Musser, *Mormonism in Dialogue*, 209.
Barber mentions problems in denying human agency in the process of interpretation
(Barber, "Literalist Constraint," 21–22).

be construed in accord with its intended sense."[160] When the prophet, as a reader, makes a theological declaration supposedly based on a biblical text, but in reality not moored to the text, one wonders to what extent LDS hermeneutics respects the rights of texts.

8.2.4. *Philosophical and LDS Hermeneutics: The Text Itself*

Gadamer insisted that "all correct interpretation" would "direct its gaze" on the text.[161] If the content of the text is ignored, it is more likely that it will be abused by the "located" interpreter.[162] We have noted several ways to focus on the text. For instance, a reader can demonstrate respect for the text as "other," acknowledge the ontological realism of the text, investigate the intended sense of the text, as well as explore the intention of the implied author.

While the LDS Church does, in fact, look to the biblical text, it does so inconsistently. We noted the randomness in chapter 3 with their selective literalism. We also saw the use of isolated phrases and words that highlight the promotion of the institution through re-authoring. Overall, the five uses of the Bible demonstrate a neglect of a textual focus. Instead, attention is centered on the modern institution. Additionally, as Davies and Madsen put it, "(a)bove the authority of the written record stands the authority of the living prophet."[163] An *in the text* focus is overshadowed by the modern LDS prophet. In fact, given the LDS lack of engagement with hermeneutical realities such as self-awareness, locatedness, and self-interest as it relates to the living Prophet, LDS interpretation yields several questionable hermeneutical implications. For instance, since the living voice of the prophet needs to be interpreted, it is certainly possible that this voice leads to *less* understanding than textual interpretation. The displacement of the text by the living voice does not solve the problem of interpretation. The LDS might respond that the living voice is an empirical reality to which they have access. However, in biblical interpretation, the living voice still needs to reconstruct the implied world of the ancient text. Yet, this voice does not appear interested in doing this. Thus, the

---

160. See Meyer, *Critical Realism*, xi, 17.
161. Gadamer, *Truth and Method*, 236.
162. Dunn, *Jesus Remembered*, 114.
163. Davies and Madsen, "Scriptures," 1278.

preoccupation of the LDS with *modern realities*, i.e., the interpreter, ends up subverting the empirical realities of the *ancient text*.

Earlier, we queried whether it is possible to honor the deep concern for contemporary contextualization while at the same time respecting the textual horizons of the scriptures. By attending to as many hermeneutical locations of the text as possible, the interpreter significantly increases the likelihood of not only (1) honoring this deep concern for contemporary contextualization and the textual horizons of the scriptures, but also (2) plausible interpretation of the meaning *in the text*, and the transformative power of the text in the life of the interpreter.[164] To the extent that we attend to the various hermeneutical locations, we can more successfully avoid a distorted, myopic self-interest. However, the LDS does not appear to execute in a hermeneutically sound way and does not appear interested in these geographical locations.

8.3. Methodological Possibility

8.3.1. Philosophical Hermeneutics: Method

Our investigation of philosophical questions and issues—such as ontology and presuppositions, and the exploration of location of meaning issues within hermeneutical geography—has alerted us to some very useful methodological tools. In fact, *some* type of methodology needs to be in place to combat the tendencies toward self-deception and self-interest.[165] We noted in the first chapter the need for methodological *parameters* to investigate another religious system. An "appropriate method is not ruled out," for it is not "Truth *or* Method."[166] Wright mentions the need for "proper tools."[167] Others describe a "theory of rules;"[168] a "framework of interpretation;"[169] the need for an eclectic model;[170] a "general body of

---

164. See Porter and Stovell, *Hermeneutics*, 201–5.

165. However, we acknowledge that any method will unavoidably reflect pre-understandings, as well as cultural and temporal embeddedness (see Porter, "Biblical Hermeneutics," 49).

166. Selby, *Comical Doctrine*, 146; cf. Gadamer, "On the Scope and Function," 84.

167. Wright, *Scripture*, 120; cf. Wright, *People of God*, 96.

168. Paul Ricoeur, in Palmer, *Hermeneutics*, 43.

169. Shipps, *Mormonism*, xi.

170. See Brown, *Scripture as Communication*, 31.

methodological principles;"[171] or a systematic and careful methodology.[172] Even nineteenth-century Mormon apologist Parley Pratt advocated for the use of a definite, infallible rule of interpretation.[173] One final methodological approach will give us another lens from which to evaluate LDS hermeneutics: a storied (narratival) hermeneutic.

8.3.2. Storied (Narratival) Hermeneutic

An important element in interpretation is the narratival dimension of engaging a text. This draws attention to the storied background that every individual possesses. We use narratival foundations to navigate the complex environments we find ourselves in daily. We interpret stories, words and events in light of "all sorts of other stories that we habitually carry about with us."[174] We have a unifying web of stories that allow us to make sense of the events, texts and interactions surrounding us.[175] We possess "deep-level human perceptions of reality" that consist of our own stories and through which we view all events and texts we encounter.[176] When we read the biblical text, then, there is a transformation as the careful interpreter is drawn into the story projected by the text.[177] Wright reminds his readers, "interpretation is storied and relational."[178] Even propositional knowledge does not exist in a vacuum, but is infused with foundational narratives. Indeed, all communication is narratival, given that the process assumes the reality of often-unnoticed interlocking stories.[179] Subjective interpreters, according to Critical Realism, can assume that there is an objective reality. In a narratival hermeneutic, we see our subjectivity allowing our storied background to engage with the biblical

---

171. So say adherents of the tradition of Schleiermacher and Dilthey (see Palmer, *Hermeneutics*, 46).

172. See Klein, *Biblical Interpretation*, 86. Also, it is argued that "everyone relies on some type of method to learn anything" (Van Gelder, "Method in Light of Scriptures," 44).

173. Pratt, *Voice of Warning*, 1.

174. Wright, *People of God*, 66.

175. See Moritz, "Scripture and Theological Exegesis," 126.

176. See Wright, *People of God*, 123.

177. Moritz, "Scripture and Theological Exegesis," 138.

178. See Moritz, "Critical but Real," 185.

179. See Thiselton, *Hermeneutics*, 236–43.

narrative for a transformative, "story-changing" result.[180] In fact, Critical Realism "succeeds better than alternative approaches in accounting for the storied nature of our universe, [as it] presents us with the best opportunity to renew our understanding of history, literature and theology."[181]

8.3.3. LDS Narratival Hermeneutics

LDS interpreters would assuredly welcome a narratival focus related to biblical interpretation, since, again, they view their own community as the continuation of the biblical narrative, not only as the restoration of the New Testament, but also of the Old Testament. Because of these perspectives, it is at least theoretically possible that they have found fresh points of entry into the ancient texts. This possibility gains traction precisely because they claim to "liken the Scripture to themselves." Also, the transformative nature of narrative should find consonance with the LDS focus on a hermeneutics of praxis. In short, a narratival focus would seem to add some legitimacy to LDS interpretation.

However, given the complex and varied assumptions needed to sustain the focus on the community embodying the biblical narrative, it appears that their hermeneutical practice does not actually fulfill that promise. This communal concept illustrates one of the significant sociological factors that account for the apparent inconsistencies in their interpretive methods. The hermeneutical issue is not that they see themselves as being in continuity with the biblical narrative, something that is true of most Christian traditions. Rather, the problem is that the LDS goes beyond this by "discovering" themselves in the biblical narrative. Their understanding of being narratival consists of simply finding themselves in the text. In other words, they import referentiality—the text refers to them. *They* claim to be the embodiment of the narratival biblical movement, when in contrast, one should be arguing that narratival hermeneutics allows the text to stand within its own narratival context, being interpreted and respected only within this context.

---

180. Moritz, "Critical Realism," 149. However, Critical Realism insists that the authorial intentionality of the IA, as an external reality, must be the controlling factor in interpretation. Again, determinate meaning exists, "even if it is not objectively accessible" (Moritz, "Critical Realism," 149; cf. Wright, *People of God*, 44–46; Moritz, "Scripture and Theological Exegesis," 136–37).

181. Moritz, "Critical but Real," 174.

8.4. Conclusion: Interpretive Practice of the LDS

In this book, my intention has been to present LDS hermeneutics as a worthwhile object of study. Even to the extent that it is impossible to articulate "one, satisfactory" LDS hermeneutic, I have proposed tentative, yet synchronic and heuristic depictions. Throughout this process, I have utilized Critical Realism as a framework to direct us, one that does justice to the relationship between objectivity and subjectivity. I acknowledge that we are subjective interpreters who assume there is an objective reality. Our pre-understandings are transformed by the objective reality of the biblical text, and we are transformed as we "perform" the text. We have also been assisted by the insights of Hans-Georg Gadamer.

We noted overlap in our five categories and have acknowledged that numerous LDS texts can rightly be cited in more than one of these categories. We also noted the impossibility of comprehensively categorizing any tradition's hermeneutics, given the artistic aspect of interpretation. Nonetheless, a focus on general hermeneutical advances, especially those elucidated by Gadamer, such as the inescapability of interpretation, the concepts of ontology, presuppositions, community, and application, assisted us in the examination of the five uses of the Bible by the LDS. Additionally, our investigation benefited from the perspectives garnered from the "geographical" locations of meaning, as well as the methodological framework of narratival hermeneutics. Based on the evaluation of the five categories—literal, allegorical, sociological and emendatory, and "re-authoring"—I have investigated the hermeneutical plausibility of the uses of the Bible by the LDS.

After surveying the LDS asymmetrical viewpoint regarding the Bible, we noted the importance of continuing revelation, manifested specifically in personal and prophetic revelation and interpretation. Several literalistic interpretations emerged that ignored the illocutionary intent of the ancient biblical author. Allegorizations performed by the LDS imported a modern historical referent into biblical narratives. Their sociological interpretations highlighted institutional needs to justify their separation as a "new-reform movement" from the Christian church affected by the Great Apostasy ("the parent community"). An emendatory approach reflected contemporary adjustments and purported improvements. A re-authoring hermeneutic elevated Joseph Smith, advanced LDS doctrines, and promoted the modern LDS institution. We note with these examples a lack of a merging of the ancient and modern horizons.

We also note that LDS hermeneutics demonstrates a prioritization not to the ancient biblical text, but to the modern LDS institution.

I began this chapter with the question: what potential do the concepts of philosophical hermeneutics have for our evaluation of their hermeneutics? We acknowledged several ways that their hermeneutical practices, at least initially, align themselves with accepted hermeneutical concerns. Examples of such resonance include a respect given to the ancient text evinced in a desire to restore it, an ontological focus on the interpreter, the need to consider the community in the interpretive process, and the important role of narrative, with narratival realities from Scripture reflected in the interpreter's life. However, our final conclusions regarding the uses of the Bible by the LDS cannot overlook significant aspects of their hermeneutics that are hermeneutically implausible.

First, interpretive language is used as a substitute for actual interpretation, most notably in the assertions by Joseph Smith and Brigham Young that they *believed* the Bible, reading it "just as it was" (i.e., literally), in contradistinction to other traditions that held to "interpretations" of the Bible. There is also a consistent claim to avoid the practice of hermeneutics. However, despite the lack of acknowledgement from LDS authors on the need to "practice" hermeneutics,[182] they are nonetheless active in interpretation. As much as this observation seems obvious, it needs to be restated, because the LDS operates under the assumption of being able to avoid discussions concerning the process of understanding biblical texts. Our consideration of accepted conclusions in philosophical hermeneutics is helpful to adequately account for the complexities of biblical interpretation—and for keeping accountable any reading of the Bible, LDS or otherwise. However, precisely because of the lack of hermeneutical reflection inherent in the LDS perspective, it is reasonable to conclude that their use of the Bible largely falls outside of the boundaries of accepted conclusions.

Besides a purported claim to be free of "hermeneutics," our second conclusion regards the individualistic emphasis in LDS personal and prophetic interpretation. This subjective, methodological posture masks the ontological realism of the biblical texts, obscuring the conceptuality embodied in the text. Despite the insistence on a "literal" interpretation,

---

182. Again, LDS author James Siebach considers it problematic "to assume that systemic philosophical thought—even the application of hermeneutical categories— ought to be employed in order to clarify the content of revelation" (Siebach, "Dialogue on Theology," 467).

for example, the illocutionary intent of the implied author is neglected. The JST translation also illustrates this subjectivity, as words are added, changed or deleted according to the limited perspective of Joseph Smith.

Thirdly, interpretive freedom and flexibility is a hallmark of claimed LDS privilege. On the one hand, thorough attention is given to the minutiae of word meanings in Gen 1:1 or Heb 6:1, yet on the other hand, ancient texts exhibit allegorization to validate modern perspectives. We saw that passages are sociologically interpreted to justify a separate existence of the new reform movement, verses are updated to avoid unwelcome interpretation, and phrases and words are re-authored to elevate their founder. Because of such interpretive freedom and flexibility, responsible hermeneutical execution is lacking.

Fourthly, given the LDS propensity to "inspire" and "motivate,"[183] this casts doubt on the LDS ability to execute hermeneutically. Considering the complexity of interpretation, and the impossibility of "just reading" the text, one wonders to what extent LDS interpreters avoid being seduced by self-interest.[184] We all need "outside assistance" to help us see our blind spots,[185] but the LDS Church does not seem interested in this assistance.

Our fifth conclusion centers on the "systemic parameters" of the LDS. The church's hermeneutic claims positional priority over the biblical text. The use of the Bible appears to be a mining of the ancient text not for the interpretation of authorial meaning; nor for a listening to the text as "other"; nor for a validation of the ontological realism of the ancient text; but for the support of a hermeneutic that is centered on the LDS itself. They are quite willing to deploy hermeneutical language and biblical words. Yet they reduce the sum of biblical documents to a single repository of locutions, and such locutions are adjusted—with their referentiality often ignored, sometimes quite willfully. What remains in view, however, is the LDS.

The hermeneutical plausibility of many of the uses of the biblical text by the LDS needs to be questioned. The *de facto* disallowance of hermeneutics is ultimately unsustainable. Rather than acknowledging every interpreter's epistemic relativity as an inevitable and potentially fruitful factor in the interpretation of "the other," it has been used by the LDS as

---

183. Oman, "Living Oracles," 2.

184. See Thiselton, *Hermeneutics*, 5.

185. Brown, *Scripture as Communication*, 123.

a way of turning "the other" into a mirror. Ultimately, the real object of interpretation appears to be the LDS, and not the biblical text. To that extent, LDS hermeneutics reveals more about institutional parameters and motivations than it does about any interpretive commitment to the ancient biblical text. Any modern legitimacy and relevancy must be based on ancient authorial intention. The conclusion, then, of this brief introduction into Mormon hermeneutics: LDS Bible interpretation says more about the modern LDS church than it does the ancient meaning of Scripture. We noted earlier that there has emerged "a type of believer whose only interest in the Bible is what *he gets out of it for himself and his own comfort* . . . His aim is self and his own particular experience . . . In a subtle way it keeps this sort of person *pre-occupied with himself,* instead of being occupied with Christ and God's great and glorious redemptive plan."[186] May all Bible believers honor the ancient *and* modern horizons, live out the biblical text, and be occupied with Christ and God's glorious plan.

186. Allen, in Thiselton, *New Horizons*, 193, emphasis added.

Appendix

Five Categories of Uses of the Bible by the LDS

Literalistic (Chap 3)

1. "If any of you lack wisdom" (Jas 1:5)

2. "The head one of the Gods brought forth the Gods" (Gen 1:1)

3. *Deification:* "participating in the divine nature" (2 Pet 1:4); "heirs" of God (Rom 8:16–17); "we shall be like him" (1 John 3:2); "perfect" (Matt 5:48); "gods" (John 10/Ps 82; John 17)

4. *Divine corporeality:* Gen 1:27, 5:1, 9:6, 18:1f; 32:30, Exod 24:9–10, 31:18, 33:11, Luke 24:39, John 14:9, 2 Cor 4:4, Phil 3:21, 1 John 3:2, Rev 22:4; cf. Isa 6; Exod 33); Jesus as "image of the invisible God" (Col 1:15); in the "form of God" (Phil 2:6); the "express image of the (Father)" (Heb 1:3)

5. *Image of God:* Gen 1:26–27; 5:3

6. *Interpretation with/by Spirit:* 1 Cor 2:10–11; 2 Cor 3:8; 2 Pet 1:20–21

7. *Burning bosom:* Luke 24:32

8. *Guidance to Prophets:* "the Sovereign Lord does nothing without revealing his plan to his servants the prophets" (Amos 3:7; 2 Pet 1:20–21)

9. *Prophetic Interpretation:* 2 Pet 1:19–21; Eph 4:11–16; Acts 6–12

10. *Apostles*: Eph 4:11

11. *Polygamy*: Gen 16:1–11; 29:28; 30:4, 9, 26; Exod 2:21; Num 12:1

12. *"Other" books*: "Book of the Wars of the Lord" (Num 21:14; cf. 1 Cor 5:9, Col 4:16, 2 Chr 16:11; 25:26; 27:7; 32:32; Josh 10:13; 2 Sam 1:18)

13. *Canon*: Deut 4:2; Rev 22:18–19

Allegorization (Chap 4)

1. *Two sticks (BoM and Bible)*: Ezek 37

2. *Sealed book speaking from ground (BoM)*: Isa 29

3. *LDS as "Israel"*: Jer 23:3; 31:8, 9

4. *LDS as NT church*

5. *LDS Church as continuation of biblical narrative*

6. *LDS hermeneutical filter*: "Systemic Parameters"

Sociological Approach (Chap 5)

1. *Continuing revelation*: Matt 16:16, 17; Gal 1:12; 2 Cor 12:1; cf. Gen 22; Gal 3:24; 1 Cor 13:9–10

2. "dispensation of the fulness of times" (Eph 1:10)

3. *Premortal existence*: chosen "before the foundation of the world" (Eph 1:4; cf. 1 John 4:19; Job 38:4, 7; Jer 1:5; Acts 17:29; Rom 8:16; John 9:2)

4. "baptism for the dead" (1 Cor 15:29; Zech 9:11)

5. *Aaronic/Melchizedek priesthood*: Gen 14:18–20; Acts 6:1–6

6. *Coming apostasy becomes Great Apostasy*: Acts 20:29–31; 2 Thess 2:1–5, 7–11; 1 Tim 1:15; 4:1–3, 2 Tim 3:1–7; 3 John 9–10; Jude 17–18; cf. Isa 29:10; Amos 8:11

7. *Angel bringing Gospel*: "And I saw another angel fly in the midst of heaven, having the everlasting gospel to preach unto them that dwell on the earth" (Rev 14:6 KJV)

8. "times of restoration" (Acts 3:20)

Emendatory Practices (Chap 6)

1. "uniformity of the gospel" (Gal 3:8)

2. "without father or mother" (Heb 7:3, explained in Alma 13)

3. "other sheep" (John 10 in 3 Nephi 15:21)

4. *Book of Mormon expansions* (Moroni 7:44–46; 1 Cor 13).

5. *Adam and Eve died "spiritually":* Gen 2:17; D&C 29:41

6. *New Jerusalem in Missouri:* Rev 21:2 in D&C 57:1–3

7. *Universalism:* John 5:28–29

8. *The "gods" of Ps 82:* Book of Abraham 3:22–23

9. *Creation Accounts:* Gen 1, 2 in Book of Moses, PGP

10. *Singleness changed to eternal marriage:* JST of 1 Cor 7:7–8

11. *Discrepancies with number of angels:* Mark 16:3, 4; John 20:12

12. *Number of demoniacs healed:* Matt 8:28, 29; Mark 5:2

13. *Noah repented, not God:* Gen 6:6 (Gen 8:13 JST).

14. *Calvinist" reading changed:* Acts 13:48

15. *Misunderstanding of biblical word:* "elementary principles" (Heb 6:1)

16. "be ye therefore wise *servants,* and as harm-less as doves" (Matt 10:14 JST)

17. *LDS hermeneutical filter:* "Systemic Parameters"

Re-Authoring: Locutionary Reassignment (Chap 7)

1. "the same yesterday, and to day, and for ever" (Heb 13:8 KJV)

2. "Father working out kingdom in fear/ trembling" (Phil 2:12)

3. "Here am I" (Isa 6:8)

4. "Son of Man" (Dan 7:13)

5. "first estate" (Jude 6)

6. "no respecter of persons" (Acts 10:34)

7. *Nephi reinterpreting:* 2 Nephi 26:16; Isa 29

8. "seventy" (Exod 24:1; Luke 10:1)

9. "levels"—three in heaven (1 Cor 15:40–42; 2 Cor 12:2)

10. "sealing" (Matt 16:19; Eph 1:13, 4:30, 2 Cor 1:22)

11. "keys" (Luke 11:52)

12. "Urim and Thummim" (Exod 28:30; Lev 8:8; Num 27:21; Deut 33:8; Ezra 2:63; Neh 7:65)

13. *Seerstone like divination cup:* Gen 44:5

14. "precept upon precept, line upon line" (Isa 28:10).

15. *LDS hermeneutical filter:* "Systemic Parameters"

Bibliography

Abanes, Richard. *One Nation under Gods: A History of the Mormon Church.* New York: Four Walls Eight Windows, 2002.

Abbott, T. K. *The Epistles to the Ephesians and to the Colossians.* ICC. Edinburgh: T. & T. Clark, 1977.

Adams, Nicholas, et al., eds. *The Oxford Handbook of Theology and Modern European Thought.* Oxford: Oxford University Press, 2013.

Ahlstrom, Sydney. *A Religious History of the American People.* 2nd ed. New Haven: Yale University Press, 2004.

Alexander, Joseph Addison. *Commentary on the Prophecies of Isaiah.* Grand Rapids: Zondervan, 1980.

Alexander, Thomas G. *Mormonism in Transition: A History of the Latter-day Saints, 1890–930.* Urbana: University of Illinois Press, 1986.

———. "The Reconstruction of Mormon Doctrine: From Joseph Smith to Progressive Theology." *Sunstone* 5.4 (1980) 24–33.

Alford, Henry. *Alford's Greek Testament: An Exegetical and Critical Commentary.* Vol. 2. Grand Rapids: Guardian, 1976.

Allison, Dale C., Jr. "Eschatology." In *DJG*, edited by Joel B. Green and Scot McKnight, 206–9. Downers Grove, IL: InterVarsity, 1992.

Alter, Robert. *The Art of Biblical Narrative.* New York: Basic, 1981.

———. *The World of Biblical Literature.* New York: Basic, 1992.

Andersen, Francis I., and David Noel Freedman. *Amos: A New Translation with Introduction and Commentary.* AB 24a. New York: Doubleday, 1989.

Anderson, Ross J. "The Virtues of Hard Work and Self-Reliance Rooted in Biblical versus Latter-day Saint Worldviews." *Trinity Journal* 27.1 (2006) 63–75.

Arbaugh, George Bartholomew. *Revelation in Mormonism: Its Character and Changing Forms.* Chicago: University of Chicago Press, 1932.

Archer, Margaret S., et al. *Transcendence: Critical Realism and God.* London: Routledge, 2013.

Arndt, William, et al. *A Greek-English Lexicon of the New Testament and Other Early Christian Literature*. Chicago: University of Chicago Press, 2000.

Arnold, Clinton E. *Ephesians*. ZECNT. Grand Rapids: Zondervan, 2010.

Arrington, Leonard J. *Brigham Young: American Moses*. Urbana: University of Illinois Press, 1986.

Arrington, Leonard J., and Davis Bitton. *The Mormon Experience*. 2nd ed. Urbana: University of Illinois Press, 1992.

Arthur, Christopher E. "Gadamer and Hirsch: The Canonical Work and the Interpreter's Intention." *Cultural Hermeneutics* 4.2 (1976–77) 183–97.

Association for Religious Data. "Church of Jesus Christ of Latter-day Saints." https://www.thearda.com/Denoms/D_1117.asp.

Attridge, Harold W. *The Epistle to the Hebrews*. Hermeneia. Philadelphia: Fortress, 1989.

Bailey, David H. "Mormons and the Omnis: The Dangers of Theological Speculation." *Dialogue* 37.3 (2004) 29–48.

Baker, Jacob T., ed. *Mormonism at the Crossroads of Philosophy and Theology: Essays in Honor of David L. Paulsen*. Salt Lake City: Kofford, 2012.

Baldridge, Kenneth W. "Pearl of Great Price." In *EM*, edited by Daniel H. Ludlow, 1070–72. New York: MacMillan, 1992.

Ballard, Melvin J. *Three Degrees of Glory*. Odgen, UT: Neuteboom, 1922.

Barber, Ian G. "Beyond the Literalist Constraint: Personal Reflections on Mormon Scripture and Religious Interpretation." *Sunstone* 20 (1997) 20–26.

Barker, Kit. "Speech Act Theory, Dual Authorship, and Canonical Hermeneutics: Making Sense of *Sensus Plenior*." *JTI* 3.2 (2009) 227–39.

Barlow, Philip L. "Before Mormonism: Joseph Smith's Use of the Bible, 1820–829." *Journal of the American Academy of Religion* 57.4 (1989) 739–71.

———. *Mormons and the Bible*. Updated ed. Oxford: Oxford University Press, 2013.

Barney, Kevin L. "Examining Six Key Concepts in Joseph Smith's Understanding of Genesis 1:1." *BYU Studies* 39.3 (2000) 107–24.

———. "Joseph Smith's Emendation of Hebrew Genesis 1:1." *Dialogue* 30.4 (1997) 103–35.

———. "Line upon Line." *By Common Consent* (blog). https://bycommonconsent.com/2006/03/11/line–upon–line/.

Barr, James. "Allegory and Historicism." *JSOT* 69 (1996) 105–20.

———. *The Bible in the Modern World*. London: SCM, 1973.

———. "The Literal, the Allegorical, and Modern Biblical Scholarship." *JSOT* 44 (1989) 3–17.

———. *The Semantics of Biblical Language*. 1961. Reprint, Eugene, OR: Wipf & Stock, 2004.

Barrett, C. K. *The Acts of the Apostles: A Critical and Exegetical Commentary*. Vol 1. ICC. Edinburgh: T. & T. Clark, 1994.

Barth, Markus. *Ephesians 1–3*. AB 34. New York: Doubleday, 1967.

Bartholomew, Craig G. "Three Horizons: Hermeneutics from the Other End—An Evaluation of Anthony Thiselton's Hermeneutic Proposals." *European Journal of Theology* 5.2 (1996) 121–35.

Barton, Stephen C. "Social-Scientific Criticism." In *DTIB*, edited by Kevin J. Vanhoozer et al., 753–55. Grand Rapids: Baker Academic, 2005.

Bauckham, Richard J. *2 Peter, Jude*. WBC 50. Dallas: Word, 1998.

Beale, G. K. "Eschatology." In *DLNT*, edited by Ralph P. Martin and Peter H. Davids, 330–45. Downers Grove, IL: InterVarsity, 1997.

————. *A New Testament Biblical Theology: The Unfolding of the Old Testament in the New.* Grand Rapids: Baker Academic, 2011.

Beam, Alex. *American Crucifixion: The Murder of Joseph Smith and the Fate of the Mormon Church.* New York: PublicAffairs, 2014.

Beckwith, Francis J., and Stephen E. Parrish. *The Mormon Concept of God: A Philosophical Analysis.* Lewiston, NY: Mellen, 1991.

Beckwith, Francis J., et al., eds. *The New Mormon Challenge: Responding to the Latest Defenses of a Fast-Growing Movement.* Grand Rapids: Zondervan, 2002.

Bergera, Gary J., ed. *Conflict in the Quorum: Orson Pratt, Brigham Young, Joseph Smith.* Salt Lake City: Signature, 2002.

Berkouwer, G. C. *Man: The Image of God.* Grand Rapids: Eerdmans, 1962.

Best, Ernest. *Ephesians.* Sheffield: Sheffield Academic, 1997.

Biblia Hebraica Stuttgartensia. Edited by Rudolf Kittel et al. Stuttgart: Deutsche Bibelgesellschaft, 1990.

Bietenhard, H. "Beginning, Origin, Rule, Originator." In *NIDNTT*, edited by Colin Brown et al., 1:164–69. Grand Rapids: Zondervan, 1986.

Bigg, Charles. *Epistles of St. Peter and St. Jude.* ICC. Edinburgh: T. & T. Clark, 1956.

Bitton, Davis, ed. *Historical Dictionary of Mormonism.* 2nd ed. Lanham, MD: Scarecrow, 2000.

Bitton, Davis, and Thomas G. Alexander. *The A to Z of Mormonism.* Lanham, MD: Scarecrow, 2009.

Black, Susan Easton, ed. *Expressions of Faith: Testimonies of Latter-day Saint Scholars.* Salt Lake City: Deseret, 1996.

Blenkinsopp, Joseph. *Isaiah 1–39: A New Translation with Introduction and Commentary.* AB 19. New York: Doubleday, 2000.

Blomberg, Craig L. "Historical-Critical/Grammatical Response." In *Biblical Hermeneutics: Five Views,* edited by Stanley E. Porter and Beth M. Stovell, 27–47. Downers Grove, IL: InterVarsity, 2012. Kindle.

Blomberg, Craig L., and Jennifer Foutz Markley. *A Handbook of New Testament Exegesis.* Grand Rapids: Baker, 2010.

Blomberg, Craig L., and Stephen E. Robinson. *How Wide the Divide? A Mormon & an Evangelical in Conversation.* Downers Grove, IL: InterVarsity, 1997.

Bloom, Harold. *The American Religion.* 2nd ed. New York: Hartley, 2006.

Blum, Edwin A. *1 Peter.* EBC 12. Grand Rapids: Zondervan, 1981.

Boda, Mark J., and J. Gordon McConville, eds. *Dictionary of the Old Testament Prophets.* Downers Grove, IL: IVP Academic, 2012.

Bohn, David. "The Larger Issue." *Sunstone* 16.8 (1994) 45–63.

————. "Unfounded Claims and Impossible Expectations: A Critique of New Mormon History." In *Faithful History: Essays on Writing Mormon History,* edited by George D. Smith, 227–56. Salt Lake City: Signature, 1992.

Book of Mormon. https://www.lds. org/scriptures/bofm?lang=eng.

Booth, Wayne C. *The Company We Keep.* Berkeley: University of California Press, 1998.

————. "Resurrection of the Implied Author: Why Bother?" In *A Companion to Narrative Theory,* edited by James Phalen and Peter J. Rabinowitz, 75–88. Malden, MA: Blackwell, 2005.

————. *The Rhetoric of Fiction.* Chicago: University of Chicago Press, 1961.

Bovon, Francois. *Luke 3: A Commentary on the Gospel of Luke 1:28—24:53.* Hermeneia. Translated by James Crouch. Minneapolis: Fortress, 2012.

Bowman, Matthew Burton. "History Thrown into Divinity: Faith, Knowledge, and the Telling of the Mormon Past." *Fides et Historia* 45.1 (2013) 76–91.

———. *The Mormon People: The Making of an American Faith*. New York: Random House, 2012.

Bowman, Robert M., Jr. "The Book of Hebrews and the Joseph Smith Translation." https://mit.irr.org/book-of-hebrews-and-joseph-smith-translation.

Boylan, Robert. "On Not Understanding the Book of Mormon." *FARMS Review* 22.1 (2010) 181–89.

Brady, Christian M. M. "Targum." In *DTIB*, edited by Kevin J. Vanhoozer et al., 780–81. Grand Rapids: Baker Academic, 2005.

Bray, Gerald "Allegory." In *DTIB*, edited by Kevin J. Vanhoozer et al., 34–36. Grand Rapids: Baker Academic, 2005.

Bringhurst, Newell G., and Darron T. Smith, eds. *Black and Mormon*. Urbana: University of Illinois, 2004.

Brodie, Fawn M. *No Man Knows My History: The Life of Joseph Smith the Mormon Prophet*. 2nd ed. New York: Knopf, 1971.

Brown, Francis, et al. *Enhanced Brown-Driver-Briggs Hebrew and English Lexicon*. Oxford: Clarendon, 1977.

Brown, Jeannine K. *Scripture as Communication: Introducing Biblical Hermeneutics*. Grand Rapids: Baker, 2007.

Brown, Raymond E. "The History and Development of the Theory of a *Sensus Plenior*." *Catholic Biblical Quarterly* 15 (1953) 141–62.

———. "The *Sensus Plenior* in the Last Ten Years." *Catholic Biblical Quarterly* 25 (1963) 262–85.

Bruce, F. F. *The Acts of the Apostles: The Greek Text with Introduction and Commentary*. 3rd ed. Grand Rapids: Eerdmans, 1990.

———. *The Book of Acts*. Rev. ed. NICNT. Grand Rapids: Eerdmans, 1988.

Brueggemann, Walter. *Isaiah 1–39*. Louisville: Westminster John Knox, 1998.

Bultmann, Rudolf. "Is Exegesis without Presuppositions Possible?" In *Existence and Faith: Shorter Writings of Rudolf Bultmann*, 289–96. Cleveland: Word, 1965.

Busch, Austin. "Presence Deferred: The Name of Jesus and Self-Referential Eschatological Prophecy in Acts 3." *Biblical Interpretation* 17.5 (2009) 521–53.

Bushman, Richard Lyman. *Joseph Smith and the Beginnings of Mormonism*. Urbana: University of Illinois Press, 1984.

———. *Joseph Smith: Rough Stone Rolling*. New York: Vintage, 2005.

Caird, G. B. *The Language and Imagery of the Bible*. London: Duckworth, 1980.

Campbell, W. S. "Church as Israel, People of God." In *DLNT*, edited by Ralph P. Martin and Peter H. Davids, 211–12. Downers Grove, IL: InterVarsity, 1997.

Cannon, George. "Persecution." http://jod.mrm.org/14/163.

Carmack, John K., ed. *The New Testament and the Latter-day Saints*. Orem, UT: Randall, 1987.

Carrigan, Cky John. "The Mormon Mirage: A Closer Look at the Teachings of the Church of Jesus Christ of Latter-day Saints." *Southwestern Journal of Theology* 46.2 (2004) 1–14.

Carson, D. A. "Contemporary Challenge to Inerrancy." https://www.thegospelcoalition.org/essay/contemporary-challenges-to-inerrancy/.

———. "Recent Developments." In *Hermeneutics, Authority and Canon*, edited by D. A. Carson and John D. Woodbridge, 1–48. Eugene, OR: Wipf & Stock, 1986.

Chatman, Benjamin Seymour. *Story and Discourse: Narrative Structure in Fiction and Film.* Ithaca, NY: Cornell University Press, 1980.

Cheung, Luke Leuk. *The Genre, Composition, and Hermeneutics of the Epistle of James.* Milton Keynes: Paternoster, 2003.

Childs, Brevard S. *Biblical Theology of the Old and New Testaments.* Minneapolis: Fortress, 1992.

———. *Isaiah.* Louisville: Westminster John Knox, 2001.

Chilton, Bruce D. *The Isaiah Targum: Introduction, Translation, Apparatus and Notes.* The Aramaic Bible 11. Wilmington, DE: Glazier, 1987.

Ciampa, Roy E., and Brian S. Rosner. "1 Corinthians." In *CNTOT*, edited by G. K. Beale and D. A. Carson, 695–752. Grand Rapids: Baker Academic, 2007.

Cole, Graham A. "God, Doctrine of." In *DTIB*, edited by Kevin J. Vanhoozer et al., 259–63. Grand Rapids: Baker Academic, 2005.

Cole, Zachary J. "Myths about Copyists." In *Myths and Mistakes in New Testament Textual Criticism*, edited by Elijah Hixson and Peter J. Gurry, 132–51. Downers Grove, IL: InterVarsity, 2019.

Compton, Todd. *In Sacred Loneliness: The Plural Wives of Joseph Smith.* Salt Lake City: Signature, 1997.

Connelly, Matthew R., and BYU Studies Staff. "Sizing Up the Divide." *BYU Studies* 38.3 (1999) 163–90.

Conzelmann, Hans. *Acts of the Apostles: A Commentary on the Acts of the Apostles.* Hermeneia. Translated by James Limburg et al. Philadelphia: Fortress, 1987.

———. *Die Apostelgeschichte.* Handbuch Zum Neuen Testament 7. Tübingen: Mohr, 1963.

Cook, J. A. "Hebrew Language." In *DOTP*, edited by Mark J. Boda and J. Gordon McConville, 307–18. Downers Grove, IL: IVP Academic, 2012.

Crowther, Duane S. *The Prophecies of Joseph Smith.* Salt Lake City: Bookcraft, 1963.

Cummings, Brian. "The Problem of Protestant Culture: Biblical Literalism and Literary Biblicism." *Reformation* 17.1 (2012) 177–98.

Cummings, Richard J. "Quintessential Mormonism: Literal-Mindedness as a Way of Life." *Dialogue* 15.4 (1982) 93–102.

Dart, John. "Counting Mormons: Study Says LDS Numbers Inflated." *Christian Century* 124.17 (2007) 26–29.

Davids, Peter H. *The Letters of 2 Peter and Jude.* PNTC. Grand Rapids: Eerdmans, 2006.

Davies, Douglas J. *An Introduction to Mormonism.* Cambridge: Cambridge University Press, 2003.

———. *The Mormon Culture of Salvation: Force, Grace, and Glory.* Aldershot: Ashgate, 2000.

Davies, W. D. "Reflections on the Mormon 'Canon.'" *Harvard Theological Review* 79.1–3 (1986) 44–66.

Davies, W. D., and Truman G. Madsen. "Scriptures." In *EM*, edited by Daniel H. Ludlow, 1277–80. New York: Macmillan, 1992.

deSilva, David A. *Perseverance in Gratitude: A Socio-Rhetorical Commentary on the Epistle 'to the Hebrews.'* Grand Rapids: Eerdmans, 2000.

Detweiler, Robert, ed. "Reader Response Approaches to Biblical and Secular Texts." *Semeia* 31 (1985) 1–228.

Detweiler, Robert, and Vernon K. Robbins. "From New Criticisms to Poststructuralism: Twentieth-Century Hermeneutics." In *Reading the Text: Biblical Criticism and Literary Theory*, edited by Stephen Prickett, 247–72. Oxford: Blackwell, 1991.

Dibelius, Martin. *James: A Commentary on the Epistle of James.* Revised by Heinrich Greeven. Translated by Michael A. Williams. Hermeneia. Philadelphia: Fortress, 1976.

Doctrine and Covenants. https://www.churchofjesuschrist.org/study/scriptures/dc-testament?lang=eng.

Dodd, B. J. "Universalism." In *DLNT*, edited by Ralph P. Martin and Peter H. Davids, 1188–89. Downers Grove, IL: InterVarsity, 1997.

Dornisch, Loretta. "Biblical Hermeneutics." *Semeia* 4 (1975) 27–148.

Dostal, Robert J., ed. *The Cambridge Companion to Gadamer.* Cambridge: Cambridge University Press, 2002.

Doxey, Roy W. "Doctrine and Covenants: Overview." In *EM*, edited by Daniel H. Ludlow, 405–7. New York: Macmillan, 1992.

Draper, Richard D., and Michael D. Rhodes. *Paul's First Epistle to the Corinthians: Brigham Young University New Testament Commentary.* Provo, UT: BYU Studies, 2017.

Duffy, John-Charles. "Mapping Book of Mormon Historicity Debates: A Guide for the Overwhelmed—Part I." *Sunstone* 151 (2008) 36–62.

Dunn, James D. G. *Jesus Remembered.* Grand Rapids: Eerdmans, 2003.

Dyer, Alvin R. *The Meaning of Truth.* Salt Lake City: Deseret, 1961.

Easter, Matthew C. *Faith and the Faithfulness of Jesus in Hebrews.* Cambridge: Cambridge University Press, 2014.

Eliason, Eric A., ed. *Mormons and Mormonism: An Introduction to an American World Religion.* Urbana: University of Illinois Press, 2001.

Ellis, E. Earle. "Perspectives on Biblical Interpretation: A Review Article." *JETS* 45.3 (2002) 473–95.

England, Breck. *The Life and Thought of Orson Pratt.* Salt Lake City: University of Utah Press, 1985.

Ericson, Loyd. "The Challenges of Defining Mormon Doctrine." *Element* 3.1–2 (2007) 69–87.

Esplin, Scott C. "Wondering at His Words: Peter's Influence on the Knowledge of Salvation for the Dead." In *The Ministry of Peter, the Chief Apostle*, edited by Frank F. Judd Jr. et al., 296–312. Salt Lake City: Deseret, 2014.

Evans, Craig A. "Jewish Exegesis." In *DTIB*, edited by Kevin J. Vanhoozer et al., 380–84. Grand Rapids: Baker Academic, 2005.

———. "Midrash." In *DJG*, edited by Joel B. Green and Scot McKnight, 544–47. Downers Grove, IL: InterVarsity, 1992.

Evans, Richard L., ed. *Gospel Ideals: Selections from the Discourses of David O. McKay, Ninth President of the Church of Jesus Christ of Latter-day Saints.* Salt Lake City: Improvement Era, 1953.

Faulconer, James E. "Advice for a Mormon Intellectual, Part 2." *Patheos* (blog), December 11, 2013. https://www.patheos.com/latter-day-saint/advice-mormon-intellectual-james-faulconer-12-12-2013.

———. "Are Mormons Christians?" *Patheos* (blog). August 29, 2012. https://www.patheos.com/latter-day-saint/are-mormons-christians-james-faulconer-08-30-2012.

———. "Dialogue on Theology as Hermeneutics." In *Mormonism in Dialogue with Contemporary Christian Theologies*, edited by Donald W. Musser and David Paulsen, 468–78. Macon, GA: Mercer University Press, 2007.

———. "Introduction: Thinking Transcendence." In *Transcendence in Philosophy and Religion*, edited by James E. Faulconer, 1–10. Bloomington: Indiana University Press, 2003.

———. *The New Testament Made Harder: Scripture Study Questions*. Provo, UT: Neal A. Maxwell Institute for Religious Scholarship, 2015.

———. "Philosophy and Transcendence: Religion and the Possibility of Justice." In *Transcendence in Philosophy and Religion*, edited by James E. Faulconer, 70–84. Bloomington: Indiana University Press, 2003.

———. "Recovering Truth: A Review of Hans-Georg Gadamer, *Truth and Method*." *The Mormon Review* 2.2 (2010) 1–7.

———. "Review of 'Rethinking Theology: The Shadow of the Apocalypse.'" *FARMS Review* 19.1 (2007) 175–99.

———. "Scripture as Incarnation." In *Historicity and the Latter-day Saint Scriptures*, edited by Paul Y. Hoskisson, 17–62. Provo, UT: Brigham Young University Press, 2001. https://rsc.byu.edu/historicity-latter-day-saint-scriptures/scripture-incarnation.

———. *Scripture Study: Tools and Suggestions*. Provo, UT: Foundation for Ancient Research and Mormon Studies, 1999.

———. *Transcendence in Philosophy and Religion*. Bloomington: Indiana University Press, 2003.

Faulconer, James E., and Mark A. Wrathall, eds. *Appropriating Heidegger*. Cambridge: Cambridge University Press, 2000.

Fielding McConkie, Joseph. "The 'How' of Scriptural Study." In *By Study and by Faith: Selections from the Religious Educator*, edited by Richard Neitzel Holzapfel and Kent P. Jackson, 51–68. Provo, UT: Brigham Young University Press, 2009.

Firth, David G., and Jamie A. Grant, eds. *Words and the Word: Explorations in Biblical Interpretation and Literary Theory*. Downers Grove, IL: InterVarsity, 2008.

Fitzmyer, Joseph A. *Acts of the Apostles: A New Translation with Introduction and Commentary*. AB 31. New Haven: Yale University Press, 1998.

Flake, Kathleen. "The Four Books of Mormonism: The Bible Plus." *Christian Century* 129.17 (2012) 28–31.

———. "Translating Time: The Nature and Function of Joseph Smith's Narrative Canon." *Journal of Religion* 87.4 (2007) 497–527.

Fluhman, J. Spencer. *"A Peculiar People": Anti-Mormonism and the Making of Religion in Nineteenth-Century America*. Chapel Hill: University of North Carolina Press, 2012.

Forsberg, Clyde R., Jr. *Equal Rites: The Book of Mormon, Masonry, Gender, and American Culture*. New York: Columbia, 2004.

Fowl, Stephen. "Effective History and the Cultivation of Wise Interpreters." *JTI* 7.2 (2013) 153–61.

———. "The Importance of a Multivoiced Literal Sense of Scripture: The Example of Thomas Aquinas." In *Reading Scripture with the Church: Toward a Hermeneutic for Theological Interpretation*, edited by A. K. M. Adam et al., 35–50. Grand Rapids: Baker, 2006.

Frame, John M. *Salvation Belongs to the Lord: An Introduction to Systematic Theology*. Phillipsburg, NJ: P&R, 2006.

Frei, Hans W. *The Eclipse of Biblical Narrative: A Study in Eighteenth and Nineteenth Century Hermeneutics*. New Haven: Yale University Press, 1974.

Fuller, Michael E. *The Restoration of Israel: Israel's Re-gathering and the Fate of the Nations in Early Jewish Literature and Luke-Acts*. Berlin: de Gruyter, 2006.

Furnish, Victor Paul. *The Theology of the First Letter to the Corinthians*. Cambridge: Cambridge University Press, 1999.

Gadamer, Hans-Georg. "On the Scope and Function of Hermeneutical Reflection." *Continuum* 8.1–2 (1970) 77–95.

———. *Philosophical Hermeneutics*. Edited and Translated by David E. Linge. Berkeley: University of California Press, 2004.

———. "The Science of the Life-World." In *The Later Husserl and the Idea of Phenomenology: Idealism-Realism, Historicity, and Nature*, edited by Anna-Teresa Tymieniecka, 173–85. Dordrecht: Reidel, 1972.

———. *Truth and Method*. 2nd rev. ed. New York: Seaberry, 1975.

———. *Wahrheit und Methode: Grundzüge einer philosophischen Hermeneutik*. Tübingen: Mohr Siebeck, 2010.

Gardner, Brant A. "I Do Not Think That Word Means What You Think It Means." *Interpreter* 7 (2013) 49–55.

Garland, David E. *1 Corinthians*. BECNT. Grand Rapids: Baker Academic, 2003.

Gaustad, Edwin S. "History and Theology: The Mormon Connection." *Sunstone* 5.6 (1980) 44–50.

Gibbons, Ted L. "Paul as a Witness of the Work of God." In *Go Ye into All the World: Messages of the New Testament Apostles*, edited by Thomas A. Wayment and Jerome M. Perkins, 27–40. Salt Lake City: Deseret, 2002.

Givens, Terryl L. *By the Hand of Mormon: The American Scripture That Launched a New World Religion*. Oxford: Oxford University Press, 2003.

———. "Mormons at the Forefront." *First Things* 264 (2016) 19–21.

———. *People of Paradox: A History of Mormon Culture*. Oxford: Oxford University Press, 2007.

———. *The Viper on the Hearth: Mormons, Myths, and the Construction of Heresy*. Updated ed. Oxford: Oxford University Press, 2013.

———. *Wrestling the Angel: The Foundations of Mormon Thought: Cosmos, God, Humanity*. New York: Oxford University Press, 2015.

Givens, Terryl L., and Philip L. Barlow, eds. *Oxford Handbook on Mormonism*. Oxford: Oxford University Press, 2015.

Goff, Alan. "How Should We Then Read? Reading Mormon Scripture after the Fall." *The FARMS Review* 21.1 (2009) 137–78.

Goldsworthy, G. "Relationship of Old Testament and New Testament." In *New Dictionary of Biblical Theology*, edited by T. Desmond Alexander and Brian S. Rosner, 81–89. Downers Grove, IL: InterVarsity, 2000.

Goppelt, Leonhard. *Typos: The Typological Interpretation of the Old Testament in the New*. Grand Rapids: Eerdmans, 1982.

Gorman, Michael J. "A 'Seamless Garment' Approach to Biblical Interpretation?" *JTI* 1.1 (2007) 117–28.

Graham, David. "Defending Biblical Literalism: Augustine on the Literal Sense." *Pro Ecclesia* 25.2 (2016) 173–99.

Gray, George Buchanan. *The Book of Isaiah*. Vol. 1. ICC. Edinburgh: T. & T. Clark, 1962.

Greaves, Sheldon. "The Education of a Bible Scholar." *Dialogue* 42.2 (2009) 55–78.

Green, Joel B. *The Gospel of Luke*. NICNT. Grand Rapids: Eerdmans, 1997.

———. *Practicing Theological Interpretation: Engaging Biblical Texts for Faith and Formation*. Grand Rapids: Baker Academic, 2011.

Greenberg, Moshe. *Ezekiel 21–37: A New Translation with Introduction and Commentary.* AB 22a. New Haven: Yale University Press, 1997.

Greene-McCreight, Kathryn. "Literal Sense." In *DTIB*, edited by Kevin J. Vanhoozer et al., 455–56. Grand Rapids: Baker Academic, 2005.

Griffin, Carl W., and David L. Paulsen. "Augustine and the Corporeality of God." *Harvard Theological Review* 95.1 (2002) 97–118.

Grogan, Geoffrey W. *Isaiah.* EBC 6. Grand Rapids: Zondervan, 1986.

Grondin, Jean. *Introduction to Philosophical Hermeneutics.* New Haven: Yale University Press, 1994.

Grudem, Wayne A. "Scripture's Self-Attestation and the Problem of Formulating a Doctrine of Scripture." In *Scripture and Truth*, edited by D. A. Carson and John D. Woodbridge, 15–59. Grand Rapids: Baker, 1992.

Grünfeld, Joseph. "Gadamer's Hermeneutics." *Science et Esprit* 41.2 (1989) 231–36.

Gundry-Volf, J. M. "Paul and Universalism." In *DPL*, edited by Gerald F. Hawthorne et al., 956–60. Downers Grove, IL: InterVarsity, 1993.

Gutjahr, Paul C. *The Book of Mormon: A Biography.* Princeton: Princeton University Press, 2012.

———. "Measuring the Measuring Stick." *Dialogue* 25.4 (1992) 205–6.

Habermas, Jürgen. *On the Logic of the Social Sciences.* Translated by Sherry Weber Nicholsen and Jerry A. Stark. Cambridge: Polity, 1988.

Haenchen, D. Ernst. *The Acts of the Apostles: A Commentary.* Philadelphia: Westminster, 1971.

———. *Die Apostelgeschichte.* Göttingen: Vandenhoeck & Ruprecht, 1968.

Hardy, Grant. *Understanding the Book of Mormon: A Reader's Guide.* Oxford: Oxford University Press, 2010.

Harrell, Charles R. *"This Is My Doctrine": The Development of Mormon Theology.* Salt Lake City: Kofford, 2011.

Harrington, Daniel J. *1 Peter, Jude, and 2 Peter.* SP 15. Collegeville, MN: Liturgical, 2003.

Harris, Matthew L., and Newell G. Bringhurst, eds. *The Mormon Church & Blacks: A Documentary History.* Urbana: University of Illinois, 2015.

Hatch, Edwin. *The Influence of Greek Ideas and Usages upon the Christian Church.* 5th ed. Peabody, MA: Hendrickson, 1996.

Hays, Christopher B. "The Covenant with Mut: A New Interpretation of Isaiah 28:1–22." *Vetus Testamentum* 60.2 (2010) 212–40.

Hays, Richard B. *The Conversion of the Imagination: Paul as Interpreter of Israel's Scripture.* Grand Rapids: Eerdmans, 2005.

Heidegger, Martin. *Being and Time.* Translated by Joan Stambaugh. Albany: University of New York Press, 2010.

———. *On the Way to Language.* Translated by Peter D. Hertz. San Francisco: Harper & Row, 1971.

Henry, Carl F. H. *God, Revelation, and Authority.* 6 vols. Wheaton: Crossway, 1999.

Hicks, Lester J. Review of *Scripture as Communication*, by Karel van der Toorn. *JETS* 50.4 (2007) 816–18.

Himes, Paul A. "Peter and the Prophetic Word: The Theology of Prophecy Traced through Peter's Sermons and Epistles." *Bulletin for Biblical Research* 21.2 (2011) 227–43.

Høgenhaven, Jesper. *Gott und Volk bei Jesaja: Eine Untersuchung zur biblischen Theologie.* Leiden: Brill, 1988.

Holladay, William Lee, and Ludwig Köhler. *A Concise Hebrew and Aramaic Lexicon of the Old Testament*. Leiden: Brill, 2000.

Holland, Jeffrey R. "Daddy, Donna, and Nephi." https://www.churchofjesuschrist.org/study/ensign/1976/09/daddy-donna-and-nephi?lang=eng.

Holzapfel, Richard Neitzel, and Thomas A. Wayment. *Making Sense of the New Testament*. Salt Lake City: Deseret, 2010.

Hopkins, Richard. *Biblical Mormonism: Responding to Evangelical Criticism of LDS Theology*. Bountiful, UT: Horizon, 2006.

———. *How Greek Philosophy Corrupted the Christian Concept of God*. 2nd ed. Bountiful, UT: Horizon, 2009.

Hovey, Craig, and Cyrus P. Olsen, eds. *The Hermeneutics of Tradition*. Eugene, OR: Cascade, 2014.

Huff, Benjamin I. "Theology in the Light of Continuing Revelation." In *Mormonism in Dialogue with Contemporary Christian Theologies*, edited by Donald W. Musser and David Paulsen, 478–87. Macon, GA: Mercer University Press, 2007.

Huff, Peter A. "A Gentile Recommends the Book of Mormon." *Dialogue* 43.2 (2010) 206–12.

Huggins, Ronald V. "Joseph Smith and the First Verse of the Bible." *JETS* 46.1 (2003) 29–52.

———. "Joseph Smith's 'Inspired Translation' of Romans 7." *Dialogue* 26.4 (1993) 159–82.

———. "Lorenzo Snow's Couplet: 'As Man Now Is, God Once Was; As God Now Is, Man May Be': No Functioning Place in Present-Day Mormon Doctrine? A Response to Richard Mouw." *JETS* 49.3 (2006) 549–68.

Hughes, Philip Edgcumbe. "The Truth of Scripture and the Problem of Historical Relativity." In *Scripture and Truth*, edited by D. A. Carson and John D. Woodbridge, 169–94. Grand Rapids: Baker, 1992.

Hummel, Charles E. "Interpreting Genesis One." *Journal of American Scientific Affiliation* 38.3 (1986) 175–85.

Humphrey, Edith M. "Jesus and Scripture." In *DTIB*, edited by Kevin J. Vanhoozer et al., 358–63. Grand Rapids: Baker Academic, 2005.

Hutchinson, Anthony A. "LDS Approaches to the Holy Bible." *Dialogue* 15.1 (1982) 99–124.

———. "A Mormon Midrash? LDS Creation Narratives Reconsidered." *Dialogue* 21.4 (1988) 11–74.

Ing, Michael D. K. "Ritual as a Process of Deification." In *By Our Rites of Worship: Latter-day Saint Views on Ritual in Scripture, History, and Practice*, edited by Daniel L. Belnap, 349–67. Salt Lake City: Deseret, 2013.

Inspired Version (Joseph Smith Translation). https://www.centerplace.org/hs/iv/default.htm.

Irving, Gordon. "The Mormons and the Bible in the 1830s." *BYU Studies* 13 (1973) 473–88.

Iser, Wolfgang. *The Range of Interpretation*. New York: Columbia University Press, 2000.

Jackson, Kent P. "Latter-day Saints: A Dynamic Scriptural Process." In *The Holy Book in Comparative Perspective*, edited by Frederick Mathewson Denny and Rodney L. Taylor, 63–83. Columbia: University of South Carolina Press, 1985.

———. "New Testament Prophecies of Apostasy." In *Sperry Symposium Classics: The New Testament*, edited by Frank F. Judd Jr. and Gaye Strathearn, 394–406. Salt Lake City: Deseret, 2006.

Jacobson, Cardell K., et al., eds. *Revisiting Thomas F. O'Dea's 'The Mormons':
Contemporary Perspectives.* Salt Lake City: University of Utah Press, 2008.

Jervell, Jacob. *Die Apostelgeschichte.* Göttingen: Vandenhoeck & Ruprecht, 1998.

Jessee, Dean C., et al., eds. *Joseph Smith Papers: Histories.* Vol. 1. Salt Lake City: Church
Historian's, 2012.

Johnson, Dennis E. *The Message of Acts in the History of Redemption.* Phillipsburg, NJ:
P&R, 1997.

Johnson, Frank J., and William J. Leffler. *Jews and Mormons: Two Houses of Israel.*
Hoboken, NJ: Ktav, 2000.

Johnson, Luke Timothy. *The Acts of the Apostles.* SP 5. Collegeville, MN: Liturgical,
1992.

————. *The Letter of James.* AB 37a. New York: Doubleday, 1995.

Joseph Smith Translation. https://www.centerplace.org/hs/iv/default.htm.

Jospe, Raphael, et al., eds. *Covenant and Chosenness in Judaism and Mormonism.*
Denver: University of Denver, 2001.

Journal of Discourses. https://jod.mrm.org/.

Kaiser, Otto. *Isaiah 1–39: A Commentary.* Philadelphia: Westminster, 1974.

Kaiser, Walter C., Jr., and Moisés Silva. *Introduction to Biblical Hermeneutics: The Search
for Meaning.* Rev. ed. Grand Rapids: Zondervan, 2007.

Kee, Howard Clark. *Knowing the Truth: A Sociological Approach to New Testament
Interpretation.* Minneapolis: Fortress, 1989.

Keener, Craig S. *Acts: An Exegetical Commentary. Introduction and 1:1—2:47.* Grand
Rapids: Baker Academic, 2012.

————. *Acts: An Exegetical Commentary 3:1—14:28.* Grand Rapids: Baker Academic,
2013.

Keller, Roger R. "The Latter-day Saint (Mormon) Theology of Being: A Response to
Social Fragmentation." *Encounter* 56.2 (1995) 189–98.

Kenney, Scott. "The Triumph of Conservative Biblical Criticism." *Dialogue* 28.2 (1995)
163–66.

Kissling, Paul. *Genesis.* 2 vols. The College Press NIV Commentary. Joplin, MO:
College, 2004.

Kittel, Gerhard, and Gerhard Friedrich, eds. *TDNT.* Translated by Geoffrey W. Bromiley.
10 vols. Grand Rapids: Eerdmans, 1964–76.

Klein, William W., et al. *Introduction to Biblical Interpretation.* Dallas: Word, 1993.

Koester, Craig R. *Hebrews: A New Translation with Introduction and Commentary.* AB
36. New York: Doubleday, 2001.

Kurz, William S. *Acts of the Apostles: Catholic Commentary on Sacred Scripture.* Grand
Rapids: Baker, 2013.

Larson, Stan, and Samuel J. Passey, eds. *The William E. McLellin Papers, 1854–1880.* Salt
Lake City: Signature, 2007.

Lassetter, Courtney J. "Dispensations of the Gospel." In *EM,* edited by Daniel H.
Ludlow, 388–90. New York: Macmillan, 1992.

LDS. "Approaching Mormon Doctrine." https://newsroom.churchofjesuschrist.org/
article/approaching-mormon-doctrine.

————. "Be Ye Therefore Perfect." In *Messages for Exaltation: Eternal Insight from the
Book of Mormon,* 236–42. Salt Lake City: Deseret Sunday School Union, 1967.

————. "Divine Revelation in Modern Times." http://www.mormonnewsroom.org/
article/divine-revelation-modern-times.

———. *Gospel Principles*. Salt Lake City: LDS, 2009.

———. "Growth of the Church." https://newsroom.churchofjesuschrist.org/topic/church-growth.

———. "Global Leadership of the Church." https://www.churchofjesuschrist.org/learn/global-leadership-of-the-church?lang=eng.

———. "How Do I Study Effectively and Prepare to Teach?" In *Preach My Gospel: A Guide to Missionary Service*, 17–27. Salt Lake City: LDS, 2004.

———. *Joseph Smith: History, Extracts from the History of Joseph Smith, the Prophet*. Salt Lake City: LDS, 1982.

———. "Joseph Smith Translation (JST)." https://www.churchofjesuschrist.org/study/scriptures/bd/joseph-smith-translation?lang=eng.

———. "Marriage." https://www.churchofjesuschrist.org/study/manual/gospel-topics/marriage?lang=eng.

———. "A Mormon Worldview." https://newsroom.churchofjesuschrist.org/ldsnewsroom/eng/commentary/a-mormon-worldview.

———. *New Testament Seminary Teacher Manual*. Salt Lake City: LDS, 1999.

———. *Old Testament Seminary Teacher Manual*. https://www.churchofjesuschrist.org/study/manual/old-testament-seminary-teacher-manual/introduction-to-the-book-of-ezekiel/lesson-142-ezekiel-37?lang=eng.

———. *Preach My Gospel: A Guide to Missionary Service*. Salt Lake City: LDS, 2019.

———. *Primary 5: Doctrine and Covenants; Church History, Ages 8–11*. Book 2. Salt Lake City: LDS, 1996.

———. "Sealing." https://www.churchofjesuschrist.org/study/manual/gospel-topics/sealing?lang=eng.

———. "Sustaining the General Authorities of the Church." *Improvement Era* 48.6 (1945) 354.

Leone, Mark P. *The Roots of Mormonism*. Cambridge.: Harvard University Press, 1979.

Lincoln, Andrew T., and A. J. M. Wedderburn. *The Theology of the Later Pauline Letters*. Cambridge: Cambridge University Press, 1993.

Link, H.-G. "Reconciliation, Restoration, Propitiation, Atonement." In *NIDNTT*, edited by Colin Brown et al., 3:145–76. Grand Rapids: Zondervan, 1986.

The Literary Critic. "Thursday, June 26, 2003." *Metaphysical Elders* (blog), June 26, 2003. https://elders.blogspot.com/2003_06_22_archive.html.

Lohfink, Gerhard. *Jesus and Community*. Translated by John P. Galvin. Philadelphia: Fortress, 1984.

Lohse, Eduard. *Colossians and Philemon*. Translated by William R. Poehlmann and Robert J. Karris. Hermeneia. Philadelphia: Fortress, 1971.

Lonergan, Bernard J. F. *Method in Theology*. London: Darton, Longman, & Todd, 1971.

Longenecker, Richard N. *The Acts of the Apostles*. EBC 9. Grand Rapids: Zondervan, 1981.

Ludlow, Daniel H., ed. *EM: The History, Scripture, Doctrine, and Procedure of the Church of Jesus Christ of Latter-day Saints*. New York: Macmillan, 1992.

Ludlow, Victor L. "Bible." In *EM*, edited by Daniel H. Ludlow, 104–8. New York: Macmillan, 1992.

MacDonald, Neil B. "Illocutionary Stance in Hans Frei's *The Eclipse of Biblical Narrative*." In *After Pentecost: Language and Biblical Interpretation*, edited by Craig Bartholomew et al., 312–28. Scripture and Hermeneutics Series 2. Grand Rapids: Zondervan, 2001.

MacKay, Michael Hubbard, and Nicholas J. Frederick. *Joseph Smith's Seer Stones.* Salt Lake City: Deseret, 2016.

Malcolm, Matthew R. "Biblical Hermeneutics and *Kerygmatic* Responsibility." In *The Future of Biblical Interpretation: Responsible Plurality in Biblical Hermeneutics,* edited by Stanley E. Porter and Matthew R. Malcolm, 71–84. Downers Grove, IL: InterVarsity, 2013.

Malina, Bruce J. "Rhetorical Criticism and Social-Scientific Criticism: Why Won't Romanticism Leave Us Alone?" In *The Social World of the New Testament: Insights and Models,* edited by Jerome H. Neyrey and Eric C. Stewart, 5–21. Peabody, MA: Hendrickson, 2008.

Marshall, I. Howard. *The Acts of the Apostles.* Sheffield: Sheffield Academic, 1997.

———. *The Epistles of John.* NICNT. Grand Rapids: Eerdmans, 1978.

———. *New Testament Theology: Many Witnesses, One Gospel.* Downers Grove, IL: InterVarsity, 2004.

Martins, Marcus H. Review of *All Abraham's Children: Changing Mormon Conceptions of Race and Lineage,* by Armand L. Mauss. *Sociology of Religion* 65.4 (2004) 423–24.

Matthews, Robert J. "Joseph Smith Translation of the Bible (JST)." In *EM,* edited by Daniel H. Ludlow, 763–69. New York: Macmillan, 1992.

———. *"A Plainer Translation": Joseph Smith's Translation of the Bible: A History and Commentary.* Provo, UT: Brigham Young University Press, 1975.

———. "The Restoration of All Things: What the Doctrine and Covenants Says." In *Sperry Symposium Classics: The Doctrine and Covenants,* edited by Craig K. Manscill, 68–91. Provo, UT: Brigham Young University Press, 2004.

———. "The Role of the Joseph Smith Translation in the Restoration." In *Plain and Precious Truths Restored: The Doctrinal and Historical Significance of the Joseph Smith Translation,* edited by Robert L. Millet and Robert J. Matthews, 37–54. Salt Lake City: Bookcraft, 1995.

Mauss, Armand L. "Refuge and Retrenchment: The Mormon Quest for Identity." In *Contemporary Mormonism: Social Science Perspectives,* edited by Marie Cornwall et al., 24–42. Urbana: University of Illinois Press, 2001.

Maxwell, Neal A. "From the Beginning." https://www.churchofjesuschrist.org/study/ensign/1993/11/from-the-beginning?lang=eng.

McConkie, Bruce. *Mormon Doctrine.* 2nd ed. Salt Lake City: Bookcraft, 1966.

———. *A New Witness for the Articles of Faith.* Salt Lake City: Deseret, 1985.

———. "What Think Ye of the Book of Mormon?" https://www.churchofjesuschrist.org/study/ensign/1983/11/what-think-ye-of-the-book-of-mormon?lang=eng.

McGuire, Ben. "Understanding the Book of Mormon? He 'Doth Protest Too Much, Methinks.'" *The FARMS Review* 22.1 (2010) 163–80.

McKnight, E. V. "Literary Criticism." In *DJG,* edited by Joel B. Green and Scot McKnight, 473–80. Downers Grove, IL: InterVarsity, 1992.

McKnight, Scot. "Israel." In *DTIB,* edited by Kevin J. Vanhoozer et al., 344–46. Grand Rapids: Baker Academic, 2005.

McLaughlan, James, and Loyd Ericson, eds. *Discourses in Mormon Theology: Philosophical and Theological Possibilities.* Salt Lake City: Greg Kofford, 2007.

McLean, B. H. *Biblical Interpretation and Philosophical Hermeneutics.* Cambridge: Cambridge University Press, 2012.

McMurrin, Sterling M. "Some Distinguishing Characteristics of Mormon Philosophy." *Sunstone* 16.4 (1993) 35–46.

————. *The Theological Foundations of the Mormon Religion*. Salt Lake City: University of Utah Press, 1965.

Metcalfe, Brent Lee, ed. *New Approaches to the Book of Mormon: Explorations in Critical Methodology*. Salt Lake City: Signature, 1993.

Meyer, Ben F. *Critical Realism and the New Testament*. Allison Park, PA: Pickwick, 1989.

————. *Reality and Illusion in New Testament Scholarship: A Primer in Critical Realist Hermeneutics*. Collegeville, MN: Liturgical, 1994.

Michaelsen, Robert S. "Enigmas in Interpreting Mormonism." *Sociological Analysis* 38.2 (1977) 145–53.

Midgley, Louis. "The Challenge of Historical Consciousness: Mormon History and the Encounter with Secular Modernity." In *By Faith and By Study: Essays in Honor of Hugh W. Nibley*, edited by John M. Lundquist and Stephen D. Ricks, 2:502–51. Salt Lake City: Deseret, 1990.

Millet, Robert L. *A Different Jesus? The Christ of the Latter-day Saints*. Grand Rapids: Eerdmans, 2005.

————. *Getting at the Truth: Responding to Difficult Questions about LDS Beliefs*. Salt Lake City: Deseret, 2004.

————. "Joseph Smith's Translation of the Bible: Impact on Mormon Theology." *Religious Studies and Theology* 7.1 (1987) 43–53.

————. "'The Most Correct Book': Joseph Smith's Appraisal." In *Living the Book of Mormon: Abiding by Its Precepts*, edited by Gaye Strathearn and Charles Swift, 55–71. Salt Lake City: Deseret, 2007.

————. "What Do We Really Believe? Identifying Doctrinal Parameters within Mormonism." In *Discourses in Mormon Theology: Philosophical and Theological Possibilities*, edited by James M. McLaughlan and Loyd Ericson, 265–81. Salt Lake City: Kofford, 2007.

————. *Within Reach*. Salt Lake City: Deseret, 1995.

Millet Robert L., and Gregory C. V. Johnson. *Bridging the Divide: The Continuing Conversation between a Mormon and an Evangelical*. Rhinebeck, NY: Monkfish, 2007.

Millet, Robert L., et al. *LDS Beliefs: A Doctrinal Reference*. Salt Lake: Deseret, 2011.

Miscall, Peter D. *Isaiah*. Readings, a New Biblical Commentary. Sheffield: JSOT, 1993.

Moberly, R. W. L. *The Bible, Theology, and Faith: A Study of Abraham and Jesus*. Cambridge: Cambridge University Press, 2000.

Monson, Dwight E. *Shared Beliefs, Honest Differences: A Biblical Basis for Comparing the Doctrines of Mormons and Other Christians*. Springville, UT: Horizon, 2010.

Moo, Douglas J. "The Problem of *Sensus Plenior*." In *Hermeneutics, Authority, and Canon*, edited by D. A. Carson and John D. Woodbridge, 175–211. Eugene, OR: Wipf & Stock, 1986.

Mootz, Francis J., III, and George H. Taylor, eds. *Gadamer and Ricoeur: Critical Horizons for Contemporary Hermeneutics*. London: Continuum, 2011.

Moritz, Thorsten. "Critical but Real: Reflecting on N. T. Wright's *Tools for the Task*." In *Renewing Biblical Interpretation*, edited by Craig Bartholomew et al., 172–97. Carlisle: Paternoster, 2000.

————. "Critical Realism." In *DTIB*, edited by Kevin J. Vanhoozer et al., 147–50. Grand Rapids: Baker Academic, 2005.

————. "Mark." In *TINT*, edited by Kevin J. Vanhoozer, 39–49. Grand Rapids: Baker Academic, 2008.

———. "Scripture and Theological Exegesis." In *The Sacred Text: Excavating the Texts, Exploring the Interpretations, and Engaging the Theologies of the Christian Scriptures*, edited by Michael F. Bird and Michael W. Pahl, 119–40. Piscataway, NJ: Gorgias, 2010.

Mosser, Carl. "The Greatest Possible Blessing: Calvin and Deification." *Scottish Journal of Theology* 55.1 (2002) 36–57.

Motyer, J. Alec. *Isaiah: An Introduction and Commentary*. TOTC 20. Downers Grove, IL: IVP Academic, 1999.

Mould, Tom. *Still, the Small Voice: Narrative, Personal Revelation, and the Mormon Folk Tradition*. Logan, UT: Utah State University Press, 2011.

Moyise, Steve. "Quotations." In *As It Is Written: Studying Paul's Use of Scripture*, edited by Stanley E. Porter and Christopher D. Stanley, 15–28. Symposium Series 50. Atlanta: Society of Biblical Literature, 2008.

Muis, Jan. "Can Christian Talk about God Be Literal?" *Modern Theology* 27.4 (2011) 582–607.

Munck, Johannes. *The Acts of the Apostles*. AB 31. Garden City, NY: Doubleday, 1967.

Muthengi, Julius. "A Critical Analysis of Sensus Plenior." *East Africa Journal of Evangelical Theology* 3.2 (1984) 63–73.

Nathan, Emmanuel. "Truth and Prejudice: A Theological Reflection on Biblical Exegesis." *Ephemerides Theologicae Lovanienses* 83.4 (2007) 281–318.

Neill, Stephen, and Tom Wright. *The Interpretation of the New Testament: 1861–1986*. 2nd ed. Oxford: Oxford University Press, 1988.

Nelson, Russell M. *Accomplishing the Impossible: What God Does, What We Can Do*. Salt Lake City: Deseret, 2015.

Nestle, Eberhard, et al. *The Greek New Testament*. 27th ed. Stuttgart: Deutsche Bibelgesellschaft, 1993.

Nibley, Hugh. *The World and the Prophets*. The Collected Works of Hugh Nibley 3. Salt Lake City: Deseret, 1987.

Nyman, Monte S., and Lisa Bolin Hawkins. "Book of Mormon." In *EM*, edited by Daniel H. Ludlow, 139–43. New York: Macmillan, 1992.

O'Dea, Thomas F. *The Mormons*. Chicago: University of Chicago Press, 1957.

Oaks, Dallin H. "Scripture Reading and Revelation." https://www.churchofjesuschrist.org/study/ensign/1995/01/scripture-reading-and-revelation?lang=eng.

Olsen, Steven L. "The Theology of Memory: Mormon Historical Consciousness." *The FARMS Review* 19.2 (2007) 25–37.

Oman, Nathan. "'The Living Oracles': Legal Interpretation and Mormon Thought." *Dialogue* 42.2 (2009) 1–19.

Orr, William F., and James Arthur Walther. *1 Corinthians*. AB 32. New York: Doubleday, 1976.

Osborne, Grant R. *The Hermeneutical Spiral: A Comprehensive Introduction to Biblical Interpretation*. 2nd ed. Downers Grove, IL: InterVarsity, 2006.

Ostler, Blake T. "The Idea of Pre-existence in the Development of Mormon Thought." *Dialogue* 15.1 (1982) 59–78.

———. *Of God and Gods*. Exploring Mormon Thought 3. Draper, UT: Kofford, 2008. iBooks.

Ostling, Richard N., and Joan K. Ostling. *Mormon America: The Power and the Promise*. New York: HarperCollins, 2007.

Oswalt, John N. *The Book of Isaiah: Chapters 1–39*. NICOT. Grand Rapids: Eerdmans, 1986.

Owen, Paul L., and Carl A. Mosser. "Mormon Scholarship, Apologetics, and Evangelical Neglect: Losing the Battle and Not Knowing It?" *Trinity Journal* 19.2 (1998) 179–205.

———. "A Review of 'How Wide the Divide? A Mormon and an Evangelical in Conversation' by Craig L. Blomberg and Stephen E. Robinson." *FARMS Review of Books* 11.2 (1999) 1–102.

Packer, Boyd K. "Scriptures." https://www.churchofjesuschrist.org/study/general-conference/1982/10/scriptures?lang=eng.

Packer, J. I. "Infallible Scripture and the Role of Hermeneutics." In *Scripture and Truth*, edited by D. A. Carson and John D. Woodbridge, 321–56. Grand Rapids: Baker, 1992.

Painter, John. *1, 2, and 3 John*. SP 18. Collegeville, MN: Liturgical, 2002.

Palmer, Grant H. *An Insider's View of Mormon Origins*. Salt Lake City: Signature, 2002.

Palmer, Richard E. *Hermeneutics: Interpretation Theory in Schleiermacher, Dilthey, Heidegger, and Gadamer*. Evanston: Northwestern University Press, 1969.

Pao, David W. *Acts and the Isaianic New Exodus*. Grand Rapids: Baker Academic, 2002.

———. *Colossians and Philemon*. ZECNT. Grand Rapids: Zondervan, 2012.

Park, Benjamin E. "Salvation through a Tabernacle: Joseph Smith, Parley P. Pratt, and Early Mormon Theologies of Embodiment." *Dialogue* 43.2 (2010) 1–44.

Parrish, Alan K. "Keys of the Priesthood." In *EM*, edited by Daniel H. Ludlow, 780–81. New York: Macmillan, 1992.

Parsons, Mikeal C. *Acts*. Paideia. Grand Rapids: Baker Academic, 2008.

Patton, Corrine L., and Stephen L. Cook. "Introduction: Jane Morse and the Fuller Sense (Theoretical Framework for a *Sensus Plenior*)." In *The Whirlwind: Essays on Job, Hermeneutics, and Theology in Memory of Jane Morse*, edited by Stephen L. Cook et al., 13–39. JSOTSup 336. Sheffield: Sheffield Academic, 2001.

Paul, Shalom M. *Amos: A Commentary on the Book of Amos*. Hermeneia. Minneapolis: Fortress, 1991.

Paulsen, David L. "Are Christians Mormon? Reassessing Joseph Smith's Theology in His Bicentennial." *BYU Studies* 45.1 (2006) 35–128.

———. "Early Christian Belief in a Corporeal Deity: Origen and Augustine as Reluctant Witnesses." *Harvard Theological Review* 83.2 (1990) 105–16.

Paulsen, David L., and Donald W. Musser, eds. *Mormonism in Dialogue with Contemporary Christian Theologies*. Macon, GA: Mercer University Press, 2007.

Payne, Philip B. "The Fallacy of Equating Meaning with the Human Author's Intention." *JETS* 20.3 (1977) 243–52.

Pearl of Great Price. https://www.churchofjesuschrist.org/study/scriptures/pgp?lang=eng.

Pelikan, Jaroslav. *Acts*. Brazos Theological Commentary on the Bible. Grand Rapids: Brazos, 2005.

Pervo, Richard I. *Acts: A Commentary*. Hermeneia. Minneapolis: Fortress, 2009.

Peterson, Daniel C. "Defending the Faith: A Lutheran Bishop's Perspective on Mormon Baptism for the Dead." *Deseret News*, February 22, 2012. https://www.deseret.com/2012/2/22/20395076/a-lutheran-bishop-s-perspective-on-mormon-baptism-for-the-dead.

Peterson, David G. *The Acts of the Apostles*. PNTC. Grand Rapids: Eerdmans, 2009.

Phelps, W. W. "Letter No. 5." http://www.centerplace.org/history/ma/v1n06.htm.

———. "Letter No. 8." http://www.centerplace.org/history/ma/v1n09.htm.

Polhill, John B. *Acts*. NAC 26. Nashville: Broadman & Holman, 1992.

Porter, Stanley C., et al. *Horizons in Hermeneutics: A Festschrift in Honor of Anthony C. Thiselton*. Grand Rapids: Eerdmans, 2013.

Porter, Stanley E. "Biblical Hermeneutics and *Theological* Responsibility." In *The Future of Biblical Interpretation: Responsible Plurality in Biblical Hermeneutics*, edited by Stanley E. Porter and Matthew R. Malcolm, 29–50. Downers Grove, IL: InterVarsity, 2013.

Porter, Stanley E., and Matthew R. Malcolm. "Remaining Hermeneutical Issues for the Future of Biblical Interpretation." In *The Future of Biblical Interpretation: Responsible Plurality in Biblical Hermeneutics*, edited by Stanley E. Porter and Matthew R. Malcolm, 157–65. Downers Grove, IL: InterVarsity, 2013.

Porter, Stanley E., and Jason C. Robinson. *Hermeneutics: An Introduction to Interpretive Theory*. Grand Rapids: Eerdmans, 2011. Kindle.

Porter, Stanley E., and Beth M. Stovell, eds. *Biblical Hermeneutics: Five Views*. Downers Grove, IL: InterVarsity, 2012.

Powell, Mark Allan. *What Is Narrative Criticism?* Minneapolis: Fortress, 1990.

Pratt, Parley P. *Key to the Science of Theology*. 5th ed. Salt Lake City: Cannon & Sons, 1891.

———. *A Voice of Warning and Instruction to All People; Or, an Introduction to the Faith and Doctrine of the Church of Jesus Christ of Latter-day Saints*. 13th ed. Salt Lake City: Cannon & Sons, 1891.

Properzi, Mauro. *Mormonism and the Emotions: An Analysis of LDS Scriptural Texts*. Lanham, MD: Fairleigh Dickinson University Press, 2015.

Quinn, D. Michael. *Early Mormonism and the Magic World View*. Salt Lake City: Signature, 1987.

———. *The Mormon Hierarchy: Extensions of Power*. Salt Lake City: Signature, 1997.

———. *The Mormon Hierarchy: Origins of Power*. Salt Lake City: Signature, 2010.

Räisänen, Heikki. "Joseph Smith as a Creative Interpreter of the Bible." *Dialogue* 43.2 (2010) 64–85.

Rahlfs, Alfred, and Robert Hanhart, eds. *Septuaginta*. Rev. ed. Stuttgart: Deutsche Bibelgesellschaft, 2006.

Rakestraw, Robert V. "Becoming like God: An Evangelical Doctrine of Theosis." *JETS* 40.2 (1997) 257–69.

Rees, Robert A. "Joseph Smith, the Book of Mormon, and the American Renaissance." *Dialogue* 35.3 (2002) 83–112.

———. "The Midrashic Imagination and the Book of Mormon." *Dialogue* 44.3 (2011) 44–66.

Resseguie, James L. *Narrative Criticism and the New Testament*. Grand Rapids: Baker, 2005.

Restoration Branches. *Evening and Morning Star*. https://www.centerplace.org/history/ems/default.htm.

———. *Messenger and Advocate*. http://www.centerplace.org/history/ma/.

———. *Times and Seasons*. http://www.centerplace.org/history/ts/default.htm.

Ricks, Stephen D. "Latter-day Saint Doctrines and the Bible." *The FARMS Review* 14.1–2 (2002) 337–40.

Riddle, Chauncey C. "Letter to Michael." https://www.churchofjesuschrist.org/study/ensign/1975/09/letter-to-michael?lang=eng.

———. "Revelation." In *EM*, edited by Daniel H. Ludlow, 1225–28. New York: Macmillan, 1992.

———. "Welcome." http://chaunceyriddle.com/welcome/.

Ridges, David J. *The New Testament Made Easier Part 1: Matthew, Mark, Luke, & John.* 2nd ed. Springville, UT: Cedar Fort, 2007.

———. *The New Testament Made Easier Part 2: Acts through Revelation.* 2nd ed. Springville, UT: Cedar Fort, 2010.

Robbins, Vernon K. "The Social Location of the Implied Author of Luke–Acts." In *The Social World of Luke–Acts: Models for Interpretation,* edited by Jerome H. Neyrey, 305–31. Peabody, MA: Hendrickson, 1991.

Roberts, J. J. M. *First Isaiah: A Commentary.* Hermeneia. Minneapolis: Fortress, 2015.

Robertson, Archibald, and Alfred Plummer. *A Critical and Exegetical Commentary on the First Epistle of St. Paul to the Corinthians.* ICC. Edinburgh: T. & T. Clark, 1950.

Robinson, Stephen E. *Are Mormons Christians?* Salt Lake City: Bookcraft, 1991.

Schmidt, Lawrence Kennedy. *The Epistemology of Hans-Georg Gadamer: An Analysis of the Legitimization of Vorurteile.* Frankfurt: Lang, 1985.

Schnabel, Eckhard J. *Acts.* ZECNT. Grand Rapids: Zondervan, 2012.

Schneiders, Sandra Marie. "Faith, Hermeneutics, and the Literal Sense of Scripture." *Theological Studies* 39.4 (1978) 719–36.

Schrijver, Georges de. "Hermeneutics and Tradition." *Journal of Ecumenical Studies* 19 (1982) 32–47.

Schweiker, William. "Sacrifice, Interpretation, and the Sacred: The Import of Gadamer and Girard for Religious Studies." *Journal of the American Academy of Religion* 55.4 (1987) 791–810.

Scott, Charles E. "Gadamer's *Truth and Method.*" *Anglican Theological Review* 59 (1977) 63–78.

Seely, David Rolph. "Prophecy in Biblical Times." In *EM,* edited by Daniel H. Ludlow, 1162–63. New York: Macmillan, 1992.

Selby, Rosalind M. *Comical Doctrine: An Epistemology of New Testament Hermeneutics.* Milton Keynes: Paternoster, 2006.

Selms, Adrianus van. "Isaiah 28:9–13: An Attempt to Give a New Interpretation." *Zeitschrift Für Die Alttestamentliche Wissenschaft* 85.3 (1973) 332–39.

Shannon, Nathan D. "His Community, His Interpretation: A Review of Merold Westphal's 'Whose Community? Which Interpretation?'" *The Westminster Theological Journal* 72.2 (2010) 415–25.

Shepard, William, and H. Michael Marquardt. *Lost Apostles: Forgotten Members of Mormonism's Original Quorum of Twelve.* Salt Lake City: Signature, 2014.

Shepherd, Gordon, and Gary Shepherd. "The Doctrinal and Commitment Functions of Patriarchal Blessings in Early Mormon Development, 1834–45." *Journal of the American Academy of Religion* 80.3 (2012) 718–49.

———. *A Kingdom Transformed: Early Mormonism and the Modern LDS Church.* 2nd ed. Salt Lake City: University of Utah Press, 2016.

Sherlock, Richard. "Faith and History: The Snell Controversy." *Dialogue* 12.1 (1979) 27–41.

Shipps, Jan. *Mormonism: The Story of a New Religious Tradition.* Chicago: University of Illinois Press, 1987.

Siebach, Jim. "Dialogue on Theology as Hermeneutics." In *Mormonism in Dialogue with Contemporary Christian Theologies,* edited by David L. Paulsen and Donald W. Musser, 458–67. Macon, GA: Mercer University Press, 2007.

Smith, Christopher C. "Joseph Smith in Hermeneutical Crisis." *Dialogue* 43.2 (2010) 86–108.

Smith, George Albert. *History of the Church of Jesus Christ of Latter-day Saints.* 7 vols. https://byustudies.byu.edu/further-study/history-of-the-church/.

Smith, Joseph. "Inspired Version." https://www.centerplace.org/hs/iv/default.htm.

———. "The King Follett Discourse." http://mldb.byu.edu/follett.htm.

Smith, Joseph Fielding, ed. *Teachings of the Prophet Joseph Smith.* Salt Lake City: Deseret, 1977.

———. *Essentials in Church History.* Salt Lake City: Deseret, 1979.

Smith, Julie M. "Five Impulses of the Joseph Smith Translation of Mark and Their Implications for LDS Hermeneutics." *Studies in the Bible and Antiquity* 7 (2015) 1–21.

———. *The Gospel according to Mark.* BYU New Testament Commentary Series. Provo, UT: BYU Studies, 2018. Kindle.

———. "LDS Hermeneutics." *Times and Seasons* (blog), April 20, 2004. https://www.timesandseasons.org/harchive/2004/04/lds-hermeneutics/.

———. "She Hath Wrought a Good Work: The Anointing of Jesus in Mark's Gospel." *Studies in the Bible and Antiquity* 5 (2013) 31–46.

Snodgrass, K. R. "Parable." In *DJG*, edited by Joel B. Green and Scot McKnight, 591–601. Downers Grove, IL: InterVarsity, 1992.

Soards, Marion L. *The Speeches in Acts: Their Content, Context, and Concerns.* Louisville: Westminster John Knox, 1994.

Southerton, Simon G. *Losing a Lost Tribe: Native Americans, DNA, and the Mormon Church.* Salt Lake City: Signature, 2004.

Stamps, Dennis L. "The Use of the Old Testament in the New Testament as a Rhetorical Device: A Methodological Proposal." In *Hearing the Old Testament in the New Testament,* edited by Stanley E. Porter, 9–37. Grand Rapids: Eerdmans, 2006.

Stapley, Delbert L. "The Gift of the Holy Ghost." https://emp.byui.edu/SATTERFIELDB/Talks/GiftofHolyGhostDLS.htm.

Stark, Rodney. *The Rise of Mormonism.* New York: Columbia University Press, 2005.

———. "The Rise of a New World Faith." *Review of Religious Research* 26.1 (1984) 18–27.

Stendahl, Krister. *Meanings: The Bible as Document and as Guide.* Philadelphia: Fortress, 1984.

———. "The Sermon on the Mount and Third Nephi." In *Reflections on Mormonism: Judaeo-Christian Parallels,* edited by Truman G. Madsen, 139–54. Provo, UT: Brigham Young University Press, 1978.

Stevens, George B., ed. *Saint Chrysostom: Homilies on the Acts of the Apostles and the Epistle to the Romans.* In vol. 11 of *A Select Library of the Nicene and Post-Nicene Fathers of the Christian Church, Series 1,* edited by Philip Schaff. New York: Christian Literature Company, 1889.

Stroup, George W. *The Promise of Narrative Theology: Recovering the Gospel in the Church.* Atlanta: John Knox, 1964.

Swanson, James. *Dictionary of Biblical Languages with Semantic Domains: Hebrew (Old Testament).* Oak Harbor, WA: Logos Research Systems, 1997.

Talmage, James Edward. *The Articles of Faith.* Salt Lake City: Deseret, 1899.

———. *The Great Apostasy Considered in the Light of Scriptural and Secular History.* Independence, MO: Zion's, 1909.

———. *Jesus the Christ.* Salt Lake City: LDS, 2006.

Tate, W. Randolph. *Handbook for Biblical Interpretation.* 2nd ed. Grand Rapids: Baker, 2012.

Terry, Roger. "Authority and Priesthood in the LDS Church, Part 1: Definitions and Development." *Dialogue* 51.1 (2018) 1–37.

———. "The Source of God's Authority: One Argument for an Unambiguous Doctrine of Preexistence." *Dialogue* 49.3 (2016) 109–44.

Thiessen, Gerd. *The Social Setting of Pauline Christianity: Essays on Corinth.* Philadelphia: Fortress, 1982.

Thiselton, Anthony C. *The First Epistle to the Corinthians: A Commentary on the Greek Text.* NIGTC. Grand Rapids: Eerdmans, 2000.

———. *Hermeneutics: An Introduction.* Grand Rapids: Eerdmans, 2009. Kindle.

———. *The Hermeneutics of Doctrine.* Grand Rapids: Eerdmans, 2007.

———. *New Horizons in Hermeneutics.* Grand Rapids: Zondervan, 1992.

Thomas, M. Catherine. "Scripture, Interpretation within Scripture." In *EM*, edited by Daniel H. Ludlow, 1283–84. New York: Macmillan, 1992.

Tidball, Derek. *The Social Context of the New Testament: A Sociological Analysis.* Grand Rapids: Zondervan, 1984.

Toussaint, Stanley D., and Jay A. Quine. "No, Not Yet: The Contingency of God's Promised Kingdom." *Bibliotheca Sacra* 164.654 (2007) 131–47.

Trebilco, P. R. "Diaspora Judaism." In *DNLT*, edited by Ralph P. Martin and Peter H. Davids, 287–300. Downers Grove, IL: InterVarsity, 1997.

Treier, Daniel J. *Introducing Theological Interpretation of Scripture.* Grand Rapids: Baker, 2008.

Troeltsch, Ernst. *The Social Teaching of the Christian Churches.* Translated by Olive Wyon. 2 vols. Louisville: Westminster John Knox, 1992.

Trueman, Carl R. *Histories and Fallacies.* Wheaton, IL: Crossway, 2010.

Tucker, Gene M. *The Book of Isaiah 1–39.* NIB 6. Nashville: Abingdon, 2001.

Tull, Patricia K. *Isaiah 1–39.* SHBC. Macon, GA: Smyth & Helwys, 2010.

Turner, John G. *Brigham Young: Pioneer Prophet.* Cambridge, MA: Belknap, 2012.

Twelftree, Graham H. *People of the Spirit: Exploring Luke's View of the Church.* Grand Rapids: Baker Academic, 2009. Kindle.

Underwood, Grant. "Book of Mormon Usage in Early LDS Theology." *Dialogue* 17.3 (1984) 35–75.

———. *The Millenarian World of Early Mormonism.* Urbana: University of Illinois Press, 1993.

———. "More than an Index: The First Reference Guide to the Doctrine and Covenants as a Window into Early Mormonism." *BYU Studies* 41.2 (2002) 116–47.

———. "The 'Same' Organization That Existed in the Primitive Church." In *Go Ye into All the World: Messages of the New Testament Apostles*, edited by Thomas A. Wayment and Jerome M. Perkins, 167–86. Salt Lake City: Deseret, 2002.

Van Gelder, Craig. "Method in Light of Scriptures and in Relation to Hermeneutics." *Journal of Religious Leadership* 3.1–2 (2004) 43–73.

Vanhoozer, Kevin J. *Is There a Meaning in This Text? The Bible, the Reader, and the Morality of Literary Knowledge.* Grand Rapids: Zondervan, 1998.

———. "What Is Theological Interpretation of the Bible?" In *TINT*, edited by Kevin J. Vanhoozer, 13–26. Grand Rapids: Baker Academic, 2008.

Wachterhauser, Brice R., ed. *Hermeneutics and Modern Philosophy.* New York: State University of New York Press, 1986.

Walters, Wesley P. "The Use of the Old Testament in the Book of Mormon." ThM thesis, Covenant Theological Seminary, 1981.

Walton, Steve. "Acts." In *TINT*, edited by Kevin J. Vanhoozer, 74–83. Grand Rapids: Baker Academic, 2008.

Warnke, Georgia, ed. *Inheriting Gadamer: New Directions in Philosophical Hermeneutics.* Edinburgh: Edinburgh University Press, 2016.

Watson, Duane F. *The Second Letter of Peter.* NIB 12. Nashville: Abingdon, 1998.

Watson, Francis. *Paul and the Hermeneutics of Faith.* New York: T. & T. Clark International, 2004.

―――. *Paul, Judaism, and the Gentiles: A Sociological Approach.* Cambridge: Cambridge University Press, 1986.

―――. *Text and Truth: Redefining Biblical Theology.* Grand Rapids: Eerdmans, 1997.

―――. "Toward a Literal Reading of the Gospels." In *The Gospels for All Christians: Rethinking the Gospel Audiences,* edited by Richard Bauckham, 195–217. Grand Rapids: Eerdmans, 1997.

Watts, John D. W. *Isaiah 1–33.* Rev. ed. WBC 24. Nashville: Nelson, 2005.

Webb, Stephen H. *Mormon Christianity: What Other Christians Can Learn from the Latter-day Saints.* Oxford: Oxford University Press, 2013.

Weinsheimer, Joel. *Philosophical Hermeneutics and Literary Theory.* New Haven: Yale University Press, 1991.

Wenham, Gordon J. *Genesis 1–15.* WBC 1. Dallas: Word, 1998.

Westphal, Merold. *Whose Community? Which Interpretation?* Grand Rapids: Baker, 2009.

White, O. Kendall, Jr. *Mormon Neo-orthodoxy: A Crisis Theology.* Salt Lake City: Signature, 1987.

Widmer, Kurt. *Mormonism and the Nature of God: A Theological Evolution, 1830–1915.* London: Mcfarland, 2000.

Wilcox, Miranda, and John D. Young, eds. *Standing Apart: Mormon Historical Consciousness and the Concept of Apostasy.* Oxford: Oxford University Press, 2014.

Wildberger, Hans. *Isaiah 28–39.* Translated by Thomas H. Trapp. A Continental Commentary. Minneapolis: Fortress, 2002.

Williams, Clyde J. *Teachings of Lorenzo Snow.* Salt Lake City: Bookcraft, 1984.

Willsky, Lydia. "The (Un)plain Bible: New Religious Movements and Alternative Scriptures in Nineteenth-Century America." *Nova Religio* 17.4 (2014) 13–36.

Winn, Kenneth H. *Exiles in a Land of Liberty: Mormons in America, 1830–1846.* Chapel Hill: University of North Carolina Press, 1989.

Witherington, Ben, III. *The Acts of the Apostles: A Socio-Rhetorical Commentary.* Grand Rapids: Eerdmans, 1998.

Wolterstorff, Nicholas. *Divine Discourse: Philosophical Reflections on the Claim That God Speaks.* Cambridge: University of Cambridge Press, 1995.

―――. "On God Speaking." *The Reformed Journal* (1969) 7–15.

Wright, Andrew. *Christianity and Critical Realism: Ambiguity, Truth, and Theological Literacy.* New York: Routledge, 2013.

Wright, David P. "Historical Criticism: A Necessary Element in the Search for Religious Truth." *Sunstone* 16.3 (1992) 28–38.

―――. "Joseph Smith's Interpretation of Isaiah in the Book of Mormon." *Dialogue* 31.4 (1998) 181–206.

Wright, G. Ernest. *God Who Acts: Biblical Theology as Recital.* Studies in Biblical Theology 8. London: SCM, 1962.

Wright, N. T. *Acts for Everyone: Part One: Chapters 1–12.* Louisville: Westminster John Knox, 2008.

————. *Jesus and the Victory of God.* Christian Origins and the Question of God 2. London: SPCK, 1996.

————. *The New Testament and the People of God.* Christian Origins and the Question of God 1. London: SPCK, 1992.

————. *The Resurrection of the Son of God.* Christian Origins and the Question of God 3. London: SPCK, 2003.

————. *Scripture and the Authority of God: How to Read the Bible Today.* HarperCollins e-books, 2013. Kindle.

Young, Brigham. "Effects and Privileges of the Gospel." https://jod.mrm.org/1/233.

————. "Intelligence." https://jod.mrm.org/7/282.

————. "Remarks on a Revelation." https://jod.mrm.org/3/333.

————. "Texts for Preaching." https://jod.mrm.org/13/261.

————. "Unbelief." https://jod.mrm.org/16/40.

Young, Edward J. *The Book of Isaiah: Chapters 19 to 39.* Grand Rapids: Eerdmans, 1999.

Young, Francis. "The Pastoral Epistles and the Ethics of Reading." *JSNT* 14.45 (1992) 105–20.

Zabala, Santiago. "The Anarchy of Hermeneutics: Interpretation as a Vital Practice." In *Inheriting Gadamer: New Directions in Philosophical Hermeneutics,* edited by Georgia Warnke, 67–77. Edinburgh: Edinburgh University Press, 2016.

Zimmerli, Walther. *Ezekiel 2: A Commentary on the Book of the Prophet Ezekiel Chapters 25–48.* Translated by James D. Martin. Hermeneia. Philadelphia: Fortress, 1983.

Zucker, Louis. "Joseph Smith as a Student of Hebrew." *Dialogue* 3 (1968) 41–55.

Subject Index

(selected)

223

Name Index

(selected)

Scripture Index